SOUTH AFRICA IN TRANSITION

Also by Aletta J. Norval

DECONSTRUCTING APARTHEID DISCOURSE

South Africa in Transition

New Theoretical Perspectives

Edited by

David R. Howarth
Lecturer in Political Theory
Staffordshire University

and

Aletta J. Norval
Lecturer in Political Theory
University of Essex

First published in Great Britain 1998 by
MACMILLAN PRESS LTD
Houndmills, Basingstoke, Hampshire RG21 6XS and London
Companies and representatives throughout the world

A catalogue record for this book is available from the British Library.

ISBN 0–333–67156–2

 First published in the United States of America 1998 by
ST. MARTIN'S PRESS, INC.,
Scholarly and Reference Division,
175 Fifth Avenue, New York, N.Y. 10010

ISBN 0–312–21430–8

Library of Congress Cataloging-in-Publication Data
South Africa in transition : new theoretical perspectives / edited by
David R. Howarth and Aletta J. Norval.
p. cm.
Includes bibliographical references and index.
ISBN 0–312–21430–8 (cloth)
1. South Africa—Politics and government—1994– I. Howarth,
David R. II. Norval, Aletta J.
DT1974.S73 1998
968.06'4—dc21   98–11004
                                                      CIP

This book is printed on paper suitable for recycling and made from fully managed and
sustained forest sources.

10   9   8   7   6   5   4   3   2   1
07   06   05   04   03   02   01   00   99   98

Printed and bound in Great Britain by
Antony Rowe Ltd, Chippenham, Wiltshire

Contents

Contents

List of Abbreviations

ALRA	Agricultural Labour Relations Act
ANC	African National Congress
AVF	Afrikaner Volkswag
BCEA	Basic Conditions of Employment Act
CASE	Community Agency for Social Enquiry
CCC	Cape Town City Council
CODESA	Conference for a Democratic South Africa
Cosatu	Congress of South African Trade Unions
COSAW	Congress of South African Writers
ERS	Education Renewal Strategy
FF	Freedom Front
Fosatu	Federation of South African Trade Unions
GNU	Government of National Unity
HRC	Human Rights Commission
IFP	Inkatha Freedom Party
KZP	KwaZulu Police
MK	Umkhonto we Sizwe
NAD	Native Administration Department
NEPI	National Education Policy Investigation
NEUM	Non European Unity Movement
NIS	National Intelligence Service
NMS	National Management System
NP	National Party
PAC	Pan Africanist Congress
PRA	Participatory Rural Appraisal
RDP	Reconstruction and Development Programme
SAAM	South African Association of Men
SABRA	Suid-Afrikaanse Buro vir Rasse-Aangeleenthede
SACP	South African Communist Party
SADF	South African Defence Force
SAIDE	South African Institute for Distance Education
SAP	South African Police
SDU	Self Defence Unit
SSC	State Security Council
SWAPO	South West African People's Organization
TBVC	Transkei, Boputhatswana, Venda, Ciskei (former 'independent homelands')

TRC   Truth and Reconciliation Commission
UDF   United Democratic Front
UDUSA   Union of Democratic University Staff Associations
UIA   Unemployment Insurance Act
WCAB   Western Cape Administration Board

Notes on the Contributors

Antony Altbeker is Deputy Director-General of the Department of Finance. He completed a joint Honours degree in the Departments of Economics and Politics at the University of the Witwatersrand, and is working on a Master's degree in economics.

Debby Bonnin teaches in the Department of Sociology at the University of Natal, Durban. She is a founding member of the editorial collective of the journal *Agenda*. She is an active member of the ANC's Women's Movement, and was a delegate to the Beijing conference.

Roger Deacon teaches in the Education Department, University of Natal, Durban. He is editor of *Theoria*, and has published widely on historiography, education and development, and the politics of postmodernism.

Mark Devenney is currently working on a PhD at the University of Essex. He has a Master's degree (by research) from the University of Witwatersrand and has taught philosophy and literature at the University of Durban-Westville, South Africa. He has published articles on various aspects of Southern African literature and its connection to emancipatory politics.

Andries du Toit is Director of a research project on land reform and its policy implications in South Africa. He has completed a Master's degree (by research) at the University of Cape Town, and has taught politics at the University of the Western Cape. He has published articles on the 'land question' and agrarian reform in South Africa. He has recently completed a PhD at the University of Essex on wine farmworkers in the Western Cape.

Sean Field is currently involved in setting up an oral history research project in Cape Town, South Africa. He has a Master's degree from the University of Cape Town and has taught sociology at that university. He has completed a PhD at the University of Essex on African and coloured identity in Guguletu township.

Daryl Glaser teaches political theory at the University of Strathclyde. He has taught and studied in South Africa. He completed a Master's degree at the University of Witwatersrand on industrial decentralization, and has obtained his PhD at the University of Manchester on the normative theorization of democracy and democratization. He has published numerous articles on questions of socialism and democracy in the South African context.

David Howarth teaches political theory at the University of Staffordshire. He has studied and taught in South Africa, where he completed a Master's degree (by research) at the University of Natal. He has obtained a PhD from the University of Essex on the Black Consciousness Movement in South Africa. He has published articles on various aspects of South African politics and political theory.

Robert Morrell teaches history and gender-related courses in the Education Department, University of Natal. He has completed a PhD at the University of Natal. He has published articles on South African agrarian history, gender and education policy in contemporary South Africa, as well as on the historical formation of masculinity in a colonial setting. During the 1980s he taught at the universities of Transkei and Durban-Westville, where he was active in staff politics. He has edited a book entitled *White but Poor: Essays on the History of Poor Whites in Southern Africa* (Pretoria, 1992).

Aletta Norval is director of the MA programme in Ideology and Discourse Theory at the University of Essex. She has studied, taught and conducted research in South Africa, before taking up a post at the University of Essex. She obtained a Master's degree (by research) from the Rand Afrikaans University and a PhD from the University of Essex on the construction and dissolution of apartheid discourse. She has recently published *Deconstructing Apartheid Discourse* (London, 1996).

Ben Parker has taught in the Philosophy Department, University of Durban-Westville. He has published on social theory, philosophy and education and governance. He is now Chair of the Department of Education, University of Natal, Pietermaritzburg.

Jennifer Robinson teaches in the Department of Geography, London School of Economics. She has published in the field of urban politics and history, and gender studies. She has recently published *The Power of Apartheid: State, Power and Space in South African Cities* (Oxford, 1996).

Mark Shaw is a senior researcher and head of the Crime and Police Policy Project at the Institute for Security Studies in Johannesburg, and a research associate at the Centre for Policy Studies. He is currently completing his PhD at the University of the Witwatersrand.

Jonny Steinberg is a doctoral student at Oxford University. He has completed a Master's degree (by research) in the Department of Politics at the University of the Witwatersrand. He taught politics at that university and worked for the Goldstone Commission of Inquiry.

Rupert Taylor teaches political science at the University of the Witwatersrand, Johannesburg. He completed a Master's degree at Queens University, Belfast before doing a PhD at the University of Kent. He has published numerous articles on aspects of contemporary South African politics. His current concerns centre on questions of violence and ethnicity in South Africa's townships. He was a fellow at the New School for Research in New York.

Chronology

March 1989	Mandela sends memorandum on ANC–government talks to P. W. Botha
5 July 1989	P. W. Botha meets Mandela in prison
14 August 1989	Botha resigns and is succeeded by F. W. de Klerk
21 August 1989	Adoption of Harare Declaration
13 December 1989	De Klerk discusses preconditions for negotiation with Mandela
2 February 1990	Unbanning of the ANC, SACP and other proscribed organizations
11 February 1990	Mandela released after 27 years in prison
16 February 1990	ANC agrees to talks with de Klerk government
2–4 May 1990	ANC and de Klerk government agrees the first pact, the 'Groote Schuur Minute'
July 1990	National Party and Inkatha each opens their party membership to all races; violence in Natal escalates
6–7 August 1990	Second round of formal talks ends with the 'Pretoria Minute'
September 1990	Conflict between IFP and ANC supporters spreads from Natal to townships on the Witwatersrand
8 January 1991	ANC calls for an All-Party Congress
31 January 1991	Joint ANC–IFP delegations meet in Durban
15 February 1991	The government and ANC conclude the 'D. F. Malan Minute'
March 1991	ANC releases 'Constitutional Principles and Structures for a Democratic South Africa'
6 April 1991	ANC ultimatum links talks to diminution of violence
18 May 1991	ANC withdraws from negotiations
17 June 1991	Population Registration Act repealed
22 June 1991	Business and church leaders plan national peace conference
19 July 1991	The *Weekly Mail* publishes reports detailing police funding of IFP rallies
8 September 1991	Just before the National Peace Conference 18 are killed and 14 wounded in violence near Johannesburg; by the end of the week, 121 die and 550 wounded in factional violence

14 September 1991	National Peace Accord signed
20 December 1991	CODESA, the first formal constitutional negotiation, is convened
17 March 1992	White voters back de Klerk's reforms overwhelmingly (67.8 per cent)
March 1992	Widespread violence in townships
April 1992	Working Groups set up by CODESA negotiate transition path
15–16 May 1992	CODESA II results in deadlock
17 June 1992	Boipatong massacre; 49 dead; ANC withdraws from negotiation
August 1992	Following secret talks with the government, the PAC agrees to attend relaunched multi-party talks; the CP agrees to talks
3 August 1992	Cosatu spearheads three-day general strike
7 September 1992	ANC protesters march on Ciskei capital Bisho; 28 killed by Ciskei security forces, after which government–ANC bilateral talks resume
26 September 1992	Government–ANC agree to the 'Record of Understanding' which charts the path of further transition
6 October 1992	Buthelezi, some 'homeland' leaders and white right-wing groups form a rejectionist front, the Concerned South Africans Group (COSAG)
12 February 1993	Government–ANC agreement on SACP document 'Negotiation: A Strategic Perspective'
17 February 1993	Government–IFP negotiation fail to win IFP backing for power-sharing deal
5 March 1993	Multi Party Negotiation Process (MPNP) planned
1 April 1993	MPNP first session at the World Trade Centre in Johannesburg
10 April 1993	Chris Hani, SACP leader assassinated
3 June 1993	Tentative agreement on 27 April 1994 as election date; objections by IFP and COSAG
25 June 1993	Armed right-wingers invade MPNP forum
2 July 1993	MPNP affirm 27 April 1994 election date
July 1993	600 die in political violence
18 July 1993	IFP withdraws from MPNP over election date
26 July 1993	MPNP present first draft of an interim constitution
8 September 1993	Negotiating Council agrees on transitional structures

24 September 1993	Parliament adopts the transitional executive council legislation
7 Ocotber 1993	Black and white rejectionist groups form Freedom Alliance
15 October 1993	De Klerk and Mandela win the Nobel Peace Prize
16 November 1983	De Klerk and Mandela conclude final power-sharing agreements
18 November 1993	Interim constitution adopted by the Negotiating Council of the Multi Party Negotiating Process
March 1994	Boputhatswana battle
4 March 1994	General Constand Viljoen's FF registers for election just minutes before deadline; white right-wing splits
	IFP march in Johannesburg city centre to ANC head offices; ANC security guards kill 53
8 April 1994	Four-way summit between de Klerk, Mandela, Buthelezi and King Zwelithini; summit ends in impasse
19 April 1994	IFP agrees to participate in election after intervention by Kenyan mediator, Washington Okumu
24 April 1994	Right-wing bombings just prior to elections killed nine
27–29 April 1994	General election inaugurates democracy
2 May 1994	De Klerk concedes victory to Mandela
6 May 1994	Final election results released; election declared 'substantially free and fair' by Independent Electoral Commission

Introduction: Changing Paradigms and the Politics of Transition in South Africa

David R. Howarth and Aletta J. Norval

> There is a past to be learned about, but the past is now seen, and it has to be grasped as a history, as something that has to be told. It is narrated. It is grasped through desire. It is grasped through reconstruction. It is not just a fact that has been waiting to ground our identities.[1]

South Africa has undergone momentous changes over the past ten years. At the end of 1989, the National Party (NP) embarked on a process that ended white minority rule. The dramatic unbanning of the African National Congress (ANC), the South African Communist Party (SACP) and other proscribed organizations on 2 February 1990 took place in an international and domestic context in which there were both new opportunities and pressures for democratization. These events are well documented, and it is not our aim to rehearse them here.[2] Rather, our more limited aim is to contextualize the various chapters in this book, all of which deal concretely with different aspects of the transition, by situating them in the broader theoretical and intellectual context from which they have emerged.

The dismantling of apartheid and the creation of a democratic system of representation has not been a singular process. Just as the characterization of apartheid excited much discussion, so has the nature of the transition process and its outcome. We do not wish to adjudicate on these disputes and interpretations, as it is important not to close down these hard-won spaces of discussion too soon. Doing so would be to succumb to the pressures of providing a singular characterization which would rule out all other interpretations, and the process of transition is much too uneven to take such unitary stances. Moreover, while some scholars seem to agree that it is now necessary to shift attention away from the transition process to questions of democratic consolidation,[3] this is to presume that the transition process has been completed. This precludes the continued problematization and investigation of areas of social and political life, such as issues of rural development, in which there has been little, if any, evidence of change. It would also omit seemingly marginal issues, such as gender and sexuality, from consideration. Thus, while we do not dispute the necessity

1

and urgency of democratic consolidation, we would argue that there is also a need to keep open spaces for critical investigation. In this respect, a possible analytical strategy would be the refusal to confer to the transition process the status of a clearly delimited and defined period, and instead engage with its dynamic and complex character. The different contributions to this book, each in its own way, seek to record what has already been achieved, and to examine the indeterminate transition process, as well as the possibilities and obstacles for extending and deepening democracy in South Africa.

*   *   *

> We must begin somewhere, but there is no absolutely justified beginning. . . . One cannot, for essential reasons . . . return to a point of departure from which all the rest could be constructed following an order of reasons . . . nor following an individual or historical evolution. . . . At most one can give a *strategic* justification for the procedure. A (metaphysical) thought, which begins by searching for origins or foundations and proceeds to a reconstruction in order, infallibly finds that things have not happened as they ought. . . .[4]

The democratic transition has affected those theoretical idioms used to make sense of South Africa's changing political situation. It has renewed thinking and created fissures in the sclerotic dogmas of academic writing, as old certainties are reworked, and new positions articulated. Crucial to this process has been the growth of 'post-isms', such as post-structuralism and postmodernism, which have challenged and undermined the certainties and exclusions of existing paradigms. For instance, the narrow strictures of the so-called 'race-class debate' have been deconstructed and reworked under the rubrics of post-structuralism, postmodernism, post-Marxism, post-colonial and critical theory.[5] Writers from these perspectives suggest that it is no longer sufficient merely to question the 'either-or' status of the debate, while affirming a 'both-and' approach.[6] Rather, the presuppositions of each side of the debate have been called into question such that supposedly irreconcilable positions have been shown to share some significant modernist assumptions. These include an unquestioned belief in linear historical progress, the positing of fully constituted social identities, the presumption of mechanical models of causality, and the possibilities of complete human emancipation. More particularly, the givenness and objectivity of categories such as 'race' and class have been questioned, giving rise to a lateral displacement in research problematics and agendas. Thus, instead of inquiring into the assumed class or economic interests of political agents, attention has shifted to an investigation of how interests are constructed discursively in and through political struggle. Interests are no longer considered as objectively given, but neither are they merely subjective. As a consequence, the division between objectivity and subjectivity has been problematized, so that what appears to be necessary and given is shown to be the result of political creation and historical sedimentation. Further, instead of either reducing 'race' to class, or assuming race to have the status of a natural category, analyses have increasingly begun to focus on processes of 'racialization', that is, on the historical and political *formation* and deployment of categories of race and ethnicity.

Nevertheless, it should be noted that the emergence and development of new research questions have not led to a simple rejection of the questions posed by previous paradigms. Quite the contrary. Problematizing some of the central modernist assumptions underpinning both liberal and neo-Marxist analyses, such as the givenness and objectivity of racial or class identity, has led to a renewed investigation of the politico-historical processes through which these identities are produced and have structured the political landscape. Moreover, this questioning has exposed new areas of investigation previously considered uninteresting or unimportant. The relatively recent interest in gender and religious forms of identification are two significant examples of this.[7]

However, it is important to emphasize that the adoption of non-essentialist and non-foundationalist forms of inquiry means that some of the older certainties, which either consciously or unintentionally inform substantive analyses, need to be questioned. Thus, it is inadequate simply to supplement existing categories, without transforming their original meanings and implications.[8] For instance, it is necessary to account theoretically for the assertion that subjects are criss-crossed by racial, class, gender, ethnic and religious forms of identification, and from a post-structuralist perspective this is made possible by emphasizing the structurally incomplete nature of human subjectivity, and the multiple and overdetermined forms which social identity takes. A further implication of post-structuralist and postmodernist perspectives concerns the character of theory, as well as the role of the theorist. As opposed to the view that the theorist has a privileged access to reality, performing the role of an 'objective external observer', the analyst is viewed as constitutively entangled in relations of power and knowledge, which have to be made explicit and acknowledged.[9] In this way, the character of reality itself is problematized,[10] as more careful attention has to be paid to the discourses which people construct to make sense of their own reality, rather than imputing objective sets of relations upon them.

The cumulative effect of these considerations is that the singularity and universality of theoretical work has been put into question. As Jacques Derrida argues, one can no longer presume that there is a possibility of 'totalising all theoretical phenomena, all theoretical productions . . . in a legible surface, which would, like any stable and stabilized table, allow for the reading of the taxonomic tabularity, the entries and the places, or else the genealogy, finally fixed in a tree of theory, of identities. . . .'[11] However, it should be stressed that the questioning of universalist pretensions, which quite often did nothing more than mask a Western framework of judgement, need not lead inevitably to relativism. The latter, as Richard Rorty argues, still retains the questionable supposition of a single reality in relation to which one has a series of different, but equally true, perspectives.[12] Taking the constructed character of reality seriously, retains the idea that in a given context there are regimes of truth which make certain things and statements possible, while ruling others out. It does not warrant, therefore, an 'everything goes' or 'everything is possible' position. As Michel Foucault has argued forcefully, what is at stake, here, are the conditions of existence of the true and the false, and the manner in which discursive regimes delineate what may count as truth or falsity.[13]

In line with these considerations, the chapters in this book do not share a singular theoretical framework or approach. Rather, what links them together are a series of family resemblances, a certain overlapping of themes and approaches, which display an openness to new forms of theoretical thinking inspired, or at the very least marked, by post-structuralism and postmodernism. Thus, they are best judged on the grounds of their deployment in substantive areas of analysis, rather than in terms of any single overarching theoretical schema. The chapters aim to analyse the different aspects of the transition to democracy in South Africa and, in the process, they defamiliarize what was thought to be transparent, and render visible areas of politics not previously explored.

* * *

By creating the possibility of a critical re-reading of modernity, postmodernism offers us the chance to reconsider all that was 'left unsaid' and to inject its areas of opacity and resistance with the potential for new, as yet undiscovered, meanings.[14]

The transition to democracy in South Africa has been accompanied by extreme violence, with over 16 000 lives being lost between 1990 and 1994. It is therefore appropriate that the book starts with a discussion and explanation of this violence. In Chapter 1, Rupert Taylor and Mark Shaw set out to investigate this phenomenon, attempting to account for its multiple forms, and the sources from which it sprang. In so doing, they take issue with commentators who argue either that it is a 'natural' part of the process of political change, or who provide over-personalized arguments which attempt to analyse it via an identification of the political affiliations of perpetrators and survivors. Two central questions frame their investigation. First, to what extent can the violence be interpreted as a natural continuation of apartheid violence? Second, to what extent can it be firmly linked to the political will of the state? In addressing these questions, they stress the role of state strategy, including its involvement in destabilization, and low-intensity warfare to explain the violence. Instead of merely random acts of violence, they find clear evidence for patterns of systematic and co-ordinated state complicity, which have since been confirmed by other investigations. Taylor and Shaw argue that the Boipatong massacre functioned as a turning-point for the state, forcing a loosening of the NP's relations with the Inkatha Freedom Party (IFP), and an accommodation with the ANC. This was borne out in the decline in violence towards the end of 1992. They argue that any adequate account of South Africa's transition to democracy must engage with the systematic character of political violence, or otherwise run the risk of building a polity based on a lack of respect for the rule of law.

In Chapter 2, Daryl Glaser analyses the discourses that have historically informed Left political strategy and ideology in South Africa during the 1980s and 1990s. Arguing from a perspective which accepts that a plausible articulation of democracy and socialism is feasible, Glaser provides a challenging critique of oppositional discourses in the South African context. He shows that Leftist discourses prior to the 1970s, most clearly evident in the ideas and programmes of the SACP and the Non European Unity Movement (NEUM), downplayed democratic goals and methods in favour of socialism, a tendency which was replicated in the novel theoretical and strategic debates of the 1970s and 1980s. The latter period saw the emergence of what he calls a 'prefigurative councillism' amongst the independent trade union movement and the civic organizations associated with the United Democratic Front (UDF), and centred around a form of participatory socialist democracy. Providing a detailed critique of this democratic deficit, he then draws attention to significant changes in Leftist discourse during the 1990s. In this period, he stresses the abandonment of the authoritarian and dogmatic commitments of the earlier periods, and the 'discovery' of the importance of constitutionalism, civil rights, political pluralism and an autonomous civil society. However, despite the embracing of democracy as an end in itself, Glaser concludes that this has still not resulted in an articulation of democratic and socialist objectives in Leftist discourse, as the focus on 'building up the countervailing power of civil society' effectively concedes the formulation of socialist demands and policies to the ANC in government.

The socio-political and economic contours of post-apartheid South Africa are shaped, in significant respects, by the structuring of political space under apartheid. In Chapter 3, Antony Altbeker and Jonny Steinberg address the role of the NP in delimiting the terrain of struggle during the key period of 1990–92, which, in many respects, set the limits and informed the agenda for further negotiations between the NP and the ANC. Treating the NP as a narrator, and the field of party politics as structured by competing 'truth claims', Altbeker and Steinberg argue that if political forces are constituted through their self-representations, then the importance of narrative analysis cannot be underestimated. Their chapter then analyses the manner in which consociational constitutional principles were justified in the discursive universe of the NP. It investigates the role of two distinct conceptions of history – one rationalist and the other culturalist – operative in that discourse, and outlines the consequences they have for the conception of democracy and identity upheld by the NP. Altbeker and Steinberg show through their analysis of documents and speeches how the rationalist narrative presents the past as an ideological aberration, while the 'culturalist' conception underwrites past identities as an 'immutable substratum stretching back to time immemorial'. Drawing on Etienne Balibar's analysis they show how, through a subtle mutation, the NP's culturalist discourse degenerates into neo-racism, that is, a racism which trades on, but does not invoke, the existence of 'races'. In this manner, the tensions between these two conceptions or discursive strains are 'resolved' by the precise manner in which they are entangled.

Chapters 4 and 5 also address the difficult question of the relation to the past. The central theme of Sean Field's chapter concerns the role of memory and myth in the identities of the former residents of the Windermere community who were forcibly removed to Guguletu between 1958 and 1963. Using oral history, Field unravels the complex interrelations between the interviewer and the interviewee, as well as the interviewees' memories of their past and their relation to the 'changing present'. He gives specific attention to the way in which memories of a mythically 'whole' community enable people to come to terms with the uncertainties of the present. The analysis reveals some of the effects that the imposition of apartheid had upon an ethnically mixed community, especially the rupturing of community networks and generational relations, while also problematizing the violence experienced in contemporary Guguletu. Through his sensitive analysis, the author shows the specific utility of oral resources for the historian. He argues that its potency lies not so much in the preservation of the past, but in the changes wrought by memory on the past–present relation; the past is given a certain meaning which contributes, simultaneously, to the meaning of the present. As against an empiricist conception of history, and of a certain conception of oral history, Field analyses the role 'myth-making' plays in the lives of the interviewees, arguing that oral history has an important political role to play in documenting and interpreting the untold stories of the wounds of apartheid.

The use and reconstruction of the past is also a theme that runs through Aletta Norval's analysis of the discourse of the Freedom Front (FF) in contemporary South Africa. In Chapter 5, she investigates the structure of the FF's discourse, arguing that the degree to which it has succeeded in becoming an acceptable political participant in the negotiation process, can, to a large degree, be ascribed to the fact that it has mobilized the language of 'cultural recognition' to gain legitimacy for its struggle. Utilizing available discourses demanding cultural recognition in established liberal democracies by groups aiming to extend and deepen these democracies, the FF argues that 'the Afrikaner's' position in the new South Africa – as a cultural minority – requires special forms of protection. Norval discusses the arguments which justify this position, and investigates the discursive mechanisms through which the identity of the 'Afrikaner' community is delimited. She develops a critique of their exclusivist conception of culture – along much the same lines as Altbeker and Steinberg's discussion of the neo-racisms of the NP's discourse – arguing that legitimate demands for cultural recognition would have to take the idea of a (non-racial) democracy seriously.

Drawing on Derridean insights, as well as on writers such as James Tully, she argues that it no longer makes sense in the contemporary world to think of cultures as 'billiard balls'. Rather, any adequate engagement with cultural identity needs to recognize that cultures are closely interdependent in their formation, and their identities are subject to contestation and negotiation. A recognition of this entanglement could lead to a deepening of democratic discourses, and a constitutional association in which there is a mutual recognition of cultures of citizens could engender allegiance to such associations. This is for two reasons. Firstly, citizens identify with a constitutional association in so far as they have a say in its formation and functioning and, secondly, in so far as they see their own cultural ways publicly acknowledged and affirmed by it. One's own identity as a citizen, as Tully puts it, is inseparable from a shared history with other citizens who are irreducibly different. In such a context, an ethic of critical freedom may be sustained, which is crucial to the spirit of democracy.[15] In the period of transition, South Africa has made some tentative movements in the direction of a polity which could in the future sustain and enhance difference. The very fact of the ongoing negotiations between the FF and the ANC is indicative of this. However, apartheid has left in its wake a deep sense of mistrust of any affirmation of 'cultural difference'. If South Africa is to institutionalize its new and fragile democracy, it will have to come to terms with the implications of democratic demands for the recognition of cultural difference, just as it will have to deepen the institutional practices which may sustain other forms of difference. This is one of the themes of Chapter 6, which deals with questions of identity and the changing politics of gender.

As a result of the nodal points around which both the NP and the ANC's discourses have been structured historically, the terrain of gender politics has been neglected in terms of its visibility in political struggle and in academic analysis. 'Identity and the Changing Politics of Gender in South Africa', contributed by Debby Bonnin, Roger Deacon, Robert Morrell and Jenny Robinson, stands as a corrective to the latter, offering an analysis of the terrain of gender politics during the period of transition, which reflects both an engagement with international debates and a response to the specific dynamics of the transition. With regard to the former, the chapter analyses the consequences of the extensive theoretical debates between 'feminists' and 'postmodernism' for gender politics in South Africa. The authors examine the implications of the critique of essentialism for feminist discourses premised upon the category of 'woman', arguing that the postmodern challenge and the post-colonial turn in theorizing have led to an investigation of previously unexplored class and racial biases in feminist discourses. The authors go on to assess the implications of this for the structuring of gender politics in the South African context, charting the emergence of the Woman's National Coalition, and showing how local feminist politics have worked creatively on the tensions between identity and difference. Widening the discussion, the chapter provides a rich survey of the changing conceptions of masculinity discernible in South Africa, giving attention both to masculinist discourse and counter-hegemonic constructions of masculinity. The final section of the chapter engages with debates on representation within academic feminist circles, giving special attention to the cross-cutting effect of race in the construction of gender identities. In conclusion, they show how the South African case exemplifies more general feminist dilemmas, and may, simultaneously, offer insights into gender politics elsewhere.

Education has consistently been at the centre of political struggle in South Africa. In Chapter 7, Roger Deacon and Ben Parker examine the assumptions of educational and developmental discourses in the early 1990s. They argue that the conditions which have obtained in this period make possible a radical rethinking of the nature of the political and educational struggle, and of the relations between education, development and democracy. Drawing attention to the common presuppositions of the apartheid state and the Government of National Unity's views on education – their firm belief, for example, in Enlightenment values – they argue that a postmodern sensitivity may facilitate a reconceptualization of South Africa's recent educational history in a manner which does not stand aloof from the paradoxes of identity and difference. In particular, their chapter investigates education policy research from 1991–94, including the NP's Education Renewal Strategy, the ANC's Policy Framework for Education and Training which drew on earlier initiatives, most notably the National Policy Investigation, and proposals by the Congress of South African Trade Unions (Cosatu), the South African Institute for Distance Education (SAIDE), and the Union of Democratic University Staff Associations (UDUSA). The authors argue that the education programme constructed in post-apartheid South Africa, framed as it is within the transition from confrontation to negotiation, whilst being more democratic and open, is no less *dirigiste* than education policy under apartheid, subservient as it is to the nation-building programme. In this respect, the analysis focuses specifically on the extent to which this programme ignores, and so reinforces, deep spatio-temporal inequalities and divisions, exemplified in the exclusion of rural people and rural issues from the negotiation of the new order.

Chapter 8 investigates the 'fruits of modernity' from the perspective of the relation between law, power and paternalism on wine farms in the Western Cape. These, Andries du Toit shows, have been left almost unchanged by the process of transition; low wages, poor working conditions, poor housing and a disregard for basic human rights are, thus, still prevalent. He argues that the process of rural change has to be understood as political. In other words, changes are not to be seen as the result of any modernization teleology, but of discontinuity, contingency and social conflict. The chapter is structured around an analysis of four organizing frameworks of social and labour relations in the Western Cape, all of which constitute particular sites of struggle. They are the white moral economy of racial paternalism; the subaltern spaces of the 'black underground'; the changing technologies of production and 'human resource management'; and the regulatory machinery of the law, and discourses of rights and entitlement centred on the new Constitution. Whilst new areas of struggle have been opened up in the course of the transition, du Toit argues that it is necessary to be aware of the ways in which formally non-racial discourses of administration, and the seemingly neutral languages of 'governance' can perpetuate and excuse from challenge 'the racialized and gendered hierarchies of power and privilege bequeathed by apartheid'.

In Chapter 9, Mark Devenney argues that post-apartheid literature challenges discourses of nationhood implied in the national liberation struggle. A literature beyond nationalism, he argues, finds itself potentially in tension with the project of nation-building, and will inevitably move beyond the image of a reconciled nation. He explores this tension via a discussion of Mandla Langa's short story, 'The Naked Song', Nadine Gordimer's *A Sport of Nature* and J. M. Coetzee's *Age of Iron*. Drawing on Adorno and Roman Jakobson's work, Devenney analyses the complex relationship between literary forms of representation and reality, concluding that literature is not just about an attempt to represent and offer support to a political struggle. Rather, he suggests, a literature proper to a democratic South Africa is, and ought to be, one which begins to explore genres beyond politics, and in so doing thematizes the politics of language itself. In this respect, post-apartheid literature begins to question the easy certainties of opposition. The uncertain language of literature may begin to explore the tensions, sedimentations and indeed repressions constitutive of the national democratic imaginary. But the end of this exploration should in no way be limited by the borderlines and frontiers established in political struggle. This could mean a literature of transgression; it may even mean a literature with no interest, other than itself.

The concluding chapter of the book examines whether or not the proliferation of recent writings on democratic transition and democratization has resulted in the establishment of new theoretical paradigms for the analysis of South African politics and history. David Howarth isolates and compares five different approaches which have been put forward to explain democratic transition, and pinpoints a number of theoretical and substantive weaknesses in each of the accounts considered. He also highlights two sets of problematic assumptions concerning the relationship between social structures and political agency, and the conceptualization of democracy, democratic transition and democratization. Drawing on recent developments in post-structuralist theories of discourse, as well as new conceptions of democracy put forward by Claude Lefort and Bill Connolly, he concludes by outlining an alternative theorization of the structure/agency dichotomy, and articulating a set of theoretical criteria by which to evaluate the pressures, process and prospects for democratic consolidation. This elaboration of a more complex understanding of democracy and democratization as an incomplete process opens up the space in which many of the concerns regarding the limited nature of the transition raised in the various contributions to this book, may be articulated together. This may facilitate, both in theory and in practice, a deepening of the democratic horizon which is so crucial to the future of a post-apartheid South Africa.

NOTES

1   S. Hall, 'The local and the global: globalization and ethnicity', in A. D. King (ed.), *Culture, Globalization, and the World System*, London, 1991, p. 36.
2   For a survey of this literature, see Chapter 10.
3   See A. M. Faure and J.-M. Lane, *South Africa: Designing New Political Institutions*, London, 1996; H. Giliomee, 'Democratization in South Africa', *Political Science Quarterly*, vol. 10, no. 1, pp. 83–104; W. Van Vuuren, 'Transition politics and the prospects for democratic consolidation in South Africa', *Politikon*, vol. 22, no. 1, pp. 5–23.
4   G. Bennington, 'Derridabase', in G. Bennington and J. Derrida, *Jacques Derrida*, Chicago, 1993, p. 15.
5   It is important that there are significant differences between these positions, and much depends on how precisely they are articulated.
6   A critique of the 'either-or' structure of the race-class debate has been articulated by Deborah Posel, and later elaborated upon by Harold Wolpe. See D. Posel, 'Rethinking the "race-class debate" in South African historiography', *Social Dynamics*, vol. 9, no. 1, 1983, pp. 50–66; H. Wolpe, *Race, Class and the Apartheid State*, London, 1988.
7   See, for instance, J. Robinson, '(Dis)locating historical narrative: writing, space and gender in South African social history', *South African Historical Journal*, no. 30, 1994, pp. 144–57.
8   See J. Derrida, *Writing and Difference*, London, 1978, p. 289.
9   See M. Foucault, *Power/Knowledge: Selected Interviews and Other Writings 1972–1977*, Brighton, 1980.
10   Here our position is in full agreement with that of Etienne Balibar who argues that once one accepts that '*every social community reproduced by the functioning of institutions is imaginary*, that is to say, it is based on the projection of individual existence into the weft of a collective narrative. . . . this comes down to accepting that, under certain conditions, *only* imaginary communities are real.' E. Balibar, 'The nation form', p. 93, in E. Balibar and I. Wallerstein (eds.), *Race, Nation, Class. Ambiguous Identities*, London, 1991.
11   J. Derrida, 'Some statements and truisms about neologisms, newisms, postisms, parasitisms, and other small seismisms', in D. Carroll (ed.), *The States of 'Theory'*, Stanford, 1994, p. 64.

12   R. Rorty, *Consequences of Pragmatism*, New York, 1982, pp. 166–9.
13   M. Foucault, 'The order of discourse', pp. 48–78, in R. Young (ed.), *Untying the Text: A Post-Structuralist Reader*, Boston, 1981.
14   N. Richard, 'Postmodernism and periphery', *Third Text*, vol. 2, 1987–88, p. 11.
15   See W. E. Connolly, *Identity\Difference: Democratic Negotiations of Political Paradox*, Ithaca, 1991; W. E. Connolly, *The Ethos of Pluralization*, Minneapolis, 1995.

1 The Dying Days of Apartheid
Rupert Taylor and Mark Shaw

As the negotiations to establish a new constitutional order in South Africa were underway during the period 1990 to 1994, over 16 000 people were to lose their lives in violence which centred on KwaZulu-Natal and the Reef.[1] In fact, in the transition period the violence claimed far more lives than did the fight against apartheid itself. Moreover, much of this violence was not directed against the state but took myriad forms; with people, overwhelmingly those whom apartheid designated 'black', being killed day and night in their homes, in trains and taxis, at work, on the street, during attendance at political rallies or funeral vigils, or whilst drinking in beer-halls. And the list of causes has been seen to be long. As one analyst has argued, the violence should be traced to the 'presence of hostels, SDUs (Self Defence Units), proliferation of illegal arms, unrealistic political demands, "no-go" areas and political intolerance, economic competition between rival politicized taxi organizations, traditional hierarchical structures (chiefs), conflicts over control of land specifically tribal land, presence of "warlords/ strongmen" in informal settlements, embittered and frustrated Afrikaners etc.'[2]

Generally, when social scientific attention has been directed to the violence it has been viewed as a transitional phenomenon, as the violent convulsions of the apartheid state in decline, as something which is only to be expected in a rapidly changing society and the absence of clearly defined political rules.[3] A reading which has also been taken up by National Party (NP) leaders, security force personnel, and state-sponsored social research. Thus, at the height of the violence in September 1991, Hernus Kriel, the then Minister of Law and Order, stated: 'We are in a period of change in our country, of political change, of constitutional change. And history has taught us that whenever something like that happens in a country, it is always accompanied by some sort of instability.'[4]

Beyond this, though, most attempts at social scientific explanation have become overwhelmed by the general confusion and purposelessness which seemed to characterize the violence, and end up taking refuge in arguing that the violence cannot be reduced to simplistic formulations, that there are 'many truths', that the violence is best understood as multi-faceted and multi-causal.[5] Such accounts often uncritically mix in elements of it being an African National Congress (ANC)/Inkatha struggle for political control, driven by the dynamics of 'black-on-black' ethnic or 'tribal' conflict.[6]

13

And, it must be added, this is a state of understanding which the media have done much to assist. For, instead of attempting to unravel the whole picture, the focus of reporting has been event-orientated, dramatic and personalized. In place of in-depth investigative reporting the mainstream media have on the whole simply assigned racial explanations to the violence.[7]

The confusion in understanding the violence has also not been helped by the difficulty in identifying the political affiliations of aggressors and victims. In the first place, there are wildly divergent findings on identifying aggressors; whilst the South African Institute of Race Relations claimed that it found it possible to identify the agent of attack in only 13 per cent of incidents, another research organization – the Community Agency for Social Enquiry (CASE) – found it possible to attribute aggressors in 43 per cent of cases, while a prominent monitoring agency, the Human Rights Commission (HRC), arrived at a figure of just under 90 per cent.[8] And secondly, most of the dead have been found to be ordinary members of the community, which leaves much doubt as to the reasons for attack.

Not surprisingly then, as du Toit has noted, there has been a failure to make serious sense of the 'functions and significance of continuing violence . . . [and] both the larger context and the specific sense of much of this political violence remains unclear'.[9] Does the violence, however, really defy understanding?

IMPLICATING THE APARTHEID STATE

Even the most cursory examination of the statistics on where the violence has occurred points to how, at a social structural level, apartheid is implicated. In KwaZulu-Natal the vast majority of the fatalities have occurred on the former border area of where the KwaZulu Bantustan met Natal Province, particularly on the margins of the Pietermaritzburg-Durban industrial corridor where one finds densely populated informal settlements, whose very existence must be traced to how apartheid policies – through placing restrictions on freedom of movement and access to residence and employment – blocked normal processes of urbanization.[10] And on the Reef most deaths have been centred around over-crowded single-sex hostels for African migrant workers and neighbouring squatter camps, again both the outcome of apartheid designs.[11] It is no coincidence that the conflict has occurred in these particular places, for it is here that apartheid social engineering has produced the most appalling living conditions, where there is massive impoverishment, and where people have been made most vulnerable to those around them.

It is insufficient, however, merely to focus on the material inequalities and social divisions generated by apartheid. An additional step has to be taken. What needs to be taken into account is 'the evidence that apartheid [has] actually used violence to sustain itself',[12] to recognize, as one commentator has remarked that: 'It is as easy to murder a political figure in South Africa as to buy an ice cream.'[13] It has to be asked: To what extent can the violence be interpreted as a natural continuation of apartheid violence? To what extent can the violence be firmly linked to the political will of the state?

Apartheid was a system of brutality maintained by force and terror. A racialized authoritarian order, by necessity, requires the use of violent coercion, with security forces serving the state rather than the law, and willing to employ maximum force as a first resort – as witnessed in the murder and torture of political detainees, and infamous massacres such as Sharpeville (1960) and Uitenhage (1985). The security of the apartheid state *was* maintained through a system of draconian legislation and an increasingly militarized structure of control.[14] In the mid-1980s, in response to increasing pressure from township uprisings, the apartheid state imposed a State of Emergency and set up a lattice of structures, a National Management System (NMS), to bolster the security of 'white' rule. These were co-ordinated at national level through the State Security Council (SSC), which was supported by a largely military secretariat. The SSC included many, like F. W. de Klerk and Roelf Meyer, who would later be involved in negotiations.

Thus, throughout the apartheid years, violence was strategically used to enforce and uphold 'white' domination. It would not be surprising then to expect violence to *continue* to be used to the advantage of the minority when the future of the country's power structures was being negotiated. Certainly, it would be unwise to simply dissociate state strategy under de Klerk from the use of violence by the security forces.

Leading commentators, however, have preferred to read 2 February 1990 as marking a fundamental and miraculous break with the past in which the security establishment was sidelined, such that any 'alleged' state-sponsored violence after this date was really due to the military, police and intelligence officers being 'out of control', operating on their own initiative in terms of the hard-line practices of the P. W. Botha era. Thus, Adam and Moodley in their 1993 book *The Negotiated Revolution* maintained that some of the violence can be traced to the fact that, 'the hard-line ideologues had acquired a life of their own, long after the state ideology had fundamentally changed'.[15] An argument supported by the fact that the SSC and NMS were dismantled and replaced by a civil system, the National Co-ordinating

Mechanism. Moreover, at this time the Cabinet was restored to its constitutional role as the highest decision-making body in the land.

Here, however, the real problem is that social scientists have not undertaken a very rigorous investigation of the political will of the state in relation to its complicity in the violence. A situation which can be attributed to the constraints on social research into the 'art of war', the standing given to carefully worded official statements and denials (such as 'the information was never in my office'), and South Africa's narrow public realm.[16] The issue has also been clouded by different definitions of what constitutes illegal operations or what has been termed 'third force' activity; of who is the 'third force'? Is it parts of the state security establishment? Elements within the liberation movements? Far-right extremists? Also, in the early 1990s, attempts to directly link the state to the violence were dismissed by many due to the lack of incontrovertible evidence; a position upheld by various publications of the South African Institute of Race Relations, and by the Goldstone Commission – a judicial body established in September 1991 to investigate the causes of the conflict – which argued until as late as mid-1992 that there was 'no evidence of any direct [state] complicity'.[17]

To date, the few sustained attempts to make a case for state complicity have been guided by setting aggregated data on numbers killed through political violence against key political events in the transition process. In the words of one such approach: 'There is, arguably, a dramatic rise when reports of bloodshed would cause the maximum harm to the opposition and an equally dramatic drop when the image of the state, or of President de Klerk or of other symbols or figures, would otherwise be harmed.'[18] Both the Johannesburg-based CASE and the HRC have attempted such a correlation, showing, for instance, that violence is high at certain political points. Such findings, however, have been easily disputed. Why is it that some events – like the opening of Parliament or a national hunger strike by political prisoners – and not others are chosen? Nor is it adequately argued why violence should be low at some events – like the ANC/Inkatha Freedom Party (IFP) Peace Accord in February 1991 – and high at others, and how this works to benefit any party.[19] Moreover, others have shown that the pattern of massacres does not correlate with key political events.[20] So far, it has been assumed that in order to make an argument for state complicity there *need* be this specific political pattern to the violence. It should be recognized though that this need not be so, that an argument for state complicity *can* be made from the seeming unpredictable nature of the violence, whereby randomness may in fact be seen as being part of the strategy. In order to move towards unravelling this, focus must first be directed to determining the political will of the state.

STRATEGIC THINKING

Any serious explanation of the violence must place it in the context of state strategy. F. W. de Klerk assumed office in late 1989 and unbanned the ANC in February 1990, paving the way for negotiations on democratic reform. But de Klerk did not come to power and recognize the ANC without having what was seen as a 'winning' game plan. In the words of former police operative Dirk Coetzee: 'They [the NP] did not unban the ANC without deciding that they would be able to steer the course.'[21] And here the independence of Namibia in 1989 was of critical import as an example of what could be achieved. In line with a twin-track negotiations and destabilization strategy which had first been spelt out in a secret National Intelligence Service document drafted in 1988, South African securocrats covertly sought to bolster the Democratic Turnhalle Alliance, a collection of moderate to conservative parties, to prevent a landslide South West African People's Organization (SWAPO) victory, which would have allowed the liberation movement to write the new constitution. A multi-million rand campaign under General Kat Liebenberg reduced the SWAPO vote down from an estimated 70–80 per cent to 60 per cent.[22]

To adopt this approach in the South African context meant widening the NP's support base and moving to lock the ANC into a compromise agreement centred on compulsory power-sharing as opposed to majority rule, while undermining and attacking it through covert means. Thus, on one track, the NP was out to capture the entire centre-right of the political spectrum, to become the prime mover of a 'moderate' Christian democratic electoral alliance that could potentially – at some future date – achieve majority support through the ballot box. And on the other track, the military, far from being sidelined, were to remain an important and committed component of state strategy. A high-level and secret Cabinet agreement at the beginning phase of negotiations had predicted a period of instability during negotiations requiring the military to be the 'stable core' around which change would revolve, so as to ensure 'reform with security'.[23] In fact, the new National Co-ordinating Mechanism was little different to the NMS in terms of recognizing the import of the security establishment, and covert security force projects which were undertaken on a 'need to know' basis – labelled in the *'broad national interest'* – continued,[24] with the National Intelligence Service being used as de Klerk's 'personal instrument for conducting confidential presidential initiatives'.[25] Mirroring the work of Military Intelligence in Angola and Mozambique, surrogate forces were to be encouraged, so as to obscure state involvement.

Much of the basis for state strategy had in fact been laid in the years prior to 1990, when the state's thinking first came to be informed by the need to build up 'a strong force of the political middle-ground', by *consolidating* 'in-system actors' who included the whole panoply of parliamentary and Bantustan parties and *destabilizing* 'out-system actors' which included both banned and opposition political groupings.[26] This entailed the 're-moval' of anti-apartheid activists by police hit squads specifically designated for this task,[27] and the use of surrogate forces to promote violence.[28] The most significant 'in-system' ally at this time, as in 1990, was Inkatha, which under the leadership of Chief Mangosuthu Buthelezi had, through the successful mobilization of a specific Zulu ethnic identity, built up a claimed membership of over one million. As General Tienie Groenewald, then Chief Director of Military Intelligence, later admitted; 'I thought . . . at the time that it was imperative to boost organizations like the IFP if we were to have a multiparty system.'[29] To this end, in the mid-1980s the State Security Council, under the guidance of many who had co-ordinated Renamo's actions in Mozambique – including ex-SADF Chief and Cabinet Minister General Magnus Malan – took a decision, code-named Operation Marion, to set up a paramilitary unit to ensure that Inkatha could 'deal with' the growing threat from the ANC in KwaZulu-Natal, where political violence had begun in 1986. Later revelations, first uncovered by the *Weekly Mail*, showed that in 1986 the South African Defence Force (SADF) had trained some 200 Inkatha members for this purpose on the Caprivi Strip in then South West Africa.[30]

The logic of this strategy was also bolstered by survey data at the time; a March 1989 opinion poll found that then state President P. W. Botha and F. W. de Klerk were second in popularity (22 per cent) to the jailed Nelson Mandela (41 per cent) amongst urban African people. Accordingly, Giliomee and Schlemmer in their influential 1989 book *From Apartheid to Nation-Building*, argued that 'the idea of the NP as the core of a substantial multi-racial conservative alliance may not be far-fetched'.[31]

MAKING THE LINKS

The evidence clearly indicated that the apartheid state did continue to use violence from 1990 to protect itself. After 2 February 1990 sinister events still kept happening, covert activities intensified rather than declined after the negotiation phase had begun. Classic destabilization tactics, in line with the principles of 'low-intensity warfare' where the intent is to neutralize the opposition through killing off radical activists, sabotaging organizational attempts to build a support base, and generally creating a climate in which violence becomes self-perpetuating and preys on people, oblivious to either their guilt or innocence, can be detected.[32] And this is most clearly shown by disaggregating the pattern of deaths through violence, in relation to hit squads, train attacks and massacres, as in Figure 1.1.

Figure 1.1   The Pattern of Deaths, 1990–94

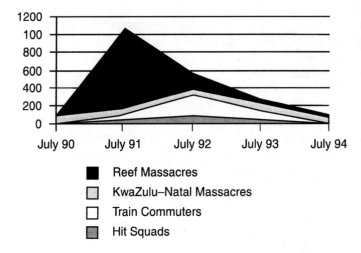

Reef Massacres
KwaZulu–Natal Massacres
Train Commuters
Hit Squads

Source: adapted from data in Human Rights Commission Reports.

It emerges that hit squad activity increased dramatically from 17 incidents leading to 17 deaths in 1990, to 56 incidents leading to 45 deaths in 1991. In fact, over January 1990 to April 1992, the HRC identified 119 people who were killed in political assassinations, and 'over 100 of these victims are clearly identifiable as belonging to the anti-apartheid camp', most occupying middle-level leadership positions.[33] Also, in the period 1990–92 around 300 people were killed in train attacks, the most notorious incident being the massacre of 26 people on a Soweto-bound train on 13 September 1990.[34] Altogether, in the two years from July 1990, there were 49 reported massacres (in which ten or more people were killed) resulting in 1250 deaths. The major massacres include: the 'Seven Days War' in the Pietermaritzburg region in March 1990; an attack on Phola Park squatter camp in August 1990; the attack on Sebokeng hostel in September 1990, when 42 people were killed; an attack on Swanieville squatter camp on 12 May 1991 which saw at least 27 people killed; fighting in Bruntville on 3–4

December 1991 in which at least 18 people were killed; and the attack centred on Boipatong's squatter area, Slovo Park, on 17 June 1992, in which 49 people were killed.

Detailed analysis of massacres reveals two main characteristics. Inkatha emerges as the most visible aggressor, and the choice of victims appears to be random, with two-thirds of victims being elderly people, women and children.[35] To a large extent, both these patterns can be explained in terms of the political will of the apartheid state.

That Inkatha members, supporters or vigilante elements were, according to the HRC, responsible for 34 of the 49 massacres reported over the two years since July 1990, with township residents/ANC supporters only being implicated in six cases, has to be put in the context of Inkatha's bid to build political hegemony through aggressive recruitment campaigns, and must be seen as confirmation of Inkatha's 'surrogate' role,[36] of the state's continuing covert support for Inkatha and for the KwaZulu Police (KZP) in the way of collusion in military training, the supplying of arms and in general logistics. Substantial evidence has emerged that the KZP had, in recent years, been supplied with weapons by senior-level members of the South African Police (SAP), and has operated a system of hit squads, comprising some of those secretly trained at Caprivi, to eliminate political figures in the ANC.[37] On the Reef, a similar pattern of complicity existed. As a security policeman has disclosed, 'On a number of occasions I was instructed by my superiors to deliver certain arms and ammunition to the IFP in Alexandra. This included shotguns, handguns and handgrenades.'[38] A SAP covert unit, C10, under the command of Colonel Eugene de Kock and operating from Vlakplaas outside of Pretoria, was engaged in propagating train and hostel violence and the manufacture of 'home-made' weapons for the IFP.[39] State support for Inkatha was most firmly demonstrated by 'Inkathagate', when in July 1991 a number of SAP Security Branch documents were leaked to the *Weekly Mail*, revealing that the police, through Colonel Louis Botha, paid over R250 000 to help Inkatha, as late as March 1990, counter the ANC. De Klerk claimed that he did not know of this, but was forced to move both Malan and Vlok from their ministerial positions.

That analysis of massacres has found it possible to readily determine the political identity of victims in only 19 of the 49 massacres (with ANC supporters targeted in ten cases, and Inkatha supporters in nine), and that many of the dead have been women and children must be seen to represent a calculated pattern of terror, where the very randomness of terror is part of overall strategy.[40] The promotion of massacres is a classic destabilization tactic. The point is that randomness serves a political agenda: for tactically, the random choice of victims works to camouflage the source of violence and '[b]y attacking individuals at random within a community known to support a particular organization, a form of collective punishment is imposed and people are terrorized into avoiding any support or contact with that which brings them such misery'.[41]

Likewise, the political assassinations undertaken by hit squads are calculated to terrorize opposition figures. As secret tapes have revealed, security police lectures given by Colonel Johan Putter in mid-1990 included the point that assassination techniques were sanctioned by then Minister of Law and Order, Adriaan Vlok. Putter stressed that Vlok had said: 'I support you in these things but you must know I will be committing political suicide if they come to light.'[42] And beyond this, a wide range of covert operations and projects were employed by the SADF's Military Intelligence and Special Forces. Military Intelligence sought to infiltrate ANC structures and criminally compromise MK(Umkhonto we Sizwe) members using a convicted murderer, drug dealers and prostitutes, and what was known as Project Echoes attempted to discredit the ANC by exposing links with the Irish Republican Army.[43] In addition, covert operations were conducted in the 'independent' Bantustans. In Ciskei, Military Intelligence, through a front organization IR–CIS (International Researchers – Ciskei Intelligence Service), which was set up six months after the unbanning of the ANC, worked to successfully 'turn' Brigadier Oupa Gqozo against the ANC, and was allegedly involved in a November 1990 failed coup attempt in Transkei.[44] Criminal gangs have also been secretly sponsored. At the beginning of 1992 three former members of a gang called the 'Black Cats', which operated in Wesselton, admitted that they had been recruited by Inkatha and given paramilitary training through a front company controlled by Military Intelligence.[45] And then there is evidence that members of SADF Special Forces participated in massacres, such as the use of 'black' troops in the 13 September 1990 attack on a Soweto-bound train in which 26 people were killed. As one informant has revealed: 'They got on the train with pangas and AK-47s, and they used the name of Inkatha. . . .They say they were not allowed to speak during that attack because most the people were Namibian and could not speak Zulu.'[46] In this context, it is worth recalling that over 1982–88 almost 500 railway workers and passengers were killed by Renamo attacks in Mozambique.[47]

The findings of various human rights reports also confirms a pattern of co-ordinated state complicity in the violence, and amounts to a chilling picture of the role of the security forces during this two-year period.[48] Time after time it emerges that the SAP, SADF and KZP consistently 'intervened or failed to intervene on a selective basis'. In KwaZulu-Natal and on the

Reef, the security forces transported, escorted and joined Inkatha offences or remained inactive during Inkatha attacks – failing to disarm the protagonists, often with the excuse that Inkatha weapons were 'cultural' or that the security forces were 'waiting for orders'. Details of individual cases in which the KZP have assaulted, murdered and tortured people were put together in 1992 by the Legal Resources Centre and HRC in Durban; their 212-page volume is a staggering indictment of the conduct of the KZP.[49] And in 1993, the Wallis Sub-Committee of the Goldstone Commission heard evidence from police officers based on the KwaZulu-Natal south coast who conceded that their role had been to support Inkatha to the detriment of the ANC.[50]

The criminal justice system continued to be manipulated by the state. Police turned a blind-eye to rigorous investigation of much of the violence; they failed to take reports placed before them seriously; they ignored or deliberately distorted or destroyed evidence; and they failed to take statements from, or to protect, key witnesses. Consider the following facts. After the Sebokeng massacre of September 1990, a judicial inquiry under Judge Stafford recommended that SADF members be prosecuted, but no action was taken. After the Swanieville massacre of 12 May 1991 only seven of some 1000 attackers were brought to trial, and subsequently acquitted. And of 172 people initially arrested by the police after the Bruntville massacre of 3–4 December 1991, none was charged. Moreover, the first conviction relating to train massacres did not come until February 1993.

There have also been clear attempts to cover up state complicity. An *Africa Watch* report, for example, found that 'it is evident that when the KwaZulu Police are being investigated, even high ranking officers allegedly resort to cover-ups to protect the police'.[51] One of the most sinister cover-ups took place in the case of the Boipatong massacre. A routine tape recording of police radio communication and telephone messages in the Internal Stability Unit's control room in Vereeniging on the night of the massacre was found to have been recorded over. While the SAP claimed that it was a mistake, British experts differed: '[t]he technical evidence suggests that this may have been done deliberately and hurriedly to obscure the contents. It is not possible to recover the original data.' Furthermore it was found that the material recorded over the original messages was at a different speed than would have been standard and some recorded backwards.[52] An outside investigation, conducted by Dr Peter Waddington from the University of Reading, into police reaction to, and investigation of, the Boipatong massacre found a number of other irregularities and slated the SAP for its poor efforts in attempting to resolve the case.[53]

THE TURNING-POINT

The Boipatong massacre led the ANC to suspend negotiations with the government. Increasingly the ANC had begun to realize that the violence was a direct result of the state's political agenda. Indeed, in 1992, Mandela, at the United Nations building in New York, openly labelled Inkatha a 'surrogate' of the government. Even before the Boipatong massacre, state strategy was crumbling under the weight of the failure, in late May 1992, to reach agreement on constitutional issues in CODESA II, where the NP and ANC became deadlocked over the percentage thresholds required to change constitutional provisions.[54] Taken together with other revelations about involvement in violence, mass action by the ANC, the poor results of IFP recruitment drives, and opinion-poll data pointing to the approval ratings for de Klerk amongst metropolitan 'black' people falling from 60 per cent in August 1991 to 27 per cent in September 1992,[55] the state's game plan was becoming self-defeating and there had to be a rethink of strategic options.

Against this background, a number of Cabinet ministers, including Roelf Meyer and Pik Botha, favoured a realignment of political forces and successfully pushed for a loosening of the NP's alignment with the IFP and accommodation with the ANC. Once this shift to advancing transition through genuine transaction with the ANC was made[56] – and which can be dated from the September 1992 Record of Understanding between the NP and ANC – de Klerk moved to rein in the security forces, with prominent securocrats reluctant to go along with the new line being retired or forced out from state security agencies.

From late 1992 new developments ensued; in August, 18 SAP generals were retired as, according to official statements, part of a rationalization process; October saw the end of destabilization tactics in Mozambique; November witnessed the start of negotiations over the future of the military at Defence Headquarters; and on 12 March 1993 the National Intelligence Service (NIS) briefed the ANC on how it functioned. In the second half of 1992 the Goldstone Commission was given wider scope for its investigations, and on 11 November 1992, in a raid on a Military Intelligence front company office in Pretoria, unearthed hundreds of incriminating files relating to state complicity in the violence. De Klerk asked SADF Chief of Staff, General Pierre Steyn, to investigate this matter, and all intelligence functions of the SADF. The outcome of Steyn's inquiry was never made public; while questions have been raised about the whereabouts of any written documentation on the matter, the general has claimed that he only reported verbally to de Klerk.[57] In any event, in December 1992, seven

SADF senior officers were placed on compulsory leave and 16 others (including two generals and four brigadiers) placed on compulsory retirement, with substantial severance packages, for 'unauthorized activities' linked to political violence which had led to killings.

As funding and support for covert projects was withdrawn, the violence that continued no longer had official sanction. Correspondingly, from the end of 1992 there was, as Figure 1.1 shows, a marked decline in some forms of violence. Hit squad activity, train attacks and the number of massacres on the Reef tail off dramatically from this time on. Hit squad activity virtually dropped off completely from the end of 1992. The number of train attacks declined from 63 in 1992, to 18 in 1993.[58] The numbers killed in massacres on the Reef started falling markedly from August 1993. In KwaZulu-Natal, however, where Inkatha continued to try and assert hegemonic control, the violence continued, with KZP hit squads remaining active.[59] And as the April 1994 election approached, anti-election elements in Inkatha and on the extreme Right produced an upsurge of violence. In the four-week period, 16 March to 15 April, 429 people were killed. But once Inkatha announced, on 19 April, that it would contest the election, the deaths subsided and only seven people were killed in political violence over the election days.[60] Violence, however, did not stop with the birth of the new democratic state. In the two years following the election over 500 people were killed in KwaZulu-Natal. Although the KZP has been incorporated into the new South African Police Service, incidents of police complicity continue, and right-wing cells in the police and military are still alleged to exist. And although state-sponsored covert operations were ordered to terminate, some did continue without authorization, especially those driven by the financial gains of gun-running.

By the end of 1995, however, the wheel had come full circle. Following extensive work by an investigative unit, appointed by the new Minister of Safety and Security, Sydney Mufamadi, to inquire into hit squad activity in KwaZulu-Natal, on 26 October 1995 the attorney-general for KwaZulu-Natal moved to indict those suspected of being responsible for an attack on a homestead at KwaMakhutha on 21 January 1987 which led to the death of 13 unarmed people, six of whom were aged ten or under.[61] Not only are the seven operatives who allegedly carried out the killings being prosecuted, but also those senior security force figures who allegedly sponsored this hit squad through Operation Marion, including General Malan, General Groenewald and General Liebenberg: all of whom, as we have seen, were intimately linked to the wider formulation and implementation of state strategy. The reaction from NP and right-wing politicians has been vocal, and the prosecutions have shaken the security establishment.

CONCLUSION

The above analysis points to a clear conclusion. Simply to see the violence as a 'necessary consequence' of the collapse of apartheid or as too multi-faceted and multi-causal to be readily understood is to mask what is in reality the central issue: the role of the apartheid state. In particular, it needs to be fully recognized that 1990 is less of a turning-point than is often assumed, that it does not make sense to talk about the 'end' of apartheid violence until late 1992 when there was a clear switch to NP/ANC pacting, that in the early 1990s South Africa was – in the words of Breyten Breytenbach – 'living through the planned horrors of the apartheid state in its death throes'.[62] The evidence continues to mount that covert operations were formulated at top level until late 1992 as an essential part of the state's reform strategy to build support around a 'moderate' coalition, at the core of which was the National Party.

In this context, the argument, as advanced by the Director of the South African Institute of Race Relations, that the violence is a result of 'Black people [becoming] victims of the *struggle against* apartheid', is totally perverse.[63] And the more balanced argument that violence assumed 'a life of its own' in the post-1990 political environment is far too weak. Explanations which seek to show that state involvement is the result of 'bad apples' or 'incompetent' individuals within the security establishment fail to link events into an overall strategy and ignore the hierarchical and structured nature of security force operations.[64] Similarly, to argue, as Brewer has, that SAP complicity in the violence was a result of the force's 'relative autonomy rather than Machiavellian manipulation by the government' is unconvincing.[65] If this was the case, which even de Klerk never argued, the government would presumably have been far more supportive of mechanisms to investigate police abuse and uphold the rule of law.

Furthermore, in this context, it is evident that social scientific accounts of South Africa's transition to democracy suffer from a failure to morally confront the evil of apartheid. The democratization literature, guided by talk of South Africa's 'miracle' and the imperatives of comparative political analysis, gives only passing attention to the violence which is seen simply as a result of political change and not intrinsically connected to the apartheid state. Studies of South Africa's democratization published in such journals as *Politics & Society* and the *Political Science Quarterly*, fail to grasp that in comparative perspective South Africa has actually been through a 'war' situation, and consign the number of deaths to their footnotes.[66] The violence must be firmly placed in the context of the inhumanity of apartheid, for it is the criminal nature of the apartheid state that is primarily responsible for the violence. A criminal state being, as Jaspers has argued, 'one which in principle neither establishes nor acknowledges the rule of law'.[67] After all, the apartheid system was, as decreed by the United Nations, 'a crime against humanity', violating key prescriptions of the Universal Declaration of Human Rights and the International Covenants on Human Rights.[68] It is not only that the dynamics of the violence are related to past policies and practices of the apartheid state which, whilst not designed to kill people off, in fact have, but also to the way in which the apartheid state has, disregarding even the rule of apartheid law, killed people through covert operations that have included assassinations and massacres. It will probably never be known just how many deaths can be directly traced to state strategy, especially given the deliberate moves to cover tracks and suppress the truth. Some 135 000 security files have been destroyed in recent years.[69] What is clear, however, is that given the right leadership the state could have acted to bring the violence under control.

In the new democratic state, a serious effort has to be made to end the continuing violence, establish the rule of law, and come to terms with the past. The trial of General Malan and others, and the recently constituted Truth and Reconciliation Commission, are clearly steps in this direction. But as the chain of command for state-sponsored violence went right to the top, and as much of the security establishment is still in the hands of those who diligently served the apartheid state and want to simply forget the past, South Africa faces a tough challenge in developing a normative framework for dealing with former human rights derogations.[70] How will South Africa work to instil and build respect for the rule of law without undermining the consolidation of democracy and political stability? The road ahead is not an easy one.

NOTES

1   The authors are grateful for the comments of: Juha Auvinen, Jacklyn Cock, George Ellis, Adrian Guelke, Jens Meierhenrich, Chris Rootes, Greg Ruiters and Elke Zuern.

2   A. Minnaar, 'The impact of political violence since 1990 on the transition to democracy in South Africa', paper presented to XVIth International Political Science Association World Congress, Berlin, Germany, 22–25 August 1994, p. 25.

3   See, for example, T. Sisk, *Democratization in South Africa: The Elusive Search for Peace*, Princeton, 1995; C. Jung and I. Shapiro, 'South Africa's negotiated transition: democracy, opposition, and the new constitutional order', *Politics & Society*, vol. 23, no. 3, 1995, pp. 269–308.

4   Hernus Kriel, quoted in *Natal Witness*, 'Kriel aims for more credible SAP', 31 September 1991. Also see A. Truluck, *No Blood on Our Hands: Political Violence in the Natal Midlands 1987–mid-1992, and the Role of the State, 'White' Political Parties and Business*, Natal Midlands Region of the Black Sash, 1992.

5   See, for example, A. Minnaar, 'Political violence in South Africa', *Journal of Theoretical Politics*, vol. 6, no. 3, 1994, pp. 389–99; M. Murray, *The Revolution Deferred*, London, 1994, chapter 5.

6   See, for example, M. Esman, *Ethnic Politics*, Ithaca and London, 1994, chapter 4.

7   Consider, for example, J. E. Fair and R. J. Astroff, 'Constructing race and violence: US news coverage and the signifying practices of apartheid', *Journal of Communication*, vol. 41, no. 4, pp. 58–74.

8   A. J. Jeffery, 'Spotlight on disinformation about violence in South Africa', South African Institute of Race Relations, *Spotlight*, no. 8, 1992; D. Everatt, 'Who is murdering the peace?', Community Agency for Social Enquiry, Johannesburg, 1991; Human Rights Commission, *HRC Special Briefing on Massacres*, Johannesburg, 1992.

9   A. du Toit, 'Understanding South African Political Violence: A New Problematic?', Discussion Paper (DP43), United Nations Research Institute for Social Development, Geneva, 1993, p. 6.

10 For further discussion, see R. Taylor and M. Shaw, 'The Natal conflict', in J. D. Brewer (ed.), *Restructuring South Africa*, London, 1994, pp. 35–52.

11 See, R. Taylor, 'The myth of ethnic division: township conflict on the Reef', *Race & Class*, vol. 33, no. 2, 1991, pp. 1–14.

12 M. E. Bennun, 'Boipatong and after: reflections on the politics of violence in South Africa', *International Journal of the Sociology of Law*, vol. 21, no. 1, 1993, p. 56.

13 P. Trewhela, 'Within the secret state: the Directorate of Military Intelligence', *Searchlight South Africa*, no. 8, 1992, p. 19.

14 International Commission of Jurists, G. Bindman (ed.), *South Africa: Human Rights and the Rule of Law*, London, 1988; K. Grundy, *The Militarization of South African Politics*, London, 1986.

15 H. Adam and K. Moodley, *The Negotiated Revolution*, Johannesburg, 1993, p.126. Also see, A. Sparks, *Tomorrow is Another Country: The Inside Story of South Africa's Negotiated Revolution*, Johannesburg, 1994, pp. 157–8; and Murray, *The Revolution Deferred*, pp. 87–9.

16 British journalist, John Carlin wrote that having detected a hidden hand in the violence, he felt 'among white South Africans' like a lunatic 'screaming in the wilderness'; see, 'Farewell to a beloved country', *Sunday Times* (Johannesburg), 19 January 1995.

17 Jeffery, 'Spotlight on disinformation'; J. Kane-Berman, *Political Violence in South Africa*, South African Institute of Race Relations, Johannesburg, 1993; P. Pereira, 'The weight of no evidence', South African Institute of Race Relations, Johannesburg, 1993. And see, for example, Goldstone Commission, *Second Interim Report to the State President*, 29 April 1992.

18 Bennun, 'Boipatong and after', p. 62. Also see, D. Everatt and S. Sadek, 'The Reef violence: tribal war or total strategy?', Community Agency for

Social Enquiry, Johannesburg 1992, p. 3; G. Ellis, ' "Third force": what is the weight of evidence?', South African Institute of Race Relations, Cape Western Region, Regional Topic Paper, no. 1, 1993; and Sisk, *Democratization in South Africa*, figure 3.1, p. 118.

19   Consider, P. Pereira, 'Switching off simplistic theories of violence', *Race Relations News*, vol. 55, no. 1, 1993.

20   A. Minnaar, T. Keith and S. Pretorius, '"Caught in the crossfire": an analysis of massacres in Transvaal and Natal, 1990–1992', paper presented to the Biennial Congress of the South African Political Studies Association, University of the Orange Free State, Bloemfontein, 20–22 October 1993.

21   Dirk Coetzee, cited in Trewhela, 'Within the secret state', p. 18.

22   See, A. Minnaar, I. Liebenberg and C. Schutte (eds.), *The Hidden Hand: Covert Operations in South Africa*, Pretoria, 1994.

23   M. Shaw, 'Biting the bullet: negotiating democracy's defence', *South African Review 7*, Johannesburg 1994, pp. 228–56, and confidential interview material.

24   R. D. A. Henderson, 'South African intelligence under De Klerk', *International Journal of Intelligence and Counterintelligence*, vol. 8, no. 1, 1994, p. 60, emphasis added.

25   Henderson, 'South African intelligence', p. 56.

26   Institute for Futures Research, *Stratcon Project: Perspectives on the Political Future of South Africa*, University of Stellenbosch, 1987.

27   J. Pauw, *In the Heart of the Whore: The Story of South Africa's Death Squads*, Johannesburg, 1990; P. Laurence, *Death Squads: Apartheid's Secret Weapon*, Johannesburg, 1991.

28   J. Cole, *Crossroads: The Politics of Reform and Repression 1976–1986*, Johannesburg, 1987; M. Kentridge, *An Unofficial War: Inside the Conflict in Pietermaritzburg*, Cape Town, 1990.

29   General Groenewald, interviewed in *Mail & Guardian* (Johannesburg), 10–16 November 1995.

30   *Weekly Mail* (Johannesburg), 13–18 December 1991.

31   H. Giliomee and L. Schlemmer, *From Apartheid to Nation-Building*, Cape Town, 1989, p. 200.

32   F. Kitson, *Low Intensity Operations: Subversion, Insurgency and Counter Insurgency*, London, 1971. And see, W. Minter, *Apartheid's Contras: An Inquiry into the Roots of War in Angola and Mozambique*, London, 1994.

33   Human Rights Commission, *HRC Special Briefing on Massacres*. Less than ten killings were linked to perpetrators within liberation movements.

34   Independent Board of Inquiry, *Blood on the Tracks: A Special Report on Train Attacks*, Johannesburg, 1992.

35   Human Rights Commission, *HRC Special Briefing on Massacres*.

36   And a content analysis of media reports by CASE found that Inkatha were cited as being responsible for 190 of a total of 370 instances in which one or other organization was blamed, and the SAP in 84 instances; as against just 13 for the ANC; see, 'The violent agenda', *New Nation* (Johannesburg), 24–29 May 1991, pp. 6–7.

37   See, for example, the video, 'Death of Apartheid', episode two: 'The Third Force', produced by the British Broadcasting Corporation, 1995.

38 Sergeant Pollock quoted in *Sunday Times* (Johannesburg), 12 February 1995.

39 Goldstone Commission, *Interim Report on Criminal Political Violence by Elements within the South African Police, the KwaZulu Police and the Inkatha Freedom Party,* 18 March 1994. De Kock is currently standing trial on eight counts of murder.

40 Human Rights Commission, *The New Total Strategy,* Special Report (SR-9), Johannesburg, 1991; Human Rights Commission, *Checkmate for Apartheid?,* Special Report (SR-12), Johannesburg, 1992.

41 Bennun, 'Boipatong and after', p. 63.

42 *Sunday Times* (Johannesburg), 'Vlok is named on secret dirty tricks tape', 5 March 1995.

43 Press statement by the Honourable Mr Justice R. J. Goldstone: Chairman of the Commission of Inquiry Regarding the Prevention of Public Violence and Intimidation, November 1992.

44 See interview with Gert Hugo, former Chief Ciskei Military Intelligence, on 'Apartheid's Last Stand: The Changing Face of South Africa', video co-produced by WGBH/Boston and BBC/Panorama for Frontline, 1993.

45 Minnaar *et al., The Hidden Hand,* pp. 342–3.

46 Felix Ndimene quoted in Trewhela, 'Within the secret state', p. 15.

47 Minter, *Apartheid's Contras,* p. 192.

48 See, in particular; Africa Watch Committee, *The Killings in South Africa: The Role of the Security Forces and the Response of the State,* New York/Washington DC/London, 1991; The International Commission of Jurists, *Agenda for Peace: An Independent Survey of the Violence in South Africa,* Geneva, April 1992; Amnesty International, *South Africa, State of Siege: Security Force Complicity in Torture and Political Killings, 1990–1992,* London, June 1992; and Africa Watch, *South Africa, Half-Hearted Reform: The Official Response to the Rising Tide of Violence,* New York/Washington DC May 1993.

49 Legal Resources Centre and Human Rights Commission, *Obstacle to Peace: The Role of the KwaZulu Police in the Natal Conflict,* Durban, June 1992. The bulk of incidents recorded in this report took place in 1990 and 1991, and the KZP were found to be implicated in the death of 219 people.

50 SAP Memorandum submitted to Wallis Committee Report, Interim Report of the Wallis Sub-Committee of the Goldstone Commission, September 1993.

51 Africa Watch, *South Africa, Half-Hearted Reform,* p. 64.

52 Reports from British Embassy in Pretoria, 29 October and 2 November 1992.

53 Waddington Report, *Report of the Inquiry into the Police Response to, and Investigation of, Events in Boipatong on 17 June 1992,* 20 July 1992.

54 On Codesa II, see S. Friedman (ed.), *The Long Journey: South Africa's Quest for a Negotiated Settlement,* Johannesburg, 1993; M. Ottaway, *South Africa: The Struggle for a New Order,* Washington DC, 1993.

55 Pereira, 'The weight of no evidence', p. 3.

56 S. Huntington, 'How countries democratize', *Political Science Quarterly,* vol. 106, no. 4, 1992, pp. 579–616.

57 Shaw, 'Biting the bullet'.

58   M. Shaw and J. Miller, *Securing the Trains? An Analysis of Train Violence and the Goldstone Commission Reports*, Institute for the Study of Public Violence, 1994, p. 10.

59   *Second Interim Report of the Transitional Executive Council Investigation Task Group into the Matter of Hit Squads in the KwaZulu Police, Dated 29 March 1994*, and *Supplementary Report of the Transitional Executive Council Investigation into the Matter of Hit Squads in the KwaZulu Police, 18 May 1994*.

60   Human Rights Committee of South Africa, 'Natal's total onslaught', Johannesburg, 1 June 1994.

61   Media release issued by the Minister of Safety and Security, 29 October 1995. This attack targeted a local ANC-aligned leader, Victor Ntuli, who was not at home at the time. Ntuli was shot dead three years later.

62   Breyten Breytenbach, quoted in *Saturday Star* (Johannesburg), 4 May 1991, p. 15.

63   Kane-Berman, *Political Violence in South Africa*, p. 12, emphasis added.

64   See, for example, D. Ottaway, *Chained Together: Mandela, De Klerk, and the Struggle to Remake South Africa*, New York, 1993, p. 238.

65   J. D. Brewer, *Black and Blue: Policing in South Africa*, Oxford, 1994, p. 348.

66   G. Adler and E. Webster, 'Challenging transition theory: the labor movement, radical reform, and transition to democracy in South Africa', *Politics & Society*, vol. 23, no. 1, 1995, pp. 75–106; Jung and Shapiro, 'South Africa's negotiated transition'; H. Giliomee, 'Democratization in South Africa', *Political Science Quarterly*, vol. 110, no. 1, 1995, pp. 83–104. Contrast this with how T. R. Gurr and B. Harff in their 1994 book *Ethnic Conflict in World Politics* (Boulder) have no difficulty in classifying the violence in South Africa as 'war' alongside 17 other countries; see, pp. 160–6.

67   K. Jaspers and R. Augstein, 'The criminal state and German responsibility: a dialogue', *Commentary*, February 1966, p. 34.

68   See, M. S. McDougal, H. D. Lasswell and L. Chen, *Human Rights and World Public Order*, New Haven and London, 1980, p. 546.

69   G. Simpson and P. van Zyl, 'South Africa's Truth and Reconciliation Commission', Centre for the Study of Violence and Reconciliation, Johannesburg, 1995, p. 12, n. 11.

70   Consider, S. Cohen, 'State crimes of previous regimes: knowledge, accountability, and the policing of the past', *Law and Social Inquiry*, March 1995, pp. 7–50.

2 Changing Discourses of Democracy and Socialism in South Africa

Daryl Glaser

South Africa is today a liberal democracy – but it is not, or not yet, socialist. The relationship between democracy and socialism has long been at the centre of South African Left debates. Is democracy a stage on the road to socialism? What is socialist democracy? Can radical forms of democracy be prefigured or must they await revolution? What kind of democracy do socialists want? I shall argue that a plausible articulation of these two goods – democracy and socialism – continues to elude the South African Left.

Focusing principally on the debates of the 1980s and the 1990s, I will show how the terms on which the democracy–socialism relationship were debated in the Left shifted ground dramatically between these decades. The debates of each decade exhibit peculiar weaknesses. The central deficit of the 1980s' debates was a failure by all principal sides to take seriously political pluralism, civil liberties and formal representative democracy. In the 1990s the dominant currents of the Left appropriated 'liberal' discourses of right, civil society and electoral competition: but they have not yet found a convincing way to link their new democratic commitments to a recognizably socialist economic programme.

BEFORE THE 1970s

Democracy has always appeared in one of two personae in the scripts of the South African Left: one national liberatory, the other socialist. The central facts of white minority rule and black resistance have vested a more immediate importance in the democracy of national liberation than in the democracy of socialism: but neither, for all their salience, received detailed or consistent specification in Left analysis over the years.

The dominant Left current in South Africa this century, the Communist Party, has since its adoption of the Native Republic slogan in 1928 viewed national liberation (and hence national democracy) as a stage on the road to socialism. In the post-Second World War decades the Communists looked

31

to the African National Congress (ANC) to deliver national democracy, and Communists (though their party was banned after 1950) played a significant role in developing the ANC's understanding of this objective. At a minimum, national democracy for the Congress camp entailed an end to white minority rule and institutionalized racial discrimination. Though still distinct from socialism, national democracy was given a social-democratic edge by the Freedom Charter, adopted by the ANC-led Congress Alliance in 1955. Charter clauses implied a significant degree of redistribution and nationalization.

While explicitly 'democratic', the Freedom Charter did not propose a particular model of democracy. It proclaimed the right of all to vote and stand in elections and to protection from a range of state abuses, but it did not unambiguously support a liberal-democratic model of multi-party democracy and free political association; nor, despite its reference to 'democratic organs of self-government', did it call for a distinctively socialist democratic model of, say, workers' councils. Democracy according to the Freedom Charter would consist in government based on popular consent coupled to respect for national minorities and redress of social inequality.[1]

The other significant, though much smaller, pre-1970s Left tradition was Trotskyism. Although initially hostile to the Native Republic slogan, Trotskyists mostly came to the view that the way to socialism lay through a minimum programme of democratic demands. Like the Communists, they found their principal political outlet under a wing of black nationalism. In the 1930s and 1940s Trotskyists worked through the All Africa Convention and, later, the Non European Unity Movement (NEUM). The NEUM called for unity of the nationally oppressed against segregationist institutions and the 'collaborators' participating in them. The NEUM's 1943 Ten Point Programme spoke not of socialism but of universal franchise, equal citizenship rights, freedoms of occupation, movement, association and speech, and redistributive land reform.

The NEUM's minimum demands seemed, like the Freedom Charter, compatible with a redistributive and non-racial social democracy. Trotskyists in the NEUM did not, as such, endorse a two-stage theory of revolution. Many believed that the struggle to realize minimum democratic demands entailed, by definition, a struggle for socialism. While Communists by contrast did endorse a two-stage theory, they veered over the decades through a series of left and right turns in their depiction of the relationship between national democracy and socialism. During its left turns the Party would insist that national liberation was inseparable from socialist revolution.[2]

If the Communists' national democracy and the NEUM's democratic programme were understood within these Left currents to be harbingers of socialism, what kind of socialism would they herald? There was then, as now, no clear answer. The clues we have leave us with little reason to believe that the Communists and Trotskyists were committed to a genuinely *democratic* socialism, if by that we mean a socialism which allies social equality and grassroots participation to political pluralism, multi-party democracy and protected civil liberties. The Communists loyally followed the dictates of the Soviet Communist Party and repeatedly endorsed the anti-democratic outrages of East bloc regimes. Many admired the Soviet system as a socialist model, its Cuban variant in particular later attracting many activists. Communists tended to regard working-class leadership as synonymous with their own leading role and treated their rivals, especially on the Left, in a spirit of intolerant sectarianism. The two-stage theory of revolution thus (in effect) raised the prospect of a socialist stage of one-party dictatorship superseding, as it did in post-war Eastern Europe, the liberal-democratic gains of a first 'stage'.

Trotskyists were not much better. Though professedly anti-Stalinist they tended, as Fine trenchantly notes, to equate Stalinism with 'two-stage theory, popular fronts and capitulation to the bourgeoisie at the expense of the working class' rather than recognizing it as a specific kind of repressive practice which could veer left as well as right.[3] Far from developing a consistent critique of Stalinism's repressive features, the Trotskyists defended the Union of Soviet Socialist Republics against capitalist powers and endorsed actions by the Soviet government against non-socialist opponents. They loudly proclaimed their anti-liberalism and revelled in denouncing their opponents.

The passionately debated issues which separated Communists and Trotskyists – differences over collaborationism for example – did not touch upon basic questions about the nature of future democratic institutions. Three such questions in particular hung in the air: How effectively would national democracy accommodate political pluralism and civil liberties? Would the final form of democracy build upon or displace its liberal-democratic features? And how participatory would socialist democracy be?

THE 1970s AND 1980s

The parameters of the democracy-socialism debate shifted in the 1970s and 1980s with the development of prominent new Left positions and the reconstruction of old ones. The period saw the emergence of black consciousness and a revived and more left-wing Trotskyism. It was also marked, from the early 1970s, by a new kind of trade unionism whose leaders and ideologists were committed to workplace democracy and independence from anti-apartheid political parties and movements. These organizational developments altered the debate about democracy and socialism in two important ways.

Firstly, they generated serious questioning of the distinction between democratic and socialist tasks. Black consciousness turned left in the early 1980s, and in 1983 allied itself with a reviving Western Cape Trotskyism oriented to a purer form of class politics. The resulting formation, the National Forum, adopted what was in effect a socialist programme, the Manifesto of the Azanian People. The Manifesto called for a 'democratic, anti-racist worker Republic' based on 'worker control of the means of production, distribution and exchange' and, implicitly, large-scale public ownership. It in effect eliminated a distinguishable democratic stage or even democratic tasks; the only democracy called for was the democracy associated with socialism itself.

Somewhat inconsistently, the movement did publicize the purely democratic task of an elected constituent assembly, but its leftist ideologues saw this prospective body as a transitional vehicle for consolidating working-class hegemony. In a manner more obviously inconsistent for an 'anti-racist' class politics movement, black consciousness ideologues continued to emphasize the unity of blacks and to oppose white involvement in the leadership of the anti-apartheid struggle. An incoherent effort was made to unite this perspective with a class one by, in practice, defining primarily white organizations as bourgeois or liberal and hence non-socialist.[4]

The main current of emerging trade unions, gathered in 1979 under the banner of the Federation of South African Trade Unions (Fosatu), also questioned the priority of national-democratic struggle. Politically non-aligned, Fosatu unions concentrated on economic battles against employers. The federation's politics, where discernible, was class-centred and socialist, defined by the suspicion that national liberation would bring to power a post-apartheid black elite hostile to socialism and independent working-class organizations. Fosatu saw its priority as building structures in the workplace capable of withstanding the assault not only of the apartheid regime but of an authoritarian post-liberation government. The federation's more politically oriented thinkers hoped these structures would provide the springboard for a future working-class political movement.

Congress-aligned socialists continued to assert a two-stage theory of national democracy first, then socialism. But leftist currents flowed also through the Congress movement. Communist Party theorist Joe Slovo could proclaim, in 1976, that there was 'no middle road' between capitalism and socialism in South Africa, and that the collapse of the country's intertwined racial and capitalist structures would generate an uninterrupted movement towards socialism.[5] The crisis of African Marxist regimes and Gorbachev's *perestroika* probably placed a brake on this sort of maximalism by the later 1980s; for its part the leadership of the ANC-aligned United Democratic Front (UDF), formed in 1983, was ideologically heterogeneous and pursued a broad alliance politics. Nevertheless township activists loudly proclaimed their reverence for socialism throughout the middle and later 1980s.[6]

A second major shift in the terms of the socialism–democracy debate involved an assertion of quasi-councillist theories of socialist democracy. By councillism I mean a range of positions envisaging strong workplace or, less commonly, neighbourhood or associational self-government, viewed potentially as the foundation of a system of higher tier political representation through instructed delegation and instant recall from below. It is classically about proletarian or producer representation, so that strictly speaking we should refer to cross-class neighbourhood or voluntary-association based variants as quasi-councillist. Councillism is often linked to the view that a future socialist democracy can be prefigured on the ground by effective democratic self-organization prior to the arrival of socialism itself. This line was most strongly developed in 'workerist' trade unions. It was also present, though more weakly, in Trotskyist and, by the mid-1980s, in Congress discourse.

The democratic content of the socialism proclaimed by National Forum affiliates was highly ambiguous. In the Manifesto of the Azanian People socialist democracy is left largely unspecified apart from (not self-evidently consistent) appeals to control by 'workers' and the 'people'. The tenor of the document is, in fact, deeply statist, replete with promises about what the future state will do in terms especially of welfare provision but saying nothing at all about either the limits of state power or the institutions of popular and proletarian control. The Manifesto apart, Trotskyists inside and outside the National Forum sought democratic inspiration in the workers' councils or soviets of Russia in 1917, which they counterposed to Stalinist bureaucratic rule.[7]

The councillism of the independent unions was more syndicalist and more prefigurative than the party-led Trotskyist version. It was more syndicalist because it vested a leading role in workplace bodies like shop stewards' councils and was suspicious of political parties, whether nationalist or socialist. Union discourse was also more prefigurative, because it assumed that current workplace practice established the organizational traditions and forms which alone made a genuinely democratic socialism conceivable in the future. A future democracy had to be rooted in strong workplace organizations established in the here-and-now, with delegates to higher tiers and structures requiring a clear mandate from below for their actions and policy decisions.

The 1980s saw a bitter dispute between independent unions and the ANC-sympathetic 'Charterists' known as the workerism-populism debate. On the one side, the independent unions argued that co-operation with community organizations and, from 1983, the UDF would result in the subordination of carefully nurtured working-class organizations to middle-class activists who mobilized their supporters in risky confrontations with the state without proper mandates from, or accountability to, base-level structures. On the other side, Charterist community and union activists charged independent unions with reformist labour practice and political abstentionism.[8]

Notwithstanding this (still quietly rumbling) dispute, prefigurative councillism entered Congress discourse as well from the mid-1980s. It did so in two forms. The formation of the Congress of South African Trade Unions (Cosatu) in 1985 brought workerist and populist currents together under a single organizational banner. This consolidated a trend, evident already in the last years of Fosatu, towards greater union–community co-operation. Cosatu's leadership adopted an increasingly pro-ANC position and the South African Communist Party (SACP) recruited prominent workerists. Councillist unionism was, in effect, co-opted into the Congress camp.

A kind of prefigurative quasi-councillism entered the community arena too. The insurrection of 1984–5 generated a vacuum of 'ungovernability' in the townships which mainly UDF-linked associations attempted to fill. Across the country organs of 'people's power' emerged, linked to civic or youth organizations or set up by freelance 'comrades'. They took many forms: the best organized were rooted in tight networks of street and area committees; some provided services, others administered popular justice. These organs were mainly conceived as instruments of insurrection presiding over liberated zones, egged on by an exiled ANC determined to up the ante of its struggle against the apartheid regime; but they were also imagined by some as prefiguring future forms of participatory self-government.[9] These were not workers' councils concerned with production, but cross-class bodies centred on issues of township collective consumption; nevertheless the parallels with union councillism were there, and unionists sometimes took a lead in building township civics.[10]

DEFICITS OF THE 1970s/1980s DEBATE

These two discursive developments – the critique of national democracy and the arrival of varieties of councillism – posed, however obliquely, the question of socialist democracy and its forms. Distilling the innovative impulses of New Left movements in Europe and America and the negative experiences of 'real socialism' in the East and Africa, union councillism in particular intimated a way to socialism that avoided the pitfalls of authoritarian nationalism and Stalinism.

Nevertheless the democratic debate of the 1970s and 1980s exhibited serious democratic deficiencies. In particular it failed to address in adequate fashion two problems for radical democratic theory: those of representational mediation and of pluralism. While councillism advertised the prospect of a non-Stalinist socialism, it could not offer a convincing account of the representative institutions of a future democratic polity, especially at regional and national centres of power. Delegates of individual workplaces or neighbourhoods would be far too numerous to assemble in provincial or national capitals; in a councillist schema, local delegates would have to elect a higher tier of delegates, and they perhaps a still higher one.

As I have argued elsewhere,[11] pyramidal representation can only be justified where the overwhelming bulk of decisions are taken by self-governing organs at the local level, with merely residual powers left at the centre. In such a scenario instructed delegates to the centre would have a status akin to, say, foreign ministers negotiating on behalf of self-contained governments. Councillism belongs properly to anarchist models of contractual federalism, not to unitary states like the new South Africa.

The other justification of indirect representation is that delegates would be accountable to electorates which, wherever they may be located in the representational pyramid, would be small, active and cohesive enough to monitor the next tier of delegates above and to administer a scheme of instructed delegation and recall. The success of such a system depends on continuously high levels of political awareness and involvement from the base through all subsequent levels. Where political activity ebbs at a particular level, so that the tier above it comes to function relatively autonomously, indirect election transmutes into a cumbersomely layered bureaucracy.

For its part rigidly instructed delegation and frequent recall might leave delegates with too little accumulated experience or tactical manoeuvring room to control effectively the permanent secretariats offering advice and implementing policies at the higher levels especially. In practice delegates would have to be accorded more autonomy than the council schema is supposed to allow, thus again weakening the rationale of indirect election.

Problems in respect of equality and proportionality of representation would be still more profound. A viable council scheme would find it hard to compute votes in a manner widely perceived as fair. The units to be represented in the council state – workplaces of various size, neighbourhoods, grassroots organizations – would differ in membership numbers, institutional character and methods of internal election. Finding a formula for representation that renders them comensurate, and which does not exclude some sectors of society, or give some individuals more or weightier votes than others, would be formidably difficult. The assemblies produced by such a system would in all probability be very poor at representing in accurate proportion the opinions and allegiances of the electorate, especially when we factor in the plurality or majority basis of council voting and its indirectness.

The councillist turn also failed to deal adequately with the issue of pluralism. Fosatu offered a kind of negative pluralism, allowing rival political groups to recruit amongst its workers; but this was the reverse side of a party-political abstentionism originating partly in a quasi-syndicalist view of political organizations as inherently elitist and bureaucratic. It was Fosatu's abstentionism and negative pluralism which allowed the 'workerists' to be wrong-footed by politically engaged forces aligned to the ANC. More seriously, Fosatu's quasi-syndicalism posited a form of political participation oriented to technical 'bread and butter' issues rather than programmatic choices on the terrain of high politics. Fosatu discourse did not permit a systematic theory of the role of political parties in a future democracy, encouraging instead either indifference to the existence and form of parties or a preference for democratic models assigning party-political debate and competition a strictly secondary role.

The quasi-councillism of the 'people's power' movement of the townships was still more problematic for pluralism. Although it encompassed a more diverse social base than the unions, its representatives tended to treat their constituency as a politically homogeneous 'people' or 'community' with a general will capable of manifestation in local assemblies or committee meetings; and the leading activists being ANC-aligned, the organs of self-government doubled up as, in effect, local ANC (or more strictly, UDF) branches, with political rivals to the ANC subject to exclusion and occasionally violence. While the better organized people's power structures managed to limit youth indiscipline, others controlled by young 'comrades' practised systematic political coercion and presided over an often brutal system of popular justice. The dominant current of the UDF, which provided an umbrella for 'people's power', had little sympathy for any notion of democracy as a 'liberal, pluralistic debating society'.[12]

The National Forum and its affiliated Trotskyists were no more promising as a source of pluralist commitment. While they espoused nonsectarianism and called for a United Front, they refused co-operation with organizations they arbitrarily labelled as 'liberal' or 'bourgeois'. While some of their thinkers spoke out in favour of pluralism, it was not clear that their envisaged democracy would accommodate bourgeois and pro-capitalist parties. Black consciousness thinkers and Trotskyists simplistically dismissed liberalism as an ideology of the bourgeoisie.

The challenge to the idea of national democracy may in some respects have compounded these deficiencies of Left democratic discourse. The SACP's espousal of national democracy was open to legitimate and necessary criticism: it did little to specify the democratic institutions and guarantees of national democracy; it situated national democracy within a stage theory which rendered the democratic gains of the first stage insecure; the organization itself exhibited neo-Stalinist practices and allegiances. Nevertheless the doctrine of national democracy did, at least, leave room for an engagement with political liberalism about the principles and institutions of political emancipation; and it allowed that there might be forms of democracy not reducible to socialist or class democracy. Prefigurative councilism established a new and necessary priority for localized self-government and grassroots participation. But it systematically downplayed a problem which the concept of national democracy posed, however awkwardly: the problem of how to build non-class specific institutions of democratic intermediation on larger spatial scales – and of how to connect these institutions to the longer-range goal of socialism.

 THE 1990s: A NEW DISCURSIVE TURN *liberal democrat. values*

From the late 1980s the leadership of the ANC and SACP began to enunciate a liberal-democratic vision of the post-apartheid polity, a discursive shift which was consolidated in the course of constitutional negotiations with the white National Party (NP) government between 1990 and 1994. There is reason to believe that this reorientation was underway by the mid-1980s, but its first public expression was the ANC's 1988 Constitutional Guidelines. This document upheld multi-party democracy and 'basic rights and freedoms, such as freedom of association, expression, thought, worship and the press', subject only to restrictions on racist, fascist and ethnically chauvinist speech; it also, importantly, recognized the right to strike.

In 1990, rebounding from the implosion of Eastern European 'Communism', the SACP's Joe Slovo disowned his party's Stalinist past and confirmed that the SACP no longer saw itself as a vanguard party but as one political tendency amongst others competing for the allegiance of a working class it still hoped to lead to socialism. Slovo offered a critique of Stalinism as 'socialism without democracy' and promised a 'thoroughgoing democratic socialism' based on multi-party democracy 'both in the national democratic and socialist phases'.[13]

The current interim constitution, endorsed by the ANC and its partners during negotiations, provides for multi-party democracy, liberal-type political and civil freedoms guaranteed by an independent judiciary and a degree of devolution to newly formed provinces. The proposed final constitution (the final draft of which is being debated in the constitutional court at the time of writing) confirms these commitments.[14]

This reorientation, though very marked at the level of public discourse and formal institutional design, should not be exaggerated. The relatively liberal positions of ANC and SACP leaders were contradicted by the continued intolerance of Congress activists on the ground who, during the April 1994 election for example, prevented NP and Democratic Party candidates from campaigning in African townships. There remained a strong Stalinist current in the SACP.

Further, a commitment to formal democracy, however necessary, does not in itself guarantee an accountable or participatory style of politics. The ANC leadership in negotiations and government has often been secretive, unilateralist and unresponsive to the input of its rank-and-file supporters. The continuing push for participatory democracy has come largely from civics, trade unions and other ANC/SACP allies threatened with marginalization under a post-apartheid political dispensation.

Moreover the ANC/SACP's liberal-democratic shift failed to reconnect democracy and socialism *in practice*. The ANC's radical social-democratic commitments steadily seeped away during negotiations and have found little expression in its post-election policies. While the socialist rhetoric of Cosatu and of the SACP remains intact, neither currently offers a convincing socialist economic programme or a believable medium- or long-term timetable for its implementation. Despite ritual claims by ANC, SACP and Cosatu sympathisers that South Africa is embarked on something called 'radical reform' or 'structural reform',[15] the truth is that the tide is all the other way, in the direction of trade and currency liberalization, privatization and a fiscal caution that does little to tackle gross social inequalities.

Nevertheless there *have* been creative efforts by theorists and activists on the Left, many of them connected to the ANC, Cosatu or township civics, to appropriate liberal-democratic insights for a socially radical and participatory politics. Though it has not yet succeeded in outlining the terms of a plausible marriage of democracy and socialism, this work has altered the terms of Left debate about their relationship. Two broad themes of the new Left debate warrant special attention: constitutionalism and rights; and civil society, with its allied sub-themes of corporatism and new social movement politics. I begin with rights.

RIGHTS AND CIVIL SOCIETY

Though increasingly won over to the language of rights, ANC thinkers like Albie Sachs[16] were keen to redefine rights in a way that extended the protection they afforded more explicitly to the poor and other subordinate social categories. The ANC's new constitutionalists proposed two types of rights extension. Instead of treating citizens as abstractly equivalent subjects, rights documents should specify categories of citizens requiring special kinds of protection or affirmative action: groups like workers, women, children, the black majority more generally. Secondly, the range of justiciable rights should be extended beyond negative and procedural rights to cover citizens' social and economic entitlements. Thus, for example, the right to free expression should be supplemented by other rights – such as to adequate nutrition or education – which would enable the poor to express themselves confidently and effectively. The ANC's 1992 Draft Bill of Rights gave clear expression to this doubly extended conception of rights. It finds expression in the list of Fundamental Rights attached to the interim constitution and in the Bill of Rights attached to the final constitution, the final draft of which insists upon 'reasonable legislative and other measures' to fulfil rights to housing, food, water, health care and education.[17]

While the ANC talked the language of constitutionalism and rights, two of its allies – the Cosatu trade unions and the township-based civic associations – demanded recognition of their autonomy from political parties and a post-apartheid state. With the collapse of black local authorities and the commencement of national political negotiations from 1990, the numbers and local importance of township civics increased dramatically. Resurgent civics had to decide how to operate both in the transition period – with its new opportunities for negotiation with state actors – and under a future dispensation of democratically elected national and local government. With their historical role as militant oppositionists seemingly concluded, civics debated a whole range of possible future roles. Almost all concurred on the need for a less partisan style, autonomy from the ANC (but with the option of a principled alliance with it or other parties) and a critically (re)constructive rather than largely oppositional role in township affairs.

Alongside this organizational debate there flourished a new discourse of civil society. Theorists close to the civics held that an autonomous civil society provided space for collective self-government and service delivery through voluntary civil associations. An effectively self-organized civil society, it was argued, could pursue egalitarian and participatory objectives in a non-statist way. Thus Mzwanele Mayekiso[18] foresaw a 'working class civil society' providing a socialist bastion against a reformist ANC and generating the embryonic institutions of a socialist mode of production. Mark Swilling[19] envisaged an 'associational socialism' in which social movements would govern themselves while negotiating externally with a democratically regulated capitalist class and strengthened local governments. Both these writers seemed to picture a civil society populated by radical and grassroots social movements akin to the civics.

After 1990 Cosatu and other trade union federations also had to adapt to an unfamiliar environment. In the past unions had perceived the state and capital as enemies; with apartheid being dismantled and the ANC preparing itself for government, they now felt obliged to seek a more constructive relationship with their former adversaries. Like the civics, they deployed a combination of negotiation and grassroots militancy to secure a role in shaping new institutions and policies. The unions' willingness to reach accords with capital and the state and to participate in sectoral and national forums fuelled an intense debate on the Left about the possibilities and dangers of corporatism in South Africa. Some feared a slide towards the subordination of union interests to those of capital and the state. Optimists vested hope in new forms of 'strategic unionism' capable of negotiating with the state and capital while preserving the autonomy of unions and securing radical reforms in alliance with a diverse array of social movements.[20]

If civics and unions were the principal actors of this new civil society emerging out of past struggles against oppression, they were far from the only ones. South Africa's burgeoning non-governmental organization (NGO) sector grew increasingly vocal in defence of its service and development role. Campaigning organizations and networks mushroomed. The women's movement in particular, refusing subordination to the national-democratic struggle, contested constitutional clauses and the internal structures of anti-apartheid organizations.[21] NGOs and campaigning movements confronted the prospect of an ostensibly sympathetic government which might seek to co-opt their causes while competing for their funding sources. Like unions and civics, they grappled for an institutional framework which would allow them access to future state resources and support without compromising their prized autonomy.[22]

AMBIGUITIES OF THE NEW DISCOURSE

This discovery of rights and civil society represents an immense advance for a Left historically attracted to the authoritarian formulae of radical nationalism and Marxism-Leninism. Protected rights and an autonomous civil realm provide a counterweight to state tyranny and bureaucratic centralism; they demarcate a space in which citizens can organize for political and cultural change, provide needed services on a self-help basis and deepen their uncoerced participation in public life. While the codification of citizen rights and free public spaces does not guarantee that power-holders will respect these goods, it does offer a powerful liberty-friendly symbolic resource which citizens and groups can draw upon to defend their autonomy and secure their proclaimed entitlements. Arguments of this sort provide fully sufficient ground for the Left's entry on to this historically liberal terrain.

What is more problematic is the way that some on the Left, in retreat from previous commitments to state-led economic planning and redistribution, have tried to recast the language of rights and civil society in radically egalitarian or socialist terms. In certain of the new talk there is a tendency to assume that rights and civil society can be vested with a socialist essence or substitute for socialist politics. Political groups on the Left quite legitimately seek to use the framework of rights and platform of civil society in their struggle to achieve a participatory and non-statist socialism. Where, however, their discourse seeks to build socialist or egalitarian goals into the basic constitution of the state or society, it threatens the pluralism which rights and civil society are supposed to underpin. At the same time it burdens these concepts with unrealistic expectations about their capacity to fulfil or assist in realizing socially radical objectives. Rights provide a framework of procedures and entitlements, civil society a legal space, in which a participatory socialist politics can be pursued; they cannot without cost codify *de facto* socialist goals (in the case of rights) or (in the case of civil society) be defined in a way that entails institutional privileges for radical social movements.

The call for socio-economic rights is not in itself especially radical (or socialist). Stated in a realistic form – as a requirement of equal treatment of citizens by the state, or as permission to engage in affirmative action or expropriate property under certain circumstances – social and economic rights seem entirely defensible. Equal treatment is already covered by the principle of rule of law, while permissive clauses about expropriation and affirmative action expand the range of social-system options available to citizens and their representatives, thus enriching democratic ideological debate.

The constitutional right to specified socio-economic goods is a more complicated matter. Where the right is codified in a weak form – that is, where it is a right to very general goods or made conditional upon resource availability (as in the draft final constitution) – it is likely to have little practical policy impact. Where social and economic rights are entrenched in a strong form – with detailed lists of the material goods to which citizens are entitled unconditionally – they become notional or else undemocratic or liberty threatening. *Notional* because they mandate outcomes which, given absolute scarcities and the unintended effects of policies, even well-intentioned politicians may be unable to produce, so that they (the politicians) could not justly be subject to any sanction for not meeting them beyond, perhaps, an obligation to justify their actions. *Undemocratic* because they vest economic policy-making in the hands of judges, illegitimately restricting the range of economic and ideological debate amongst the public and its representatives. And *liberty threatening* because their inherent unrealizability devalues rights which enjoy comparable constitutional status but which are much more obviously justiciable (such as freedom of speech).

Similar considerations apply to civil society. Normatively speaking, civil society is best understood as an empty public space, bounded by law, open to the plural purposes of free and equal citizens. It should not be equated with particular actors operating in that space (such as civics or unions) nor assigned in advance a particular collective purpose (beyond the basic ones of *accommodating* a pluralism of ends and limiting concentration of power). The conflation of civil society with radical social movements or participatory socialism – a conflation into which the South African debate occasionally slips – incurs a dual risk, one for socialism, the other for democracy.

For socialism the risk is that the role of delivering socialist goods – such as an economy based on co-operatives – is given to a civil society that cannot, by definition, deliver them. The overestimation of what civil society can do, indeed the assumption that it can, qua civil society, do *anything*, arises from a tendency in some South African Left writing (such as that of Swilling and Mayekiso) to treat the civil realm as a collective actor and a second sovereign. Civil society is assumed in this literature to mobilize around or participate in a common project (such as associational socialism), composing itself thereby into a unitary and purposive will; it is also expected to raise revenue on a large scale and issue collectively binding decisions – as though it were itself a state. In fact, of course, a civil society cannot do these things, since it is a space containing disparate projects of a more or less voluntary character.

For democracy the risk lies precisely in the effort to compose civil society into a homogeneous collective actor. The claim that, for example, township residents could be represented via interest aggregating civics transcending partisan politics – a common proposition of 1990s' civic orthodoxy – was quite understandably viewed by the civics' rivals as part of a project to bring the local political spectrum under a depoliticized ANC umbrella. Though civics and ANC alike asserted their separateness, writers like Friedman[23] could plausibly interpret this as signalling an ambition to reconstitute the state–civil society divide within a single movement. The political strength of the civics on the ground plus their historical connection to a prospective governing party raised the spectre of a future local state granting civics organizational privileges as, in effect, corporate gatekeepers interceding on behalf of township stakeholders. The tendency of civic ideologists (like Swilling and Mayekiso) to use the term civil society as a code for civic-like movements underlined this danger. The goal of nonpartisan civic forums or assemblies representing local 'communities' from the outset overestimated the representativeness of civics and naively assumed that the entire spread of local interests was containable under a single organizational rubric.

CONCLUSION

Prior to the 1990s Left discourse on socialism and democracy was marked, both in the Communist and Trotskyist Lefts, by the idea that non-socialist democratic tasks – of the kind enunciated in the Freedom Charter or Ten Point Programme – provided a necessary gateway to socialism in a society marked by the denial of elementary democratic rights. The democratic content of socialism itself remained obscure in both traditions. The practices and allegiances of the NEUM and the Communists suggested that neither envisaged a socialism of liberal-democratic institutions or guarantees.

In the 1970s and 1980s a major new tradition entered the picture, one I have characterized as prefigurative councillism, and the twofold thrust of which was to downplay, bypass or eliminate the national-democratic stage and to present participatory socialist democracy as something which could be prefigured prior to revolution in the self-organization of workers and township residents. While stressing the centrality of democracy to socialism, its ideologues appeared to envisage a councillist rather than liberal-democratic polity. The Trotskyists and black consciousness organizations for their part proclaimed the immediate priority of socialism; their depictions of socialist democracy ranged from revolutionary councillist through to statist.

In the 1990s the Left in and around the ANC, the civics and Cosatu discovered the virtues of political rights and an autonomous civil society. Some on the Left accepted these commitments and institutions as valuable in their own right, under both the first and second stages of the revolution; all hoped that their entrenchment in post-apartheid South Africa would provide new levers and spaces for advancing socially egalitarian and participatory causes.

However, some versions of the new discourse of right and civil society offered secure ground to neither democracy nor socialism. I have suggested that strong formulations of the relationship between rights and civil society on the one side, socialism on the other, are problematic for both terms of the relationship. A participatory socialism cannot be created, even embryonically, in the very definition of rights and civil society. To attempt to create it, whether by an overextended doctrine of social and economic rights or by setting up a civil society of institutionally privileged civics or unions, is to limit the space for free debate about economic programmes and open political pluralism. It is also sure to generate disappointment, for neither constitutional promises nor voluntary civil associations alone can usher socialism into being.

The long debate about the relationship between democracy and socialism in the South African Left thus remains unresolved. On the one hand the best elements of the Left have embraced what was absent from Trotskyism, Stalinism, councillism: the central importance and intrinsic value of inter-party competition, protected citizen rights and a democratic state existing alongside a separate and autonomous civil society. On the other hand these new commitments remain still to be connected plausibly, either in theory or the real world of democratic transition, to a realizable socialist project. If before the importance of formal democracy and liberties eluded the Left, today, with formal democracy in place and liberties protected, it is socialism that has receded, if not from rhetoric, then from practical politics. Unable to break through to socialism by means of state-led economic programmes in a world of global capitalist dominance, sections of the Left have sought it by other means – via rights and civil society – which have been invited to perform functions and assume natures inconsistent with their necessary ideological contingency.

One effect of the search for radically egalitarian goals via constitutional clauses and voluntary civil associations is to discourage engagement with the high politics of openly competing political parties and ideological programmes. It signals a politics which, having effectively ceded the state to the ANC and its political allies, concentrates exclusively on building up the countervailing power of civil society or binding the ANC to irrevocable constitutional obligations.

There is talk still, in dissident parts of the Left, of a new workers' party to challenge the reformist ANC on precisely the terrain of high politics. Establishing such a party may become, before long, the only way forward for socialists – though that party will require, before it can hope to succeed, a credible account of what kind of socialism, or radical social democracy, can survive and prosper in today's world. What democratic-minded socialists should *not* seek is a party conceived in the old Leninist mould, a party of insurrection, aspiring to single-party rule, the suppression of bourgeois opposition and the replacement of South Africa's new parliamentary democracy with the chimerical democracy of soviets. Though it has not yielded socialism, the discovery of rights and civil autonomy by sections of the ANC and the civic and union movements is a good thing for reasons independent of socialism – above all because it makes political tyranny less likely. The architects of any future socialist advance – whether by a new party or other means – must respect and build upon South Africa's still fragile liberal-democratic institutions and culture.

NOTES

1   The Freedom Charter of the Congress of the People, and two other documents that I will later touch upon, the Manifesto of the Azanian People and the ANC Constitutional Guidelines for a Democratic South Africa, are reproduced as Appendices A, D and E in T. Lodge and B. Nasson, *All, Here and Now: Black Politics in South Africa in the 1980s*, London, 1992, pp. 331–5, 350–6.
2   For discussions of the Trotskyists, see R. Fine, *Beyond Apartheid: Labour and Liberation in South Africa*, London, 1990; B. Hirson, 'The Trotskyist groupings in South Africa, 1932–1948', in I. Liebenberg, F. Lortan, B. Nel and G. van der Westhuizen (eds.), *The Long March: The Story of the Struggle for Liberation in South Africa*, Pretoria, 1994, pp. 52–64.
3   Fine, *Beyond Apartheid*, p. 68.
4   A discussion of the South African Far Left in the 1980s can be found in Lodge and Nasson, *All, Here and Now*, pp. 142–98, 207–29.
5   J. Slovo, 'South Africa: no middle road', in B. Davidson, J. Slovo and A. Wilkinson (eds.), *Southern Africa: The New Politics of Revolution*, Harmondsworth, 1976, pp. 103–210.

6   Lodge and Nasson, *All, Here and Now*, pp. 127–40.

7   See for example two anonymous pieces, 'South Africa: the way forward: a response', *Free Azania*, no. 2/3, 1989, pp. 32–4, especially p. 34; 'From apartheid to a post-apartheid South Africa', *Free Azania*, no. 2/3, 1989, pp. 41–7, especially p. 47.

8   Summary accounts of the workerism-populism debate can be found in P. van Niekerk, 'The trade union movement in the politics of resistance in South Africa', in S. Johnson (ed.), *South Africa: No Turning Back*, Basingstoke, 1988, pp. 153–71, especially pp. 155–9; Lodge and Nasson, *All, Here and Now*, pp. 38–9, 84–6; M. J. Murray, *The Revolution Deferred: The Painful Birth of Post-Apartheid South Africa*, London, 1994, pp. 142–6.

9   H. Barrell, 'The outlawed South African liberation movements', in Johnson (ed.), *No Turning Back*, pp. 52–93, especially p. 61.

10 M. Swilling, 'Civic associations in South Africa', *Urban Forum*, vol. 4, no. 2, 1993, pp. 15–36, especially p. 18.

11 D. Glaser, 'Paradoxes of the council state', *Studies in Marxism*, no. 1, 1994, pp. 143–77.

12 Cited in Lodge and Nasson, *All, Here and Now*, p. 131.

13 J. Slovo, *Has Socialism Failed?*, London, 1990, pp. 3, 27.

14 A copy of the draft final constitution can be located on the internet at <http://www.constitution.org.za/new.html>.

15 J. Saul, 'Structural reform: a model for the revolutionary transformation of South Africa?', *Transformation*, no. 20, 1992, pp. 1–16; G. Adler and E. Webster, 'Challenging transition theory: the labour movement, radical reform and the transition to democracy in South Africa', *Politics & Society*, vol. 23, no. 1, 1995, pp. 75–106.

16 A. Sachs, *Advancing Human Rights in South Africa*, Cape Town, 1992.

17 The ANC Draft Bill of Rights: A Preliminary Revised Text is reproduced as Appendix 1 to Sachs, *Advancing Human Rights in South Africa*, pp. 215–35.

18 M. Mayekiso, 'Working class civil society: why we need it, and how to get it', *African Communist*, second quarter, 1992, pp. 32–42.

19 M. Swilling, 'Socialism, democracy and civil society: the case for associational socialism', *Theoria*, no. 79, 1992, pp. 75–82.

20 K. Von Holdt, 'What is the future of labour?', *South African Labour Bulletin*, vol. 16, no. 8, 1992, pp. 30–7; J. Maree, 'Trade unions and corporatism in South Africa', *Transformation*, no. 21, 1993, pp. 24–54.

21 See for evidence S. Bazilli (ed.), *Putting Women on the Agenda*, Johannesburg, 1991, and the special women's struggle edition of *Transformation*, no. 15, 1991.

22 For a recent discussion see *Mail and Guardian*, July 12–18, *Reconstruct* supplement, p. 2.

23 S. Friedman, 'Bonaparte at the barricades: the colonisation of civil society', *Theoria*, no. 79, 1992, pp. 83–95.

3 Race, Reason and Representation in National Party Discourse, 1990-1992

Antony Altbeker and Jonny Steinberg[1]

Most, if not all of what has been written on the National Party (NP) since 1990 has concerned strategy, policy, ideological and organizational history and so forth. The NP has yet to be studied as a narrator. As such, we move very tentatively and modestly on to a new terrain.

We do not wish to valorize this project over others. The study of political parties as organizational complexes and as strategic actors of course occupies a formidable and irreplaceable locus in political research. Narratology too, however, has its place. The field of party politics is one of competing truth-claims, all of which are narrative in nature. These political stories, like all stories, construct a beginning, which has already happened, a middle, which is happening, and an end to be pursued. Moreover they people their respective narratives with various protagonists: 'people', party, politician or 'historical forces', or a combination thereof – thus the identity of the political actor is forged on the anvil of its own self-representation. And if political forces *are* constituted through their self-representation, then the importance of narrative cannot be underestimated. Perhaps most importantly, the political identities of ordinary people are forged through their placement of themselves in the story, through their identification with, or as, a protagonist.

This chapter was researched and written at the end of 1992. At that time the NP and its principal antagonist, the African National Congress (ANC), were engaged in negotiations to put an end to apartheid. Our aim was to examine the discursive universe out of which the NP's proposals for the new constitutional dispensation were drawn. Today, in the democratic South Africa which emerged from negotiations, the voice of the NP has mutated somewhat. Thus, despite the fact that our presentation is written in the present tense, the analysis is confined to the years 1990 to 1992. More particularly, its object is the discursive underpinning of consociational constitutional principles – principles the NP has now, in 1996, formally abandoned. Nevertheless, such mutations must reflect their origins, and perhaps with a more finely tuned analysis of what the NP

49

was, we will be able to investigate what it has become, and where it will go. In any case, the story we recount has intrinsic value. For it charts the discourse of a party which once presided over apartheid for 42 years, as it attempts to make sense of itself in the course of the dissolution of its animating project.[2]

What we found, first and foremost, is a great deal of ambiguity. There is a configuration of key words which run through NP discourse – 'democracy', 'rationality', 'reason', 'culture', 'groups', 'power-sharing', 'majoritarianism' – and yet each of these words is drawn from a multiplicity of conceptual universes. In other words, we have found entrenched in a single ensemble, a cohabitation of conceptions of history, democracy and ethics. Yet these vicissitudes are masked by the fact that they are represented by the same words. The upshot is that meaning is never fixed. Rather, there is a dynamic of linguistic play between conceptual fields perpetually deferring meaning.

Let us briefly illustrate this point in relation to the word 'group'. In NP discourse the group has become a notion simultaneously empty of all content and adaptable to every requirement. It can mean an historically determined cultural community with distinct values or an association of like-minded individuals holding a particular political view; it can mean a political party or a geographically coincident population; most importantly, it can signify a race or a freely formed assembly of individuals. A play of substitutions is permitted to lurk beneath this word. It is through the logic of this play that effects of meaning are, at once, created and concealed: races become cultural minorities, cultural minorities become political minorities, political positions become cultural values.

Simultaneously the concept of the group has become both devoid of content and the point at which a number of constructions become apparent. Its meaning always depends on its position in relation to other terms, phrases and figures of speech. The addressees of NP discourse are justified in drawing divergent conclusions about the intentions the NP evinces, precisely because this content depends so much on interpretation. This interpretation will depend on what a particular addressee has understood by previous statements and utterances and in this regard the word group has become laden with an historosophical past which it cannot renounce. Indeed there is a tacit recognition of this fact in the NP:

> From the Government's and NP's point of view, the biggest challenge is how to make the group concept acceptable in a climate with an enormous amount of scepticism and suspicion that group [sic] is only a method of continuing in a disguised way the disparities and injustice of

apartheid and the past. In arguing its case, the Government has come to realise that terminology has an important effect . . .

The challenge is to purify the group concept from the bad smell of the past caused by the dead albatross of apartheid and discrimination hanging around the neck of this concept.[3]

This is a noble endeavour. However, it is not helped by the diverse uses the term has been put to since apartheid has ceased to be the policy of the NP. In the very speech in which this commitment to 'purify' the concept is articulated, Dr Viljoen talks about negotiators as 'representative leaders of all the *population groups*', he refers to 'groups based on a pattern of alternative life-style choices' (translated from the Afrikaans), he defines negotiators elected by the black community as 'group-based representation', and finally assures us that the NP wants to negotiate 'a new definition of groups instead of the rigid statutory and prescriptive approach of the past . . . a new approach based on free association'.

This purified conception of groups still seems a mite ambiguous, covering as it does racial, political and 'life-style' associations. This is not resolved when the NP adopts phrases like 'minority groups', 'community', 'minority values' and an abundance of similarly constructed combinations.

The task which has confronted us then, is what to make of this conceptual play. At first, it seemed that we should merely demarcate the boundaries of the vicissitudes, elucidate the nature of each conceptual universe, demonstrate the rubric within which signifiers float between fields of meaning, and so on. In other words, we felt that our task was to elucidate the hidden process of deferral, and in so doing, demonstrate the magnitude of the National Party's capacity to speak in different voices.

Instead, however, we will attempt to demonstrate that the contradictory ensemble which we identify in fact effects a relatively coherent field of meaning, that what emerges from the 'conceptual collision' which constitutes NP discourse is a stable narrative. The danger of course is that this stability will appear to be forced, that an unwarranted impulse has driven our own narrative to seek closure, where in fact our object reveals nothing of the sort. We believe, however, that our course is justified. We leave the reader to assess the coherence of our presentation.

THE PAST IS A FOREIGN COUNTRY

'The past is a foreign country; they do things differently there.'
L. P. Hartley, *The Go Between*

The NP appears to be in the midst of an eschatological crisis. Some constructions of history invoked by its spokespeople determine the past an aberration and its continued impact nugatory, while others imbue the past with an indubitable and unavoidable presence, a presence, moreover, of inestimable import for the future. The future, as the old joke has it, is not what it used to be.

There are, we will argue, two distinct conceptions of history present in the discourse of the NP. In this section, our intention is to elaborate one of these primary discourses. As we will see, the conception of history which is narrated is an effect of the presence of a liberal rationalism which results in the construction of a particular conception of politics and democracy.

Briefly stated what we will advance in this section is that some constructions of the nature both of the anticipated dispensation and the process of negotiation itself, are derived from a rationalist faith in argument. Indeed these rationalist impulses, at points, render the images of the negotiation process and parts of the future institutional framework of the state, all but indistinguishable. These formulations, particularly when they are invoked in relation to the process of negotiation, adopt an almost Rawlsian 'original position' conception of the rational construction of the social. What will be of special interest in this regard, therefore, will be the interpretation of history, and its role in the future, in this discourse.

The 'intellectual core' of rationalism, argues Carl Schmitt, 'resides in its specific relationship to truth', which is construed as a mere function of the 'eternal competition of opinions'. This leads Schmitt to proclaim rationalism to be a 'consistent, comprehensive metaphysical system' in which the pursuit of the maximization of social utility is formally identical with the pursuit of truth. Both rely on the 'general liberal principle' that truth and social utility are found through the 'unrestrained clash of opinion and that competition will produce harmony'.[4]

For Schmitt the apothetically rationalist institution is parliament, the essence of which is 'public deliberation, argument and counterargument, public debate, discussion [and] parley'.[5] Parliament relies on discussion and openness. Crucially, 'discussion' is counterposed to 'negotiation' where the former 'means an exchange of opinion that is governed by the purpose of persuading one's opponent through argument of the truth or justice of something'. Negotiations, on the other hand, are characterized as a form of deliberation in which parties with pre-given interests arrive at decisions, not on the basis of what is rationally correct, but on the basis of a compromise between themselves:[6] 'I am convinced that in the negotiating process, the most successful approach towards achieving acceptable solutions would be by way of top level discussions and understandings amongst an informal group of half a dozen really influential leaders of South Africa.'[7] The NP maintains that decision-making cannot be a unilateral and one-sided business. 'The fact is that no-one in South Africa has a lease on all the answers. No-one can prescribe the ultimate solution alone. This is also not desirable.'[8] If a solution is to be found to South Africa's problems, it will involve leaders putting their heads together in a rational process of discussion and debate. Problems will be examined in the harsh light of mutual criticism, and the solutions posed by various leaders scrutinized. This rationalist discourse finds expression in the NP's constitutional proposals as well. Here a future dispensation is predicated on the need to avoid the possibility of any one political party making decisions unilaterally to the exclusion of others: minorities, and we will in a moment discuss the manner in which groups are construed in this discourse, 'must enjoy a meaningful measure of representation and of involvement in decision-making'.[9]

The imagery is rather revealing. Leaders must 'put their heads together' – not just during negotiations, but after the first elections under the new constitution.[10] Decisions will be arrived at through the consideration of options placed before the assembled intellectual and political might of South Africa's elite. There, through deep deliberation, mutual interrogation and communal consultation 'the dilemma of the conflicting claims of power-sharing and simple majority rule [will be] resolved through a process of debate and agreement'.[11]

In an interview conducted by *Leadership*, Dr Viljoen, in arguing that minorities should have a meaningful say in decision-making, was challenged by his interrogator to the effect that his vision of the future offers minorities a veto and that this would prohibit state action. The response is revealing: yes, we would need a conflict-resolving structure for questions upon which unanimity cannot be achieved – this structure should be 'a depoliticised conflict-resolving mechanism, for instance a council of influential South Africans, drawn not primarily from the political sphere but from other spheres'.[12] This captures the NP's rationalism beautifully: the most rational people are leaders from 'other spheres' – people who would, seemingly, have little personal interest in the outcome of negotiations, other than its being the most rational solution, of course.

However, we have not yet argued our point forcefully enough. It is hardly remarkable or surprising that words like 'debate', 'discussion' and 'dialogue' appear in a discourse on a process of negotiation. Indeed it is inconceivable for this not to be the case. Accordingly, it is not enough to show that 'debate' *vis-à-vis* the drafting of a new constitution takes up a core position in the NP's discourse. We must illustrate that the genealogy of these statements is governed by a 'rationalist logic', in Schmitt's specific sense of the term. Might it not be argued, for instance, that debate and discussion, though inevitable features of any process of negotiation, signify 'negotiation' in the Schmittean sense rather than (rationalist) 'discussion'?

It is precisely in this regard that the annihilation of history in the NP's discourse is revealing. It is here that its rationalist impulses emerge in full bloom and in effect establishes the 1990s as South Africa's very own Age of Enlightenment.

F. W. de Klerk, Gerrit Viljoen, Roelf Meyer, 'Pik' Botha, Tertius Delport, Adriaan Vlok – the entire leadership core of the NP – make constant references to the need to 'close the book on the past'.[13] These assertions are matched by a particular construction of the present. In this formulation, the present is deemed a radical break with the past, 'a window of opportunity' presented by history which amounts to a 'moment of truth'[14] and a 'point of no return'.[15]

In NP discourse, a new era has dawned. Transformations at the geopolitical level have had the effect of rendering social realities apparent and discernible. This conception becomes teleological when the dawn of reason is attached to the natural course of history. The present becomes a unique moment of opportunity, a moment during which the South African social body can and must collectively *carpe diem*:

> South Africans realise more and more that circumstances have changed in such a manner that the country and its people have been offered a special opportunity to move out of the corner in which we find ourselves and that we are experiencing a moment of truth which will pass if it is not seized. . .
>
> I believe that God is the master of the fortunes of peoples and nations and that the current events in Eastern Europe and in the entire world are not coincidental. Responsible leaders must, however, identify and take purposeful advantage of the opportunities that He has created in His council plan.[16]
>
> The year 1989 is destined to have as great an impact on the course of world history as the year 1789. At such times the pent up forces of economic and social reality burst through the ideological casts with which men have sought to mould the world.[17]

The present age of reason is counterposed to the age of ideology that preceded it. What has gone before, we are told in no uncertain terms, was an aberration. Societies and social actors moved to the beat of an ideological drum in defiance of the realities of social existence and of human nature.

People sought to mould the world in their own image. They constructed social orders that offended truths, they built their societies in violation of natural laws and allowed themselves to be enslaved by their own fantasies rather than submitting to the realities that, in the present Age of Enlightenment, are apparent and visible to all.

The ideologues and obscurantists, in order to construct their Utopias, had 'to force the great river of economic and social reality into the narrow channels and artificial furrows of [their] doctrines'. This may have succeeded for a time but it is in the nature of the laws of reality that they cannot long be violated – 'in due season the flood comes and washes [these] endeavours away'. South Africa, de Klerk tells us a month later, 'is currently riding the wave of history. It is a tide we must grab onto while it is still running strong.'[18]

The invocation of natural metaphors, in opposition to the 'artificial furrows of [ideological] doctrines', establishes an equivalence of socio-historical events and practices with nature itself. At one point de Klerk goes so far as to declare, seemingly without intended irony, that 'even the Inquisition could not suppress the realities that the Earth is round, that it travels around the sun and that the payment of interest is not a sin.'[19] In this way a particular social practice (the charging of interest) is deemed a reality of the same order as the shape of the Earth and its relationship to the Sun.

Rooted in any ideology was a 'worthwhile ideal', but wherever and whenever 'circumstances and people obstinately refuse to conform to the grand design, they [had to] be forced to do so'. And this is why it is, for de Klerk, that 'ideologies almost always bring about conflict'. Conflict is a direct consequence of ideological attempts to construct the world rather than letting it develop in its own, natural and innate manner. Thus it is people who, in failing to resist the temptation to fashion the world in accordance with their fantastic conceptions, lead humanity off its path, and it is this 'leading astray' that is at the root of conflict.[20]

The archetypal ideology is, of course, communism. It tries to mould humanity, in violation of its nature, into 'rigid Marxist-Leninist moulds' and to fabricate an economic system that transgresses the natural laws of the market. But apartheid too confronted insuperable truths – 'we were caught in a rising sea of economic and social reality'.

One of the realities which conflicted with the NP's policies was that the 'process of economic growth and the expansion of freedom is the natural course for mankind. . . . It has not been devised by this or that philosopher or political scientist. It is inherent in human nature and human society.' Now the 'laudable ideal' of separate states for the nations of South Africa within which different communities could exercise freedom (in the form of self-determination), could not overcome the reality of integration imposed by the exigencies of economic development. Thus the reality that the expansion of freedom is lodged in the course of history resulted, over time, in the policy of apartheid becoming an unconscionable ideology.

The past is reduced to a world of fantasy where reality exists only to subvert the intentions of those who, in succumbing to the temptations of their ideals, had tried to construct a world that could not be. De Klerk contends that the challenge confronting South African leaders, 'is to rid themselves of their favourite ideologies and to see the world as it really is and not in the light of the unrealistic Utopias of the left and right'.[21] The NP, by way of contrast, has 'painfully adapted to reality'. Through these formulations de Klerk defines the NP as centrist, not because of its location on the political spectrum, but because all those who do not see the world in this way are consigned to the category of dogmatic ideologist.

This rationalist discourse on history deems the end of the age of ideology to mean the end of irrational conflict and the possibility of normalizing the political process. The actors in the South African polity can now confront each other, not on the basis of unrealistic ideals which result in the suppression of those who would not conform, but in a normal political environment where discussion and debate dominate. 'Sterile ideological debate [can be replaced] with discussions based on reality'[22] and South Africa can 'break through from the present situation of conflict, distrust and violence into a new situation where we operate at the political level by argument and persuasion'.[23]

It is worthwhile noting the ubiquity of the imagery of light and visibility in this context. The NP rails against its Conservative opponents for their inability to see what is 'obvious to any child'.[24] De Klerk continuously reiterates that 'reasonable observers' recognize the 'new reality' in South Africa. Indeed as Gerrit Viljoen declares, 'Reality is visible to anyone with the ability to open their eyes and look around.'[25]

The realities revealed in this epiphanic moment of history can be categorized into two orders: the anthropological and the economic. The anthropological fact that individuals pursue their own self-interest has revealed itself to the NP. This, however, is deemed no bad thing. No individual, de Klerk tells his businessperson audience, could 'achieve success without the support of dedicated teams, [but] it is the individuals who provide the driving force'. He cites Adam Smith to demonstrate that it is in the individual's pursuit of maximum utility that the optimal social good is achieved.[26] This leads to a second reality, because it is only some types of economic systems which adequately reward the individual for his/her contribution.

Indeed, de Klerk tells us that 'the great debate about economic systems – which dominated global politics for the ninety years of this century – is now over. Following the collapse of communism, it has become clear that there is really only one broad formula for economic success.' He continues, without seemingly to intend the irony that 'it is no longer possible to shop around [!] and to pick and choose economic systems according to our ideological predilections'. This economic system 'rests on free markets, private ownership, individual initiative'.[27]

Thus far, for the NP, the end of the Cold War constitutes an eschatological moment. From now on, economics and politics will live in the sublimity of universal reason. But this is only one of two stories to be found in the NP's discourse. In the following section, we exposit a conception of history told by the NP which is radically incommensurable with the one above.

POSTCARDS FROM THE PAST

Bill Clinton's first words as President of the United States, delivered in Washington on 20 January 1992, were these: 'This ceremony is about the peculiar mystery of democracy. We are here today to reinvent America.' This mystery, Clinton continued, of a people whose task is its own continual redescription, is peculiar to democracy because the body politic is no longer founded upon an organic and timeless identity, but upon the principle of human rights, which subjects all hierarchies to the prospect of dissolution. Our capacity to reinvent ourselves, Clinton averred, is synonymous with 'the capacity of people to stand up for themselves', a capacity which is constitutive of the democratic experience.

While Clinton was celebrating the fluidity of a political form which can reinvent its own content, Gerrit Viljoen was speaking of democracy in a rather different register. 'There is no magic wand,' Viljoen told his Umtata audience, 'which can be waved over what has been created in the past three hundred, even the past forty or thirty years.' History is not made of the stuff which the present can remould, or destroy. We cannot have a 'blank area on which to start building a new South Africa'.[28] In contrast to Clinton's formulation, our identities in the present are cast in stone by virtue of our inscription in the past. 'History,' de Klerk commented, '[i]s more than a mere chronicle of happenings and events. It is, in fact, a living phenomenon that survives and grows in the hearts of peoples and nations; it is a looking glass which opens one's eyes to truth and reality.'[29]

In fact, to use the singular 'history' to describe South Africa would be misleading. Strictly speaking, we are talking of a multitude of histories which have no business with each other, but which had the misfortune of becoming intertwined. 'In many respects,' remarked F. W. de Klerk 'South Africa is more of an archipelago than a country. Each of our different communities lives on its own island and seldom visits neighbouring islands. . . . We live in the same geographical areas, but are divided from one another by cultural straits and economic gulfs.'[30]

As in Clinton's inaugural address, mystery is invoked in speeches such as these. But we are not talking of the mystery of a people reinventing itself. On the contrary, we are talking of entities which are mysterious precisely because their essences must elude the grasp of those in the present – they stretch back to an antiquity which is both sacred and untouchable. Viljoen, for instance, in the Transkei Republic Day speech cited above, claims to be celebrating the anniversary of a natural entity: 'Transkei was never conquered by any colonial power,' Viljoen pronounced. 'This has made it a natural entity of government, and therefore one that must not be thoughtlessly discarded at the inauguration of a new dispensation.'[31]

What is sacred about these institutions of antiquity, what requires their presence in a new dispensation, is that it is they, rather than the institutions of modernity, that constitute the guardians of our respective identities. The same is true of the ancient forms of social organization in what is today KwaZulu. 'The influence of the traditional leaders is indisputable,' De Klerk told the Kwazulu Legislative Assembly:

> Although their power bases and the traditional socio-economic circumstances of their people have changed over the years, these leaders and the authorities surrounding them have remained prominent. They are in fact, essential parts of the maintenance of authority and the social fabric in most rural areas. . . . Traditional leaders and authorities play a unique and special role. Their primary function is to regulate and control relationships and social behaviour within the tribal community. *Unlike government structures, therefore, they are people-oriented rather than service oriented* [emphasis added].

Here a 'people-oriented' institution marks the place of its privileged integrity in much the same way that the Transkei remains a 'natural' social organization. Precisely because its origin predates the advent of modernity, it is construed as organic and timeless, its character embodying the pristine essence of social identity.

In sharp contrast then to Clinton's invitation to Americans to reinvent themselves, South African identities were moulded, and indeed sealed once and for all, in the distant past. The implication, of course, is that the adoption of classical jurisprudential principles which construct an undifferentiated and homogeneous citizenship, would constitute a violation of South African identities. And indeed, as we shall see later, in the NP's constitutional proposals, the guardians of our respective identities find themselves in the legislature and executive of the new dispensation, precisely to preside over the preservation of our respective sacred histories. The archipelago metaphor is neither fortuitous nor misleading. The reference to nature qua immutable identities is precisely the conception of history which is narrated here.

Yet if this is not convincing enough, let us examine the National Party leadership's explanation of apartheid. Whatever the South African political configuration of the latter half of the twentieth century, we are told, apartheid is deemed innocent *vis-à-vis* both the genesis and reproduction of the 'cultural straits' which divide South Africans. For the divisions which characterize South Africa were there *ab initio*. De Klerk approvingly quotes P. W. Botha – a man whose name he describes as 'synonymous with the words "reform" and "just power-sharing" ':

> It was not the National Party that created the diversity of nations in this country; this is its inheritance. The God that made the Afrikaner, also made the Coloureds and Blacks. If we want to keep South Africa secure, for our children too, there must be place for God's other creations.[32]

In other words, apartheid did all that the sphere of the political can do; it read the transcendental substratum that constituted it accurately, and enshrined this reading in a set of new principles, viz. self-determination. On this level, then, apartheid was nothing more than an acute reading of reality.

Yet, if apartheid understood the right to self-determination, it miscalculated the political modalities of its attainment. More specifically, the Verwoerdian leadership failed to acknowledge the transformations wrought upon the social fabric by rapid industrialization after the Second World War. The geo-economic integration which industrialization effected rendered the democratic ideal of self-determination unimplementable. The upshot, of course, is that the logic of self-determination was thwarted by a cynical inversion; South Africans found themselves inextricably bound to territories in which they enjoyed no citizen rights:

> The best efforts of outstanding leaders and managers over almost four decades, demonstrated beyond dispute that policies of ethnic and territorial separation could not provide our country with a viable solution. More than half of South Africa's Black population lives and works

permanently outside the TBVC countries and the six self-governing territories. There is hardly a magisterial district in the country in which
Black people are not in the majority. . . . The end result is that millions
of South African citizens do not enjoy the rights citizenship normally
brings with it. And if we were to revert back to 1986, they would have no
prospect whatsoever of achieving them.[33]

The upshot is that in the age of industrial capitalism in South Africa 'absolute self-determination is impossible. . . . States for individual peoples
are not practical. The realities of our time demand a unitary state.'[34]

But what then does this mean for the fate of democracy in contemporary
South Africa? If the quintessence of democracy is, as the architects of
apartheid insisted, a configuration of ethnically homogeneous and autonomous states, what are the consequences of its impossibility?

In order to grasp the National Party's conception of democracy in a unitary state, it must be reiterated that territorial self-determination has been
abandoned, not because it misconstrued the ethico-political principles
of democracy, but, on the contrary, because it was too ambitious in the
modalities of their implementation. States for individual peoples are abandoned because 'they are not practical'. In other words, they are desirable at the
level of political ethics, but, due to an unfortunate twist of fate, are not imple-
mentable. The birth of a unitary state, then, is quintessentially an act of
resignation and compromise. What are the principles governing this compromise?

First and foremost, democracy in a new South African polity *ipso facto*
excludes the principle of 'simple majority rule'.[35] 'There are enough historical and contemporary examples of undemocratic, unfree and tyrannical
situations,' remarked Gerrit Viljoen, 'to show that simple majority rule does
not *per se* guarantee democracy. It must be understood that majority rule is
neither a necessary guarantee nor a sufficient condition of democracy.'[36] Yet
more than this, in South Africa where democracy in a unitary state is essentially constituted by a parallel configuration of discrete groups, the concept of
simple majority rule 'annuls the meaning of the entire negotiation process'.[37]
For implicit in the logic of simple majority rule is an error far greater than that
committed by the architects of apartheid; an attempt to erase South Africa's
political identity and to engage in a perilous programme of social alchemy:
'It is too much to ask a constitution to "create" its own social and cultural
substructures,' warned Viljoen. 'It is dangerous and contrary to the facts to
ascribe homogeneity to South African society.'[38]

What then is 'the meaning of the negotiation process'? Let us begin with
what it categorically is not. What is being negotiated is not a rebirth or a

reinvention. We mentioned earlier that the political is deontologized in this conception: it has no constitutive capacity. Political and social identities are an immutable substratum and are thus immune to any play of meaning. There will be no euphoric ruptures, no fissures with which to break ourselves off from the past.

In essence, the birth of a new dispensation requires, not a transformation of identities, but a transformation of inter-group relations. 'We have to establish a *modus vivendi* among all our population groups, and ensure that differences are resolved by negotiation and compromise, and above all with tolerance and understanding.'[39]

The key to the success of the negotiation process, or 'the quintessential meaning of the negotiation process', as Viljoen is fond of putting it, resides in establishing this consociational *modus vivendi*. What does this entail, in regard to the institutions of the future? First, the new constitution is to be negotiated by 'an informal gathering' of South Africa's collective leadership. If its *modus operandi* is consensus and its participants are all imbued with the ethic of power-sharing, it will tailor a constitution of consociation. And what are the principles which this constitution will embody? It will establish a citizenry imbued with the classical array of first generation rights. All will have equal access to the public sphere, all will be free to nurture their respective cultural, linguistic and religious identities.

Second, both the legislature and the executive of the new dispensation will reflect the heterogeneous character of the new order. No legislation is to be passed by a simple majority. The legislature is to be bicameral with the lower house being elected on the basis of proportional representation, and the upper, with veto powers, is to be constituted by regions, each having equal voting rights.[40] The executive will never be occupied by a single party, rather executive power is to be wielded consociationally. Moreover, neither executive nor legislative power is to be concentrated in national institutions. Federal principles will regulate its devolution. The rubric of consociation will be built into the exercise of power pervasively across the spectrum of the polity.[41]

*   *   *

It should be clear from what has gone thus far that the corpus of texts which we have cited constructs two objects, but conceals this duality by allowing the same words to slide between their two respective identities. We have structured our exposition into two discrete sections in order to render these conceptual and narrative vicissitudes palpable. In the narrative elucidated in section two, let us call it the 'rationalist narrative' for convenience, political identities of the past are exploded into oblivion by a ruptural mutation in meaning. Such is the magnitude of this rupture that the surface of reality is reduced to simple transparency. And if the object is suddenly rendered visible, it is also because the subject has been ordained with the capacity to see. The explosion of our identities has left intact only the reasonable and rational core. Reality has become so palpable that the mere discussion of the democratic process constitutes the sufficient condition of its implementation.

In the second discourse, in contrast, let us call it 'the culturalist discourse', the social is constituted by an immutable substratum stretching back to time immemorial, viz. a heterogeneity of discrete social identities. 'Rationality' designates the obviousness of this heterogeneity, 'reason' the ethical inescapability of consociation. And consociation hence designates democracy.

Most significant is that each discourse animates a conception of democracy which is incommensurable with the other. 'Culturalist' representatives – each defending a politics etched in stone – bargain and manage the compromises of a *modus vivendi*. 'Rationalist' representatives, in contrast, dissolve their erstwhile identities and, via a dialogical production of truth, converge on a single, epistemically privileged position.

Yet the relation between the two 'discursive strains', so to speak, is far more complex than appears at first sight. We have yet to examine the dynamic of their entanglement. In what follows, we hope to illustrate that despite the conceptual gulfs which separate them, the two discursive strains converge around a single political space, a space demarcated by a subtext common to both of them: that of neo-racism.

POSTCARDS FROM THE FIRST WORLD

It was a national occasion during which South Africa's First World community sent out a very clear signal.[42]

In a document called 'Constitutional Rule in a Participatory Democracy',[43] the NP outlines its plans for a future constitution. There it distinguishes two 'pillars'[44] of a future polity: (i) the establishment of a constitutional state, and (ii) a new dispensation framed in such a way as to ensure the participation of all. For the moment, we wish to focus on the second pillar.

The second pillar of the constitution will ensure 'a system of government . . . in which a number of political parties effectively participate and in which *power-sharing* therefore takes place'. This is contrasted to the Westminster model in which one party enjoys exclusive power.[45] The NP's alternative is premised on the 'reality' of a 'multiplicity of socio-economic and cultural interest groups' which do not emerge solely because they are legislated but because 'people naturally and voluntarily associate with one another because they have some kind of interest in common' and whose divergent interests are best served in the constitutional sphere through different political parties. In practical terms, the NP argues that the 'core'[46] of its proposals is that the executive should not be constituted from one party, but from members of a number of political parties. The current state president will be replaced with a collegiate presidency of the leaders of the three largest parties, and ministerial positions will be distributed to the three largest parties.[47] In addition an equal number of seats should be allocated for all regions in the second chamber of parliament, thereby mitigating against regional domination. In order to ensure that no party dominates the legislature, in the second chamber the stronger parties of each region will be allocated an equal number of seats irrespective of the actual breakdown of support for each one individually.

How, if at all, are the two historical discourses we elucidated in sections two and three, implicated in these constitutional proposals? Rationalism, which finds its constitutional expression in parliamentarianism, posits the pursuit of truth to be an effect of the conflict of opinions and perspectives. It reduces politics to a debate over the correct, most rational path for the society to follow. In doing so it demands the renunciation of interests by those involved in the process since this would merely serve to predispose them to positions that may not, in fact, represent the most rational of possible courses. It demands that the parliamentary representative be free to adopt any position he/she chooses.

Members of parliament must not be influenced by private concerns. It is demanded of them that they sever themselves from interests other than the pursuit of truth. More explicitly, they must sever themselves from the constituencies who elected them. It is, therefore, the archetypal conception of government through reason and discussion.[48]

But if this is the case, then at first glance it appears that the NP's constitutional proposals have all but obliterated its rationalist construal of history. Unambiguously consociationalist in design, the *raison d'être* of government in the NP's proposals resides precisely in the fact that its composition mirrors the configuration of identities which constitute the social formation. The gap prised open by rationalism between government and social interests, is systematically closed.

If the relation between the NP's rationalist conception of history and its constitutional proposals seems irreparably severed, what is the relation between the culturalist narrative and the constitutional principles? At first glance, the NP's culturalism offers an intelligible basis for its consociationalism. Here groups have defined identities and interests. Consociationalism conceives political activity as a process of negotiation between discrete interest groups. Here groups actually and metaphorically sit around a table and haggle. Each presents its own preferences and a reasonable compromise is reached through discussion and debate. 'It is important,' says the most ardent theoretical advocate of this model of government:

> to understand that consociationalism deals with the potential problems of a plural society not by trying to make the society less plural, but by making it more plural. . . . By explicitly recognizing the segments, by giving the segmental organizations a vital formal function in the political system, by subsidizing them on a proportional basis, and by encouraging segmental political parties through proportional representation, consociational democracy increases the organizational strength of the segments. But instead of creating conflict, the strengthened segments now play a constructive role in conflict resolution.[49]

Here, however, another problem rears its head: despite constant references to their immutable existence from time immemorial, we do not know what groups are to be represented and protected in the consociational state. The NP has remained remarkably vague about the purpose for which groups are to be represented. Its comments in this regard are limited to some tentative declarations that group rights – such as the rights to protect a particular language, culture or religion – would best be guaranteed were representatives of such communities lodged in the state. This nebulous reasoning is further complicated by the NP's establishment of a series of equivalences and identities between different conceptions of the group. On the one hand groups have retained their primordial constitutions, while on the other they have become indeterminate, based as they are on 'socio-economic and cultural interest groups' formed because 'people naturally and voluntarily associate with one another because they have some kind of interest in common' (quoted above). As if this ambiguity were not enough, an identity between groups with particular values – which are both political and cultural – and political parties, is established: 'I represent a people,'[50] de Klerk declares.

It is in this multiple conflation – the nation with the cultural group, cultural values with political ones and political values with peoples – that the implications and intentions of consociationalism become obscured. One cannot tell whether the consociational system is designed to protect parties, nations or values.

But if this is the case, if on the one hand the rationalist discourse and the constitutional proposals are logically inarticulable, and if on the other hand, the conceptual relation between the culturalist discourse and the constitutional proposals is too hybrid and too malleable to achieve a semblance of coherence, how do the two discourses make sense *vis-à-vis* the constitutional proposals? The remainder of the paper is devoted to answering this question.

The rationalist discourse, we have had cause to repeat, announces an event of cosmic significance: the dawn of the Age of Reason and the consequent closing of the (ideological) debates of the past. Henceforth the character of society is not open to debate. However, an unfortunate problem with which the NP must deal exists: some people simply refuse to see reality in spite of its transparent obviousness. Speaking to the assembled might of the international community in Davos in February 1992, de Klerk lamented that while 'it is generally accepted today that communism is dead . . . [t]his message has not yet been brought home to all South Africans'.[51] Not all of us, it would appear, are equally able to grasp the 'facts of life'; some, in spite of the historical emergence of Truth, refuse to give up the 'out-moded policies' and 'bankrupt ideologies'[52] which characterized our ideological pre-history. So, while the constitution must be constructed on the basis of an accurate reading of the world, not all are able to do this.

But why not? Let us interrupt our narrative with a brief interlude in order to answer this question. Etienne Balibar has argued that racist discourse has undergone a transformation. 'Neo-racism' consists in 'racism without races'. This 'differentialist racism' does not explicitly posit physical stigmata as signs of superiority or inferiority. Rather it conceives different cultures as incommensurate. It goes so far as to attempt to account for racist practices by arguing that when (necessarily) incompatible communities are forced to interact, conflict will develop. In doing so, it attempts to pass itself off as the true anti-racism, an anti-racism which claims to be grounded in the empirical experience of the consequences of multicultural societies, but rejects earlier articulations which were premised on the superiority of one culture over others. It is this discursive mutation away from explicit culturalist parochialism, that Balibar detects at the root of right-wing discourses on immigration in Europe.

If, however, differentialist racism does not explicitly posit the superiority of particular collectivities, to read it as a relativist discourse would be a superficial reading. Lurking in the subtext of this discourse, a distinctly hierarchical conception of the relationship between cultures manifests itself in the construal of the character of different cultures and their respective relationships to distinctly modern priorities such as progress, development and democratic tolerance.[53]

This neatly encapsulates much of the subtextual discourse on culture and cultures that emerges from the NP. 'We have,' de Klerk tells his Swiss audience, 'this large Third World component, with the typical Third World problems which are slowly strangling the rest of Africa. We have them in our midst.'[54] This formulation captures the gist of the NP's neo-racist discourse. De Klerk unashamedly constructs an us/them opposition between sectors of the South African population. 'They' designates the poor, the illiterate, the underdeveloped sector and, most importantly, those who cannot, or will not, see reason. 'We' designates the advanced, the sophisticated and the rational. The NP conceives the 'them' as a threat to the 'objective and universal' values of the first world. 'Some members of the population,' De Klerk warns, 'have come to a growing expectation that the envisaged restructuring of the constitutional system, will be coupled with an almost simultaneous ending of the relative backlog of the developing part of the population . . . I am referring to . . . the pressure on First World standards by those who are not yet in a position to make that contribution to the economy that would justify their claims.'[55]

We have already referred to a speech de Klerk made which was heralded as an apology for apartheid. In that very speech he declares that 'Winburg is indeed a living symbol of Voortrekker history . . . of the trek that brought Christian faith, Western civilization and the democratic form of government deep into South Africa's interior.'[56]

No doubt we should all be deeply grateful to those hardy pioneers who struggled against the heathen, barbarous and authoritarian(?) hordes. They have certainly left their imprint. Indeed this philanthropic impulse has not been extinguished from the heart of those who to this very day continue to uphold Christian civilization. Take the South African police – universally admired for their restraint and impartiality. 'Often,' we are told, 'it is a single policeman, or a few of them, standing between warring groups and preventing them from taking one another by the throat.'[57]

In June 1990 F. W. de Klerk had this to say about the gap between the respective political cultures of white and black voters: '[P]articularly in the 1980s, there has been a greater tendency for people [that is, the white electorate] to support a party because of its policy and its principles, whatever those people's motivation might be, and not on the basis of culture.'[58] One month later, in the same journal Gerrit Viljoen referred to the recently enfranchised voters of 'South West Africa and Rhodesia'. There was 'a tendency in the majority of the population towards supporting the strongman and not necessarily supporting a given policy'. On this basis he argues that 'it is quite clear that intimidation . . . has a tremendous effect on the immediate support for the ANC or whichever other party is dominant'.[59]

One is tempted to leave these two statements to speak for themselves. They so neatly conjure the idea that 'the majority' is an irrational force with only the white minority exhibiting reason, that comment seems unwarranted. Nevertheless, it is not sufficient to leave it there since this conception appears frequently in the NP's formulations. On one occasion, responding to a question about the potential for a right-wing revolution, de Klerk had this to say: 'I don't think that there's a threat of a widely supported revolution from the right, because the overwhelming majority of the white people of South Africa are god-fearing people with reasonable approaches to life. That sort of radicalism cannot attract large numbers of whites in supporting devastating and negative acts of violence and killing. Therefore I trust my people. They will support reasonable solutions.'[60]

On another occasion: 'Whites, who have been embedded in the political process for a long time, should set an example of how to take part in politics. The potential for violence in our country is such that it has become time that democrats set an example of staying absolutely within the rules of decency, and giving the other man an opportunity to state his case.'[61] The attributes of reason and rationality are not evenly distributed among humanity. Certainly there is a distinction to be drawn between the 'great clarity of the West and the magic and mysticism of Africa'.[62] The net effect is that the majority constitutes an irrational, inexperienced and untutored electorate. In this regard it is crucial that those with the right values continue to occupy influential and decisive positions in the state.

* * *

We have said a great deal in this chapter. Let us conclude by briefly summarizing. We have argued that two conceptions of history, one rationalist and the other culturalist, converge in their common defence of a consociational state. Yet, we found that neither tallied, so to speak, with the logic of the consociational model proposed by the National Party. In the first place, the notion of an identity between the democratic process and the reasoned pursuit of truth, *ipso facto* contradicts a conception of the state qua consociation of discrete interests. In relation to the culturalist discourse, we could not find the *raison d'être* of cultural minorities' representation in the state. More specifically, we could not find precisely what, *vis-à-vis* cultural interests, is intended to be represented.

It is only through the detection of a subtle mutation in the culturalist conception that the entire discursive ensemble's relation to consociationalism becomes apparent. We are talking here of the moment when the notion of

South Africa qua *segmented* object is silently transformed into a *hierarchical* object.

For at this point there emerges a new universe of meaning, and with it, a new dilemma. Let us call it the dilemma of the opposition between quality and quantity. Quality represents those seemingly self-apparent truths of which the rationalist discourse speaks; the notion that ideology qua artefact has given way to reality qua nature. Yet, we have seen that this 'self-appearance' is not available to all eyes. South Africa is hierarchically structured in its relation to the truths of 'Enlightenment'. We are left with the bizarre scenario in which ethico-political legitimacy must fight the popular will. The state must be structured in such a fashion that the representation of value counterposes the representation of numbers. 'Leaders of minority groups who hold these values must,' Viljoen avers, 'be represented in the state.'[63]

It is at this moment that the cohabitation of rationalism and consociationalism in the same discursive ensemble becomes intelligible. For a plurality of cultural interests have silently mutated into an opposition between the rational and the barbaric.

NOTES

1   We are indebted to Peter Hudson, Aletta Norval, and especially to Sam Mkhabela for comments on an earlier version of this paper. Responsibility for the arguments is ours alone.

2   A brief word on methodology. The most difficult methodological problem confronted by a project of this nature is, of course, the question, 'what constitutes National Party discourse?' Do we stretch into the far reaches of the National Party's periphery, giving the speeches of small-town backbenchers the same weight as a national presidential address? Or do we establish a hierarchy of statements according to the frequency of their utterance and establish a threshold under which no statement is deemed to constitute a component of NP discourse?

Our response has been to limit our object to the utterances delivered from two portfolios: those of the state President and the Minister of Constitutional Affairs. We have gathered, to the best of our knowledge, every speech and statement delivered from these two portfolios from January 1990 to December 1992. Collectively, they approximate upwards of 250 documents. To be sure, these are government, not party, portfolios and so the insistent reader may inform us that we have not read a word of National Party discourse. Yet were this principle of separation to be followed, let us assure that insistent reader that National Party discourse would consist of no more than a monthly newspaper, a miscellaneous collection of pamphlets, and a handful of interviews with the NP's former secretary-general, Stoffel van

der Merwe. From the level of national rhetoric, to the organizational foundation of its grassroots infrastructure, the NP's profile is defined in and by
its position as governing party.

Our task then has been to identify that moment of public speech which
carries the deepest and broadest symbolic efficacy qua speech of the
National Party. In the midst of constitutional transition, we believe that the
aforementioned portfolios fill that space. In addition, we have been at pains
to ensure that the statements we draw on are neither eccentric nor infre-
quent. The discursive ensemble which we identify stretches consistently
across the time-span of our study. Moreover, it is an ensemble which spans
the entire spectrum of audiences to which NP discourse is addressed: national television, the white *platteland*, black townships, international press
conferences, and so on.

A brief word on referencing: we read the vast majority of presidential
and ministerial speeches in unpublished, typescript form, courtesy of the
State President's Office. Wherever we cite an unpublished address or
speech, our source is the State President's Office.

3   G. Viljoen, 'Address to the Institute for American Studies of the Rand
    Afrikaans University', 26 February 1990.
4   Carl Schmitt, *The Crisis of Parliamentary Democracy,* trans. Ellen
    Kennedy, Cambridge, Mass., 1985, p. 35.
5   Ibid., p. 35.
6   Ibid., pp. 4–6.
7   Viljoen, 'Address to the Institute for American Studies'.
8   F. W. de Klerk, 'Address to Pretoria Press Club', 23 March 1990.
9   G. Viljoen, 'Parliamentary address', 9 May 1990.
10 F. W. de Klerk, Address to the opening of the Special Sitting of Parlia-
    ment', 13 October 1992.
11 G. Viljoen, 'The National Party', *Journal of Democracy,* Fall 1990, pp. 43–4.
12 G. Viljoen in 'The other side of the Rubicon: Interview with Gerrit
    Viljoen', in *Leadership,* vol. 9, no 3, March 1990, p. 46.
13 Adriaan Vlok, 'Press conference held at Union Buildings, Pretoria', 1 Oc-
    tober 1992.
14 F. W. de Klerk, 'Address to the National Press Club, Washington D.C.', 25
    September 1990.
15 Viljoen, 28 June 1990.
16 F. W. de Klerk, interviewed in *South African Policy Review,* August 1990,
    pp. 11–12.
17 F. W. de Klerk, 'Address to the 13th annual conference of Frankel, Kruger,
    Vinderine Inc., Cape Town', 23 January 1990.
18 F. W. de Klerk, 'Address to the Pretoria Press Club' (translated from the
    Afrikaans), 3 March 1990.
19 The last clause is particularly symptomatic. De Klerk avers that it is not sin-
    ful to pay interest. Two 'meaning effects' are buried in this peculiar formula-
    tion. On the one hand de Klerk implies that nothing that complies with reality
    is sinful; on the other, that the notion of sin and its categories might them-
    selves be used for ideological purposes. For a man who proclaims his faith
    at every opportunity, he seems to be sailing rather close to the heretical
    winds.

20   This is not to say that all conflict is a result of human intervention into an intrinsically harmonious process – we will see below that sometimes reality itself leads to conflict. However, it is striking how closely this corresponds with religious doctrines of Original Sin: God put us in the world and provided us with the wherewithal to survive, and yet we succumbed to the temptation to pluck the fruit and so we fall. This discourse finds more explicit expression in what the mainstream media have inaccurately deemed de Klerk's 'apology speech'. Speaking at the 150-year anniversary of the founding of Winburg on 9 October 1992, de Klerk painted a picture of the Afrikaner nation moving through history and said, 'Yes, we made mistakes. Yes, we often sinned and we do not deny it. . . .Like a broken reed and shattered clay pot we strayed (sic)' (translated from the Afrikaans).

21   F. W. de Klerk, 'Address to the Pretoria Press Club' (translated from the Afrikaans), 16 September 1992.

22   F. W. de Klerk, 'Address to Parliament', 17 April 1990.

23   G. Viljoen, International Press Conference, Cape Town, 6 February 1990.

24   G. Viljoen, 'Parliamentary address', 13 February 1990.

25   G. Viljoen, 'Parliamentary address' (translated from the Afrikaans), 10 May 1990.

26   F. W. de Klerk, 25 November 1991, *Sunday Times* Top 100 Companies Banquet. Another example comes from Gerrit Viljoen, 8 October 1990, speech to Cape NP Congress. There he declares that it is the NP's 'firm conviction that the individual pursuit of excellence ensures progress for the nation as a whole' (translated from the Afrikaans).

27   F. W. de Klerk, 'Address to the Pretoria Press Club', 16 September 1992.

28   G. Viljoen, 'Speech delivered to a Transkei Republic Day rally', 28 May 1990.

29   F. W. de Klerk, 'Speech delivered at the 150th anniversary celebrations of the town of Winburg', 9 October 1992.

30   F. W. de Klerk, 'Speech to the Goodwill Foundation', 9 March 1991.

31   G. Viljoen, 'Address to a Transkei Republic Day rally', 28 May 1990.

32   F. W. de Klerk, 'Speech at the 75th anniversary of the Cape National Party, Middleburg' (translated from the Afrikaans), 15 September 1990.

33   F. W. de Klerk, 'Budget vote debate, Parliament', 2 May 1991.

34   F. W. de Klerk, 'Address to a public meeting, Ventersdorp', 9 August 1991.

35   'Simple majority rule' in the discourse of the NP refers to any 'first-past-the-post' electoral system.

36   G. Viljoen, 'Speech delivered to a University of Port Elizabeth graduation ceremony', 27 April 1990.

37   G. Viljoen, interviewed in *Policy Review,* June 1991.

38   'Speech delivered to the Jeugkrag National Congress', 28 June 1990.

39   F. W. de Klerk, 'Presidential address at the opening of parliament', 24 January 1992.

40   National Party, 'Constitutional Rule in a Participatory Democracy', September 1991, p. 12: 'Each political party which has gained a specified amount of support in an election in [a] region's legislative body will be allocated an equal number of seats for that region in the Second House.'

41   See the National Party's 'Constitutional Proposals for a New Dispensation', September 1991. We will deal with the discourse of this document in far greater depth in the following section.

42 Louis Pienaar, Minister of Home Affairs and the Environment, after white South Africans sang 'Die Stem' (apartheid South Africa's national anthem) at the opening ceremony of a rugby match against New Zealand in August 1991.
43 National Party, 'Constitutional Rule in a Participatory Democracy', September 1991.
44 Ibid., p. 5.
45 Ibid., p. 8.
46 Ibid., p. 12.
47 Ibid., p. 13.
48 Schmitt, *The Crisis of Parliamentary Democracy,* chapter 2.
49 A. Lijphart, *Power-Sharing in South Africa,* Berkeley, 1985, pp. 106–7.
50 F. W. de Klerk, '75th anniversary of the Cape National Party, Middleburg', 15 September 1990.
51 F. W. de Klerk, 'Speech delivered at Davos', 2 February 1992.
52 'Pik' Botha, 'Speech to Hans Seidel Stiftung, Munich', 20 November 1990.
53 E. Balibar, 'Is There Neo-Racism', trans. Chris Turner, in E. Balibar and I. Wallerstein, *Race, Nation, Class,* London, 1991.
54 F. W. de Klerk, 'Speech to Swiss-South Africa Association, Zürich', 23 May 1990.
55 F. W. de Klerk, 'Speech to the Johannesburg Afrikaans Business Chamber, Kempton Park' (translated from the Afrikaans), 21 November 1990.
56 F. W. de Klerk, 'Winburg speech' (translated from the Afrikaans), 9 October 1992.
57 F. W. de Klerk, 'Transcript of answers to a live TV information conference broadcast on M-Net', 24 August 1990.
58 F. W. de Klerk, interview in *Leadership,* vol. 9, no. 6, June 1990, p. 34.
59 G. Viljoen, interview in *Leadership,* vol. 9, no. 7, July 1990, p. 30.
60 F. W. de Klerk, 'Address to the National Press Club, Washington', 25 September 1990.
61 F. W. de Klerk, 'Transcript of answers to a live TV information conference broadcast on M-Net', 24 August 1990.
62 F. W. de Klerk, 'Speech to Afrikaanse taalfonds, Bloemfontein' (translated from the Afrikaans), 7 June 1990.
63 Gerrit Viljoen, 'Cape NP Congress' (translated from the Afrikaans), 8 October 1990.

4 From the 'Peaceful Past' to the 'Violent Present': Memory, Myth and Identity in Guguletu[1]

Sean Field

People do not face the present as an isolated and empty space, sandwiched between the past and future. Rather, 'the present' is 'itself historical: a complex series of interlocking histories whose interactions have to be reconstructed, not assumed'.[2] 'All present awareness' as Lowenthal puts it, 'is grounded in past perceptions and acts',[3] or as Tonkin states, 'All understandings of the past affect the present. Literate or illiterate, we are our memories.'[4] The telling of a life story is crafted from these memories of the past and is both present and presented in the present.

The comparisons that 18 African interviewees make, consciously and unconsciously, between 'the past' and 'the present' are the primary focus of this chapter.[5] I will interpret the manner in which former residents of the Windermere community construct their memories as a specific way of coping with the violence of their contemporary community life in Guguletu. Windermere was an ethnically mixed, part squatter community, on the urban periphery of Cape Town. Culturally, it thrived from the 1930s until the 1950s, but was torn apart by apartheid laws between 1958 and 1963. The bulk of Windermere's African families were removed to Guguletu.

African interviewees' memories of the apartheid past reflect both their 'good times' and 'bad times'. But these memories tend to be fraught with pain, anxiety, fear and a myriad of other conflicting emotions. Furthermore, the uncertainties of social transition and violent instability tend to make the present seem far more horrifying than anything experienced before.[6] In some cases there is a longing for a rural past; in others, for a frenetic youthful past of shebeens, dance halls and various cultural activities of Windermere of the 1940s and 1950s.[7] This is neither trivial nostalgia, nor popular romanticism, which can be dismissed with intellectual cynicism. Rather, the reconstruction, and in some cases the denial or forgetting, of social memories of the past serve a vital function of enhancing and defending an ageing self delicately located within a dangerous present.

Oral history is suited to unravelling the subtle nuances of psychological mechanisms operating as interviewees narrate their memories.[8] The different ways interviewees value and relate to their memories suggest a positioning of the self to its own past and the collective past within which it has developed. I will argue that the different values that interviewees attribute to their memories, and the form, content and selection of their narrated memories, contain significant clues about identity formation. However, this theoretically informed, interpretative methodology is in contrast to the dominant empiricist uses of oral history in South Africa. These empiricist approaches rarely pay attention to complex relationships between identities, memories and narratives.[9] They also tend not to reflect on the context in which interviews take place and the personal involvement and identities of the interviewer. Acknowledging the researcher's location *in* the research process is vital to the construction of emotionally sensitive and textured interpretations of oral histories in South Africa.

I will argue that it is especially the echoes of 'racial' and ethnic identities that can be heard in the stories from the Windermere past.[10] On the one hand, there is the physical and emotional loss of an ethnically mixed community destroyed by apartheid. On the other hand, the mythical wholeness of the Windermere past reconstructed in memory provides a comforting discourse with which the uncertain present and future can be understood and faced. It is particularly through interacting with other 'Windermere people', or attentive listeners, that interviewees grasp opportunities to sustain a community-in-memory through the remembering and telling of stories about the Windermere past.[11] Furthermore, institutional forms such as burial societies provide ongoing avenues for 'Windermere people' in Guguletu to nurture their community-in-memory. The Windermere community that developed in a space called 'Windermere' no longer exists. But through the discursive construction of myth and memory the 'Windermere people' nurture a community-in-memory as a fragile form of communal identity in the present.

FROM WINDERMERE OF THE 1950s TO GUGULETU OF THE 1990s

The Windermere/Kensington community originated on farmlands on the urban periphery of Cape Town in the first decades of this century. The area at this time consisted of a few scattered brick buildings and many more iron shanties. The Cape Town City Council (CCC) boundary stopped at 6th Avenue, Kensington. People squatted in the Windermere area beyond 6th Avenue in order to avoid municipal laws and taxes.[12] During this period the bulk of these squatters were coloured, with several whites and Africans intermingled. Most of these people came from rural areas in search of work in the urban areas. However, according to oral accounts, it is clear that the major African influx from the rural areas of Transkei and Ciskei only began in the 1930s and accelerated in the 1940s. At its peak in the 1950s the Windermere/Kensington area was estimated to contain in excess of 30 000 residents although inaccurate official estimates put it at less than 20 000. During the 1950s the African majority numbered approximately 55–60 per cent, coloured people 40–45 per cent and whites 2–4 per cent of the Windermere/Kensington area.[13]

The Windermere/Kensington area was, however, notorious for its poor sanitary conditions, overcrowding, unscrupulous landowners, and high incidence of diseases, especially tuberculosis.[14] Despite these poverty-stricken and squalid conditions there was a vibrant cultural milieu of shebeens, dance halls, gangs, brothels and even a sand horse race-track where people gambled on Sunday afternoons.

Windermere was incorporated under the jurisdiction of the CCC in 1943. In the period 1943–58 the CCC and the Native Administration Department (NAD) used sections under the 1934 Slums Act and pass laws to begin clearing Africans out of the area. These initial measures seemed to have little effect on the stream of African newcomers to Windermere. During the 1950s approximately 12 000 African men (so-called 'bachelors') were forcibly removed to single-sex hostels in Langa.[15] However, it was only when the area was racially zoned a coloured area in 1958 that dramatic changes occurred. In the 1960–3 period approximately 2500 African families were removed to Nyanga West, which was later to become Guguletu. It is therefore possible to estimate that in excess of 20 000 African people (including 'bachelors') were removed from the area. During this period approximately 1000 white people were removed to areas zoned for whites in Maitland, Brooklyn and Ruyterwacht. Because Kensington/Windermere was zoned as a coloured area, most coloured residents of Windermere were rehoused into a section (13th–18th Avenue) for economic and sub-economic housing, renamed Factreton.[16] The rest of the area previously known as Windermere is today incorporated within the 'model coloured community' of Kensington (2nd–13th Avenue).

The removal of African people to Guguletu during 1960–3 met with little popular resistance. In part, this had to do with a weak African National Congress (ANC) and Pan Africanist Congress (PAC) presence in Windermere. However, a more forceful reason is that the state promised African residents of Windermere their own houses. For the thousands who were living in corrugated iron shanties in areas highly prone to floods, fires and poor sanitary conditions (and violence), a new house in a new community seemed very appealing. However, this was not to be. When they arrived in their new homes, they found, as an interviewee put it, 'a concrete shell'. No ceiling. No inside doors. No proper floor. No electricity. No hot water. No inside toilets. A powerful sense of disappointment, and in many cases anger, was felt by every interviewee. Justifiably they felt tricked.

Since 1976 Guguletu has experienced school boycotts, stayaways, mass protests and repeated periods of violent struggles between residents, police and army. From the 1980s anti-apartheid civic and youth organizations became prominent. The levels of violence have steadily increased in Guguletu with ongoing political conflicts, taxi wars, rising unemployment and waves of new arrivals from the Ciskei and Transkei. Since the abolition of influx control in 1986 there has been considerable growth of new squatter camps in vacant lots on the perimeter of, and inside, Guguletu. Local ANC political activists claim that much of the common crime comes from desperate new arrivals in the squatter camps who are less integrated into community and political networks. Ironically, in the light of the experiences of former Windermere residents, there are now divisions between squatters and house occupants in Guguletu. Many interviewees drew parallels between the sight of Windermere of the 1950s and the squatter camps of the 1990s in and around Guguletu.

On 10 April 1993 Chris Hani was murdered, which resulted in weeks of popular unrest in Guguletu (and many other African townships around South Africa). During late April–June 1993 army patrols had checkpoints at every entrance to Guguletu and my fieldwork ground to a halt. During the July/August 1993 period I conducted most of the African interviews with the help of a black research assistant, who was a former ANC activist from Guguletu. As I moved around the streets of Guguletu the angry glares of youths on street corners and the fresh scars of recent street battles were all around. An overwhelming sense of tension and fear (of violence) seemed to permeate all my discussions (and interviews) with residents.

As a white individual entering a war-torn black township I was the one under observation. Appearing too well-dressed would increase the chances of attack, and appearing untidy would be seen as a sign of disrespect by interviewees. A delicate balance in appearance and manner was constantly necessary. Given the difficult political circumstances, the presence of my research assistant offered minimal protection. However, his grasp of the Xhosa language and customs combined with a street knowledge of Guguletu were very useful. Also, he could use my ANC membership to set up the interviews.[17] However, Guguletu in 1993 was extremely tense. While my status as a 'white comrade' afforded me some protection in the

1980s, after Chris Hani's murder on 10 April 1993, it afforded none what-soever.

Just before 5 p.m. on 25 August I conducted my last interview in Langa and was on my way (alone) to conduct a final interview in Guguletu. Inex-plicably, I did not feel like doing another interview that day and went home. Perhaps it was the end-of-fieldwork tiredness. Perhaps it was the sight of the smouldering ashes of tyres in the streets of Langa. So, instead of driving down the main road (called NY1) of Guguletu at 5 p.m., I went home. At 5 p.m., 25 August 1993, a white American student named Amy Biehl was brutally murdered on NY1, Guguletu. For a few days thereafter Guguletu witnessed a series of street battles. Guguletu was once again a war zone. All the residents I interviewed bore the emotional scars of these township wars. Most of them have experienced the trauma of having had either friends, relatives or children imprisoned, shot, whipped and in some cases killed.

MOVING MEMORIES: FROM THE 'PEACEFUL PAST' TO THE 'VIOLENT PRESENT'

Portelli has argued that 'memory is not a passive depository of facts, but an active process of creation of meanings. Thus, the specific utility of oral sources for the historian lies, not so much in their ability to preserve the past, as in the very changes wrought by memory.'[18] Such change, wrought by memory, however, 'directs our attention not to the past but to *the past present relation*' (their emphasis).[19] This relationship is crucial because to the life-story narrator, as Bertaux-Wiame argues, 'the first purpose is not to des-cribe the past "as it was", or even as it was experienced, but to confer to the past experience a certain *meaning*; a meaning which will contribute to the meaning of the present' (her emphasis).[20]

In this section, I will explore how black Africans from Windermere, who under apartheid suffered considerable hurt to their sense of self and identity, have created and forged their own personal meanings in uncer-tain times. The intention here is not a historical account of what did or did not happen in the apartheid past, but an interpretation of the ambiguous truths contained in the narration of meaningful memories. As Portelli argues:

> The importance of oral testimony may lie not in its adherence to fact, but rather in its departure from it, as imagination, symbolism and desire emerge. Therefore, there are no 'false' oral sources. . . . The diversity

of oral history consists in the fact that 'wrong' statements are still psychologically 'true' . . . [21]

The overwhelming majority of the 54 interviewees (black, coloured and white individuals) spoke of Windermere in glowing terms as a place of peace and togetherness. A place where young and old from different cultures lived happily together. For African interviewees, this romantic gloss on the Windermere past had a distinctly sharper and tenser edge to it, largely because of their frequent comparisons with contemporary violence in Guguletu. The following sequence of quotes from African interviewees illustrates a series of past/present comparisons. A 92-year-old male (former gardener and security guard) compares levels of violence, cost of living and an implied loss of neighbourliness and community:

We used to live in harmony. There was no *skollies* [SF: hooligans], one could travel at anytime of the night without fear of being robbed or stabbed. Neighbours were very friendly to each other. Everything was cheap that time. If we could be allowed to go back we'll be the first to leave.

A 61-year-old female (domestic worker and shebeen keeper) makes similar references to peace and violence. She also evokes a sense of loss over what was possible when she was young:

If they say we can move back to Windermere, oh, *ja*, I can move anytime. This place is a horrible place. I mean where we stay here now, what can we do? When we were young in Windermere we used to walk 'til midnight, but here in Guguletu, uh uh, you can't! We had a nice time in Windermere.

A 60-year-old female (domestic worker) makes similar peace/violence and cheap/expensive comparisons, but also evokes the sense of community that she shared in growing up with coloured people:

We played with the coloured children there. Ah, it was nice there, the coloured people. No fighting, nothing. All just one person. No, we stay nicely with the coloured people there. Anytime they can say to us, 'Go back to Kensington' I can be the first one! Ah, ha, ha, ha. Mmm it was not so heavy like here. Here's everything is dear, there my mother, used to see donkey carts with greens, basket of greens. Five shillings a basket of greens.

One of the younger interviewees, who was born and raised in Windermere (52-year-old female domestic worker) emphasized the sadness
evoked by being forced to leave and the longing for the place and the coloured friends she had there:

> It was a sad story when everybody had to move out of Kensington. A sad
> story. Well those who were left behind were just lucky, because quite a
> few people are still there that we grew up with in Kensington. So we had
> to move out of the place man, *hê*! Even if, even if you can come back and
> say Babsie, they say, you can come back. I can be number one.

A striking repetition in all these quotes is the desire to be the 'first one' to
go back to the Windermere/Kensington area and, of course, to go back to
the days that can never be recaptured or relived. The most powerful comparative message, interwoven with the peace/violence contrast, between
the Windermere of the 1950s and the Guguletu of the 1990s, is the perceived loss of community. As the above interviewee says:

> Now in these days, it's Guguletu where your neighbour is your enemy.
> Whereas in the olden days your neighbour was your sister. You can't
> ask your neighbour now please give me some sugar. No, she hasn't got
> it and the next thing the children fight, then the big people get involved.
> Now in the olden days if we used to fight with one another in our area
> [SF: Windermere/Kensington], the big people just come and sort it out
> and take sticks and give us there. 'Now you fight!' [SF: She bangs the
> table with her hands.]

In these passages three related effects of apartheid are referred to: firstly,
the damage to elder/youth relationships; secondly, the rupture of community and neighbourhood networks; thirdly, a deepening of the gap between
politics and the private personal sphere. In a similar vein, Passerini has argued that Fascism 'accentuated the gap between the political sphere and
daily private life, thus creating wounds in the tissue of memory, which
could not easily recompose what had been forcefully separated'.[22] When
social relations between people are ruptured, the relational spaces for containing and passing on social memories are also affected. In the above passages, I would argue we can hear interviewees making assessments about
the painful effects caused by the social engineering of the apartheid system
and the repression of anti-apartheid opposition. Furthermore, while all these
interviewees were poor and lived under difficult conditions in Windermere, the limited material advances in their contemporary lives are over-

shadowed by the turbulent political and social conditions of township life through the 1970s–1990s. The romantic tone and longing for the Windermere past reflects a genuine desire for the pleasures and relative freedoms of being young in a vibrant semi-rural squatter community. As Samuel and Thompson have argued in a review of oral testimonies in community histories:

> The slum, for so many years a byword for poverty and deprivation, is transfigured into a warm and homely place, a little commonwealth where there was always a helping hand. The narrative of hard times becomes a record of courage and endurance. The characteristic note is elegiac, saying good-bye to what will never be seen again, an affectionate leave-taking . . . the slum recaptures the symbolic space of 'the world we have lost'. Many, maybe most of the facts will be true. It is the omissions and the shaping which makes these stories also myth.[23]

Yet this kind of myth is not a common-sense falsity or untruth; that is not the issue here. This myth-making is the creation of memories that help people to live their lives in difficult times. These are 'the myths we live by'[24] and they help to form the complete stories about a personal past that will always be incomplete. Furthermore, this 'Remembrance . . . in essence points to the incompleteness of the present'.[25] An 'incompleteness' born of the unfulfilled needs, wants and desires that interviewees have lived with in their struggle to survive. Therefore, when a 'revival of memories' (as one interviewee put it) occurs in the interview dialogue a tremendous array of different emotions are evoked. Many of the interviewees cried, many were on the verge of tears, and many withdrew into a silent numbness. Narrating one's life story is an emotional event. Myth-making, as an indelible element of story telling, is about pushing the limits of vocabulary and culture in order to express and understand the emotions of a traumatic past and present. It is all about putting into words and stories the diverse mixture of fragments of emotional experiences that are embedded in conscious and unconscious memory. As Bhabha puts it, 'Re-membering (sic) is never a quiet act of introspection. It is a painful remembering, a putting together of the dismembered past to make sense of the trauma of the present.'[26]

Myth-making in the process of memory recall and story telling about the past has to be situated and interpreted within this emotionally charged social milieu. The minority of interviewees who did not paint a romantic gloss on the Windermere past, tended to focus more on the harshness of the present. The following dialogue with a 70-year-old male interviewee (retired driver) reflects these patterns:

SF: And when you are at these meetings [that is, burial society meetings] do you ever talk about the Windermere days?
I: Not actually. We almost forget about the things of Windermere, Kensington.
SF: You almost forget?
I: Mmm.
SF: Why?
I: Ha, ah. What can I say? I, I don't know. There's a lot of problems here, that's why. You see?
SF: And that makes people forget?
I: Yes, we've got no time for those old things now. We must look at this, what is happening now and these days.

With more resignation the following interviewee (a 69-year-old male, former foodworker) says:

I: It was an easy life at Windermere and everything went up. *Ja*, but we gotta bigger houses here, but, although we gotta bigger houses, eh, we also struggling with the very bad things here.
SF: So you are saying, that you wouldn't want to go back to Windermere?
I: No, I wouldn't want to.
SF: Why not?
I: . . . (Sighs) Uh uh, no it's notta the same, we know *mos* [SF: why], it, even Windermere is not de same now. Not black people there, everything's change now.

For the following interviewee there is anger and resentment at both the violence (and poverty) in contemporary Guguletu. However, these experiences of hardship are additions to the horrors he saw in Windermere of the 1950s. This 70-year-old male (former railway worker) said:

We don't talk about the Kensington *dingus, besigheid* [SF: thing, business]. Because it was too bad there. Nobody like it, anymore now. To talk about that *besigheid*, because was struggle in Kensington. Everybody know, was all the people was struggle at Kensington. Sometimes you will come from work in docks, there, sometimes overtime late at night. We come home later past twelve, past one. Here come the, that fucken dingus. The band here. You know if you don't like this man, in midnight, I try to take a paraffin or petrol, we throw it over his house. Burn there. You know was *mos* a shack was too close together, no space, passage between. If you are, you burnt, this *hokkie* [SF: shack] here, that next door be burnt, then another one next door. All over. Now must wait, how many people inside there? Then you count how, one, two, you know how many people was burn inside? Ah Kensington, that place was no good there. The white people never take care, not a fucken *dingus*.

There is searing hurt expressed in this story, in contrast to the comforting tones of the earlier stories about Windermere. Life was tough then, and life is tough now. My sense is that for all interviewees there is considerable pain associated with the Windermere past. For some that pain is managed by reconstructing their memories. On the one hand, memories of pain and hardship are suppressed (and repressed); on the other hand, happy memories are exaggerated and romanticized. Sigmund Freud argues that, 'As the indifferent memories owe their preservation not to their own content but to an associative relation between their content and another which is repressed, they have some claim to be called screen memories.'[27] In several instances these romantic memory constructions of Guguletu interviewees are perhaps a form of screen memory, which conceal the displacement of significant memories laden with painful emotions.[28] In contrast, the anger and aggression of the above male interviewee towards all this hardship, past and present, is openly delivered.

Hofmeyer correctly argues that there is a gender division between male and female story telling genres.[29] However, I find her argument that men are more likely to tell 'true' historical accounts in contrast to women who tend to use fictionalized narratives less convincing.[30] Insofar as I focused on the reconstruction of memories to fulfil present needs, both female and male interviewees reconstruct their memories in fictionalized forms. I would argue that the critical issue is not how much more or less men or women fictionalize their narratives, but that there are differing fictionalized images and patterns that men and women deploy in their story telling. For example, women interviewees often draw on maternal images and spiritual dreams, whereas men often cast themselves as heroic fighters.

The different forms and degrees of pain experienced under apartheid must be dealt with, consciously or unconsciously, by both men and women. Moral judgements should not be made about which or whose coping mechanisms are most appropriate. Rather, interpreting the 'conditions for remembering',[31] and the narrative and social means people use to survive, can provide clues about the construction of memory, myth and identity.

IDENTITIES: INTERPRETING THE AGONY OF APARTHEID

> History is what hurts, it is what refuses desire and sets inexorable limits
> to individual and collective praxis, which its 'ruses' turn into grisly and
> ironic reversals of their overt intention. But this History can be appre-
> hended only through its effects, and never directly as some reified
> force.[32]

Apartheid hurt people.[33] Apartheid is 'past'. However, the wounds and
scars of apartheid live on, in the new South Africa. While major political,
social and economic reconstruction and development are crucial to the
healing of the traumas of apartheid, the emotional traces will remain in the
memories of many generations. The memories of the apartheid past, the
impact of contemporary violence, and the desires for the future, are carried
forward. As one interviewee explains (75-year-old male, former undertaker):

> The future it looks bright, although my wish is that the killings stop. The
> killings maybe stop. This is bad. This is bad. This is bad. People should
> come together black and white man. This can be a happy country. If the
> people, can just come together and be one. No complaint. It's not neces-
> sary for one to complain, it's only that is apartheid it has done a lot of
> damage. Has done a lot of damage. If it was not for this apartheid, this is
> very, very, very good country, it's the South Africa, very good. But
> apartheid has done a lot of damage.

The narrated stories of all these interviewees bear the traces of
apartheid's effects on individuals, social relations and community life. It is
also through this variety of changing social relationships and discourses
that interviewees have constituted themselves as historical subjects. However, retaining some sense of self-control within a system that was gradually destroying any sense of control and dignity was profoundly important
to interviewees. For example, for the thousands of African shanty dwellers
of Windermere their corrugated iron dwellings became relatively permanent homes. Many interviewees longed for the relative comforts of the
pondokkies (shanties) they built in comparison with the state-built houses
in Guguletu. Therefore, 'the tracing of unity of one's self thus becomes one
of the powerful impulses behind the telling of one's life story'.[34] A sense of
security, sameness and continuity over time, is a crucial element of identity
formation. However, identity formation is also constituted by a sense of
insecurity, difference and discontinuity. On the one hand, in external

terms, the public persona is forged in a struggle to create and present a co-herent and credible image of the self. On the other hand, internally, iden-tities are also a form of emotional organization of fragmentary feelings evoked by needs, wants and desires. In order to deal with and fulfil these personal needs, people have to relate to and identify with aspects of the external world. It is within the personal dialogue between internal needs, wants and desires, in relation to external demands of social relationships, that identities are consciously and unconsciously negotiated. As Weeks argues:

> Identities are not neutral. Behind the quest for identity are different, and often conflicting values. By saying who we are, we are also striving to express what we are, what we believe and what we desire. The problem is that these beliefs, needs and desires are often patently in conflict, not only between different communities but within individuals them-selves.[35]

Identities allow people consciously and unconsciously to deploy strate-gies for dealing with the conflictual demands of daily life. Identities are in this sense a shifting pattern of contradictory outcomes over time. This conflictual coexistence of conscious and unconscious patterns is reflected in the myth-making of memory recall. Craib argues that 'we create myths of and for ourselves. We build stories about ourselves and part of the mater-ial we use is our identification not only with real people, but with fantasies gained from fiction and politics and history.'[36] This myth-making is an in-tegral part of filling in the gaps and discontinuities of identity formation. The individual subject internalizes myths with the unconscious desire of suturing his or her identity. However, the perpetual failure or incompletion of this operation is due to the ineradicable 'lack of being' that the subject experiences.[37]

By drawing on collective myths and creating personal fantasies people construct a fragile logical order between interwoven conscious and uncon-scious identity patterns. As Gay puts it, 'since the unconscious has no sense of order, it casually stores contradictory thoughts side by side; since it has no sense of time, infantile deposits are as fresh as yesterday's additions'.[38] Identity formation is also about the need to belong[39] and the need for a story to give coherence and expression to this belonging. And, in the case of former Windermere residents, of stories about ethnic belonging.

> An ethnic identity is similar to a story, a way of dealing with the present through a sense of identity that is rooted in the past. . . . Whether they

are 'true' is not immediately at issue. What matters is that they are accepted as adequate to make sense of events and behaviour. However,
stories also refer to the manner in which people are called on to make
sense of the world, especially the stories that are told about why people
belong together, what makes them different from others, and what their
collective histories are.[40]

When interviews tell stories about feeling more at home in one place
than in another, or about their community or lost community, a need for
belonging is reflected. It is also reflected in their familiarity with certain
locations and groups of people. As Maré puts it, 'No matter its origin the
emotional appeal of ethnicity stresses security and familiarity.'[41] Many of
the earlier interviewee quotes contained a longing for the place and time of
Windermere. In part, this is about the laying of personal claims to a space
and social relations that 'I' belonged in and identified with. In part, this is
also a longing for a space and time before apartheid. A time when African,
coloured and white people lived in 'harmony'.[42] While Windermere was by
most accounts a vibrant ethnic and cultural mixture, it also created a complex set of identity constructions. The clear demarcation of boundaries is
crucial to ethnic identity constitution.[43] A previously quoted 52-year-old
female domestic worker recalls a conversation with a relative:

And we go to her place and when we taste *umqombuti* [SF: African
beer], she says, 'You know children, this is African tradition. If you
children leave your tradition for wanting to be coloured, you will never
make it in this world. You must always remember the African custom
and African tradition'. Now you see we couldn't talk Xhosa that time.
We couldn't. We could only talk English and Afrikaans.

In this passage it is evident how the relative plays the role of story teller
and 'ethnic broker'.[44] The interviewee goes on to talk about her ambivalent
feelings and struggles with being African, and then fixes the decisive point
in the formation of her African identity: 'But that time it never sinked in,
but when we got to Guguletu, it started sinking.' For this interviewee, and
three others who were born and raised in Windermere, the consolidation of
their African identity only happened after their removal from Windermere.
It was only in Guguletu that she learnt how to speak Xhosa. The blurring of
linguistic boundaries between Xhosa, English and Afrikaans produced an
ambiguous sense of ethnic belonging for these four interviewees. Two of
these African interviewees spoke with distinctive coloured accents. For a
male interviewee from this group, the decisive realization of his African

identity, as opposed to being coloured, was when he went to an African circumcision ritual.[45] However, his ongoing identifications with the coloured community still destabilize his sense of belonging within the African community. Many of the ambivalent feelings that these four interviewees had about their personal and cultural location can also be attributed to the rigid demarcation of ethnic boundaries under the apartheid system. In contrast, for interviewees who were born and raised in either the Ciskei or Transkei, Windermere seemed to constitute an historical half-way station between their past rural lives, and their present urban life. For these interviewees, African customs and traditions appeared to be more firmly internalized.

For all interviewees, Windermere was (for either positive or negative reasons) a very significant phase in lives filled with physical, social and emotional movement. It was especially the rural to urban movement that required complex life strategies for survival. These life strategies were vital in organizing consciousness.[46] There were physical movements of African people from Windermere of the 1950s to Guguletu of the 1990s. But there were also movements of social memories between these places and times. Apartheid destroyed Windermere, but the social memories of Windermere still speak to individuals from within themselves through dreams, fantasies and feelings.

One interviewee spoke of her parents appearing in her nightly dreams to warn her of danger in Guguletu, and telling her not to go out the next day. Another interviewee spoke of the 'spirits' warning her of the dangers in the community. These past images of Windermere, parents and childhood interweave to form both a kind of solace to the individual and also a defensive communication about approaching danger. Underlying these images, I think, are layers of personal hurt, interwoven with the fear of experiencing even more hurt. Throughout the fieldwork I could sense high levels of anxiety and stress, and as Anna Freud puts it, 'whether it be dread of the outside world or dread of the super-ego, it is the anxiety which sets the defensive process going'.[47]

Through regular interactions in Guguletu, former Windermere residents have constant reminders of the 'Windermere days' and interpolations of their identity as 'Windermere people'. I frequently found interviewees who could point out several other 'Windermere people' next door, across the road and down the street. Established in Guguletu in the late 1960s the Kensington Burial Society offered opportunities to recall the past. Burial societies originated from migrant worker networks, as a form of self-help and protection of rural cultural patterns.[48] Burial societies also 'help distinguish "genuine" community members from others; they provide community networks and support; and above all they provide assurances that death will be properly handled'.[49] While anyone can join the Kensington Burial Society today, the core membership are former Windermere residents. At monthly organizational meetings people talk about the 'Windermere days'. The former undertaker explains:

> You know people they always remind one another where they used to stay, because there is a burial society for Windermere people. If they were staying in Windermere they all come together, in the meetings here in this hall here. We know one another. We have got the burial society of Windermere. Like others in Retreat, also have people, who used to stay in Retreat, they are reminding each other and they also build up a burial society. Whoever passed away they come here. We are doing collections and burying each other, one another.

He later stressed that 'remembering is so good because we are helping one another. That's what, we are not forgetting one another, when we come together even here in Guguletu.' The splintering and ultimate destruction of communities like Windermere through apartheid laws is countered by remembering the Windermere past as a unified whole. In the process, remembering becomes an act of reaffirming social ties with people. Remembering the Windermere past, a time before apartheid, also becomes an act of solidarity against the separations and exclusions of apartheid. As Lowenthal puts it, 'we need other people's memories to confirm our own and to give them endurance. . . . In the process of knitting our own discontinuous recollections into narratives we revise personal components to fit the collectively remembered past.'[50] Memories filled with harmonious images of Windermere create a mythical wholeness of 'our community' and 'us' as a unified 'one'. The active process of remembering in the present (as distinct from the memories themselves) simultaneously reflects an unfulfilled desire for community and the symbolic creation of a community-in-memory. Interviewees' reiteration of the term 'Windermere people' affirms both their community-in-memory and their shared sense of communal identity.

The fragility of this mythical wholeness is contrasted with the ethnic fractures and 'racial' divisions of life under apartheid. An interviewee said, 'We were sent away, we must come to Guguletu. They didn't want any black person around, that coloureds must be themselves and so on. That is apartheid. That is definite, it is through apartheid.' While 'race' has limited theoretical value,[51] its significance and salience, as used by the above interviewee, do have meaning and resonance as a conceptual category within day-to-day discourses. Gilroy argues that 'the aura of authentic ethnicity supplies a special form of comfort in a situation where the history of black experience is undermined'.[52] In the Western Cape region the black experience of the relationship between coloured and African has been painfully affected by the logic of exclusionary politics pursued by the apartheid regime.

Several African interviewees reflected anger, mistrust and suspicion towards coloured people whom they believe received a better deal under apartheid. In many other cases, 'love', friendship and longing for their coloured friends of Windermere were expressed. In some cases, there were sighs of 'shame' reflecting the infantilizing view of a parent looking down on the 'child-like' coloured people. In one of the most telling comparative stories about differences between coloured and African a male interviewee said:

> You see when you grew up with coloured people, *nê*? [SF: is it not?] Look for instance in the vicinity where we lived. There was a lot of coloured people around us, *nê*? And they right next door and a lot of blacks on that yard, but it was a mixture now. Coloured people are like this; you grew up with coloured people, they come to your place, you go to their place, they eat at your place, you eat at their place. And that's why you quarrel today, tomorrow it's over. You sort of learn that way of forgiveness if somebody does something wrong to you. You know that, at the end you must forgive him. Now when you grew up somewhere else, maybe in the rural areas or somewhere in the location [SF: African township], you know? It takes a long time to forgive somebody who's done something wrong to you. That's the difference, you see the people from Kensington they got that love, you know.

This interviewee is constructing two intriguing comparisons. Firstly, that Africans who grew up in Windermere with coloureds are different from other African township dwellers. Secondly, that coloureds are more forgiving of people who have wronged them than Africans. The interviewee is also romanticizing his experiences of living with coloured people in Windermere, and seems too harsh and generalized in his criticism of Africans. A possible interpretation of his words is that because African people suffered more severely under apartheid than coloured people, Africans have more to feel angry about and hence are less likely to forgive transgressions. But there is a fine line between forgiving and forgetting. The appearance of being more forgiving conceals patterns of forgetting and silencing the past, which are prevalent within the coloured community. In a similar vein to the above interviewee, several African and coloured interviewees also claim that there was a particular 'love' for one another in the Windermere community. This reference is probably rooted in a popular perception that a greater cultural tolerance existed between coloureds and Africans in Windermere of the 1950s. In contrast, both African and coloured interviewees experienced the present (that is, 1993) as a more divided, unforgiving and intolerant time.

There is little doubt that many coloured and African people lived together happily, but the mixture of accurate observations and mythical truths are constantly woven around an unfulfilled desire for peace, tranquillity and stable community living in the Guguletu of the present. This unfulfilled desire was unconsciously projected into the past, which was reconstructed in the form of harmonious and comforting memories of the Windermere community. As Passerini puts it, 'Hopes, fears, and projections converge into shaping memory and its strategies.'[53] However, this desire for peace and togetherness within a secure communal identity is partially met within a comforting discourse of 'Windermere': their community-in-memory.

CONCLUSION

The effects of the apartheid era continue in the lives of most South Africans. While we should not dwell morbidly on past agonies the depth of emotional experiences of the apartheid past needs to be heard, recorded and interpreted. Oral history an important political role in both documenting and interpreting the untold stories of the wounds of apartheid. Sadly, many stories will remain untold, and many emotional scars will remain unhealed, since ultimately people need to move forward in and from the present. The interviewees of this study are from a significant generation who have experienced the before, during and after of apartheid. They are all former residents of the Windermere community currently living in Guguletu. By weaving a mixture of myth and memory about the Windermere past they constituted a relatively stable sense of self and identity in contemporary Guguletu.

The Windermere past, however, was seldom peaceful, and the harmonious image of Windermere that many interviewees reconstructed was at odds with the violence that they experienced there. Several interviewees also felt an ambiguous sense of ethnic belonging about their own sense of African identity, in relation to their coloured neighbours and friends. The Windermere past signifies a range of similar and dissimilar meanings for interviewees. The identification of other 'Windermere people' in Guguletu and the sharing of social memories simultaneously nurtures a fragile sense of community-in-memory and communal identity. In contrast to a present-day Guguletu community which has been repeatedly threatened by social and political violence, the community-in-memory is one significant bulwark for emotional survival used by this older generation of African people.

Finally, I am conscious of my desire to create a conclusive closure to this chapter. However, this closure is not possible because my desire to close these painful stories, is precisely that, a desire to bring an end to the pain of apartheid. This is not possible because as long as the emotional legacies of apartheid live on, consciously and unconsciously in South Africans, there is going to be conflict and negotiation over memories and identities. The loose threads of my thoughts and writing will have to remain for now, and I will carry on with the knowledge that (as an interviewee puts it) 'everyone is under the benediction of doubting because you can't be sure what is going to take place'.[54]

NOTES

1   An earlier version of this chapter, entitled 'From the "Peaceful Past" to the "Violent Present": Memories and Identities in a South African Township' was presented to the International Conference on Oral History, Columbia University, New York 1994. This chapter acknowledges the memory of all those who died in the struggle against apartheid, and the memory of Amy Biehl, who was murdered on a roadside in Guguletu on 25 August 1993.

2   J. Weeks, *Against Nature, Essays on History, Sexuality and Identity*, London, 1991, p. 91.

3   D. Lowenthal, *The Past is a Foreign Country*, Cambridge, 1985, p.185.

4   E. Tonkin, 'History and the myth of realism', in P. Thompson and R. Samuel (eds.), *The Myths We Live By*, London, 1990, p. 25.

5   These interviewees are all residents of Guguletu. These 18 interviews are drawn from 54 oral history interviews conducted for a doctoral study. See, 'The Power of Exclusion: Moving Memories from Windermere to the Cape Flats, 1920s–1990s', University of Essex, 1996. An additional seven interviews were conducted with African people living in Langa and Nyanga. The 54 interviewees consisted of 25 African, 23 coloured and six white individuals. Their ages vary from 50 to 92 years, with the majority being between 60 and 75 years. Note also that the term 'coloured' is used in the South African sense to refer to people of mixed-ethnic origin, so defined under apartheid law. The terms 'white', 'coloured' and 'African' are imbued with a mixture of positive and negative meanings from the apartheid era. However, these contested terms will be used in this chapter as they are the dominant labels used by interviewees in referring to themselves.

6   In this chapter, 'the present' (unless otherwise stated) will refer to July/ August 1993 when these interviews were conducted.

7   'Shebeens' are usually venues for illegal trade in alcohol. While some shebeens sell drugs and sex, there are other shebeens that are part of ordinary family networks and constitute an important supplement to the household income.

8   For discussion on the differences and similarities between psychotherapy and oral history, see K. Figlio, 'Oral history and the unconscious', *History Workshop*, vol. 26, 1985.

9   For useful critiques of South African oral history see I. Hofmeyer, 'Reading oral texts: new methodological directions', University of Western Cape, 1995, and G. Minkley and C. Rasool, 'Oral history in South Africa: a country report', University of Columbia, 1994.

10 The term 'race' has limited theoretical value and will therefore be used with inverted commas. P. Gilroy, *The Black Atlantic, Modernity and Double Consciousness*, London, 1993, uses the term in a similar fashion.

11 The term 'community-in-memory' refers to a sense of community which has no necessary connection to spatial or social relationships, but is primarily constructed through the process of remembering and forgetting. Throughout fieldwork I heard informants repeat the term 'Windermere people'. This was particularly used to differentiate themselves from 'Retreat people'. Retreat was also a former squatter community that was destroyed by apartheid laws. Section 2, Guguletu is dominated by former Windermere and Retreat residents.

12 C. Swart, 'Windermere, From the Peri-urban to Suburb, 1920s to 1950s', Honours Dissertation, University of Cape Town 1983.

13 Official population figures in the 14 000–20 000 range are cited by annual reports of the medical officer of the CCC, 1944–54. The percentage estimates are my speculative calculations, drawn from Western Cape Administration Board (WCAB) records and newspapers of the 1958–63 period.

14 Swart, 'Windermere, From the Peri-urban to Suburb, 1920s to 1950s'.

15 Ibid.

16 For further discussion of coloured politics and cultural formations in Factreton during the 1980s see my master's thesis, 'The Politics of Exclusion, A Case Study of the Factreton Area', University of Cape Town 1990.

17 Due to the political circumstances in Guguletu I was obliged to be open about my political identity. If a conventional neutral role had been used I would not have been granted most of the interviews. The complex mesh of power relations between myself and research subjects, particularly gender, 'race' and cultural differences, are discussed in my doctorate, 'The Power of Exclusion: Moving Memories from Windermere to the Cape Flats, 1920s–1990s'.

18 A. Portelli, *The Death of Luigi Trastulli and Other Stories, Form and Meaning in Oral History*, New York, 1991, p. 52.

19 Popular Memory Group, 'Popular Memory: Theory, Politics and Method', in Centre for Contemporary Cultural Studies, *Making Histories, Studies in History – Writing and Politics*, London, 1982, p. 211.

20 I. Bertaux-Wiame, 'The life history approach to the study of inter-racial migration' in D. Bertaux (ed.), *Biography and Society, The Life History Approach in the Social Sciences*, London, 1981, p. 257.

21 Portelli, *The Death of Luigi Trastulli,* p. 51.
22 L. Passerini, (ed.), *Memory and Totalitarianism, International Yearbook of Oral History and Life Stories,* vol. 1, Oxford, 1992, p. 13.
23 R. Samuel and P. Thompson, (eds.), *The Myths We Live By,* London, 1990, p. 9.
24 Ibid., p. 3.
25 A. Norval, 'Images of Babel: language and the politics of identity', University of York, 1994, p. 12.
26 H. Bhabha, 'What does the black man want?', *New Formations* , vol. 1, Spring 1987, p. 123.
27 S. Freud, *The Psychopathology of Everyday Life,* London, 1991, p. 83.
28 In this chapter I have not applied any psychoanalytic model but rather I have used psychoanalysis as a 'sensitizing theory' (Ian Craib in a verbal discussion, May 1994). Also, P. Gay, *Freud for Historians,* New York, 1985, correctly warns against the dangers of reductionism that have all too often beset psycho-history. I have therefore used basic psychoanalytic ideas flexibly in interpreting the uses and functions of emotionally laden memories. In this area, see J. Hunt, *Psychoanalytic Aspects of Fieldwork,* London, 1989.
29 I. Hofmeyer, *'We Spend Our Years as a Tale That is Told',* Oral Historical Narrative in a South African Chiefdom, London, 1993.
30 Ibid.
31 A. Freud, *The Ego and the Mechanisms of Defence,* London, 1968, p. 87.
32 F. Jameson, *The Political Unconscious, Narrative as a Socially Symbolic Act,* London, 1981, p. 102.
33 I initially considered the term 'damage' to be a central concept in interpreting the different painful experiences inflicted by the trauma of apartheid. However, I now think that the concept is somewhat static and could potentially evoke stigmatization. In a similar vein, see A. Levett, 'Stigmatic factors in sexual abuse and the violence of representation', *Psychology in Society,* no. 20, 1995. Rather, by directly naming the different emotional shades of hurt, pain and agony experienced one leaves space for interpreting either possible aggravation or positive change, renewal and healing.
34 Portelli, *The Death of Luigi Trastulli,* p. 129.
35 Weeks, *Against Nature,* p. 185.
36 I. Craib, *Psychoanalyses and Social Theory, The Limits of Sociology,* London, 1989, p. 91.
37 E. Laclau, *New Reflections on the Revolution of Our Time,* London, 1990. In the Lacanian sense, 'lack' is not simply the force of unfulfilled desires that shapes identity formation but a constitutive element of identity formation. Hence all identities are subject to a 'constitutive lack'.
38 Gay, *Freud for Historians,* p. 124.
39 Weeks, *Against Nature.*
40 G. Maré, *Brothers Born of Warrior Blood, Politics and Ethnicity in South Africa,* Johannesburg, 1992, p. 2.
41 Ibid., p. 12.
42 Through their memory reconstructions of the Windermere past interviewees tend to deny the oppression they suffered during the pre-apartheid segregation years. However, there is no sharp disjuncture

between the segregation and apartheid periods. See S. Dubow, *Racial Seg-regation and the Origins of Apartheid in South Africa, 1919–1936*, London, 1989.

43   F. Barth, *Ethnic Groups and Boundaries*, Boston, 1969.

44   Maré, *Brothers Born of Warrior Blood*, p. 2.

45   In contrast, I conducted an interview with a coloured male who speaks fluent Xhosa and says he feels more African than coloured. The decisive point for him was when his mother refused to let him go to a circumcision ritual with his African friends.

46   B. Bozzoli (with M. Nkotse), *Women of Phokeng, Consciousness, Life Strategy and Migrancy in South Africa, 1900–1983*, Johannesburg, 1991.

47   Freud, *The Ego and the Mechanisms of Defence*, p. 57.

48   P. Delius traces the emergence of burial societies among male migrants in 'Sebatakgomo; migrant organization, the ANC and the Sekhukhuneland revolt', *Journal of Southern African Studies*, vol. 15, no. 4, 1989. He also argues that in the face of urban pressures these rural migrants used burial societies to 'maintain their footholds in the urban areas', p. 604.

49   Bozzoli (with M. Nkotse), *Women of Phokeng*, p. 53.

50   Lowenthal, *The Past is a Foreign Country*, p. 196.

51   Gilroy, *The Black Atlantic*.

52   Ibid., p. 86.

53   Passerini, *Memory and Totalitarianism*, vol. 1, p. 12.

54   I am indebted to all the interviewees for their memories, emotions and time. Many thanks to Aletta Norval, Paul Thompson, Catherine Hall and Ian Craib for their constructive comments on various versions of this chapter. Thanks also to the Oral History Research Office (Columbia University) and the Fuller Fund (Department of Sociology, University of Essex) for the financial assistance they provided towards my participation in the New York oral history conference. I also acknowledge the following funders who have assisted my doctoral studies: The Harold Hyam Wingate Foundation, Africa Educational Trust and the Overseas Research Students Awards. Finally, loving thanks to my partner, Jane van der Riet, for her language editing and support.

5 Reinventing the Politics of Cultural Recognition: The Freedom Front and the Demand for a *Volkstaat*[1]

Aletta J. Norval

The Freedom Front (FF), the only 'far right' party to take part in the 1994 election and achieve parliamentary representation, occupies a politically significant position in contemporary South African politics.[2] While for most commentators it is merely an unpleasant relic of the apartheid era, I will argue in this chapter that their discourse raises a series of important questions which stand at the heart of contemporary theoretical and political debate on cultural diversity and recognition, and on the constitutional forms in which they may be exercised.

The history of the last two decades, and conceivably much of our century, could be organized around a narrative based on the increasing clamour – some would argue a cacophony of voices – demanding cultural recognition, be that of a nationalist, ethnicist or minoritarian form.[3] However, a cautionary note is necessary as such a history may conflate or override important features which need to be distinguished from one another. Two such areas spring to mind immediately. The first concerns the manner in which these claims are read and interpreted, including theoretical debates concerning, for instance, the status (and possibility) of community, and the relation between the individual and the community; and the second, the precise historical contexts in which these demands are voiced. Take, for example, the attempt to draw analogies between the logic of segregation at the root of apartheid discourse, and multiculturalist demands in the late 1980s in the USA. If one looks at the logic of these demands from a theoretical perspective – that is, at the sort of claims that are voiced in the name of community – a certain blurring occurs between the two contexts which makes it difficult to conceive of the important, if not crucial, differences between them. If, however, more careful attention is given to the different historico-political configurations within which these claims have been put forward, the possibility of a too close analogy between them recedes quickly.

My argument aims to avoid reflections based either on purely abstract theoretical reflection or exclusive historical contextualization. This attempt to avoid either-or forms of argumentation has its origins in the view that these forms of argumentation, characteristic of much social and political theorizing, are inadequate and tend to simplify complex interrelationships and interactions.[4] Given this, there are two propositions which inform my reading. The *first* is a historical proposition: it is no longer a question for us whether or not one or another claim to cultural recognition ought to be admitted, but whether constitutional arrangements can give recognition to the legitimate demands of the members of diverse cultures in a manner that renders everyone their due.[5] What is distinctive about our age is the recognition of those demands as always already legitimate.[6] In Michael Walzer's discussion of the principle of self-determination, he argues that even though it is reiterated in many different places and times, and always in some local idiom, there is little difficulty in recognizing the principle: '[w]hat was at stake for the Jews and the Gauls, what is at stake for us today, is the value of a historical or cultural or religious community and the political liberty of its members. . . . Their members . . . have the basic right that goes with membership. They ought to be allowed to govern themselves (in accordance with their own political ideas) insofar as they can decently do that, *given their local entanglements*.'[7] And, in their discussion of national self-determination, Margalit and Raz make a similar, if somewhat more restricted, point arguing that 'the widespread recognition of the existence of national rights to self-determination provides a welcome point of agreement'.[8] However, as they go on to argue, this core consensus is but the eye of a raging storm.

Many crucial issues remain controversial and unresolved in these views. Here I will focus only on a few of them As a point of departure, it may be useful to note that the recognition of the legitimacy of these demands cannot be merely that of the traditional nationalist recognition of one culture at the expense of excluding or assimilating all others; it cannot be in the form of so-called neutral proceduralism.[9] It also cannot be simply the recognition of each culture in the same constitutional form. As Tully argues, this assumption is based upon the questionable idea of cultures as analogous to 'nations'.[10] From this follows my *second* principle, namely that the two common assumptions operative in the view that cultures worthy of recognition should be nations and nations should be recognized as states, misidentify the phenomenon of cultural diversity at stake here.[11] The 'billiard ball' conception of cultures – the idea that a culture is separate, bounded, internally uniform[12] – embedded in the language of modern constitutionalism is fundamentally misleading if not mistaken. However, its implications remain to be elaborated, both theoretically and historically. The rest of this chapter will address some of those implications through an examination of the case of the FF, and their demands for self-determination.

THE STATUS QUO[13]

The interim South African constitution which was finalized in January 1994, entrenched a set of constitutional principles organized under five major topics, namely, the transition period, the status of the constitution, fundamental rights, democratic principles, and the form of state and government.[14] For our purposes, Principle 34, belatedly adopted on 21 February 1994, is of special importance, for it states that the general right of self-determination does not exclude the right to self-determination of any community sharing a common cultural and language tradition. Following the adoption of Principle 34, the FF, ANC and NP signed an accord on 23 April 1994 which signified their intent to address, through a process of ongoing negotiations, the idea of Afrikaner self-determination, including the concept of a *Volkstaat*.[15] These discussions resulted in three related agreements: first, a commitment to the development of a non-racial democracy; second, the rejection of racism and failed apartheid policies; and third, acceptance that South Africa should be home to all its inhabitants.

The FF's comment on this is particularly significant. They argued that it was crucial to the agreement that the concept of self-determination should in no way 'be construed as to give support to those fatal racist ideologies of the twentieth century that were based on chauvinistic excessive escalation of identities or even ethnocentrism which bred discrimination, racism and prejudices which on their part brought war, misery and death to many'.[16]

Since self-determination, as Freeman has recently argued,[17] is both a potent and paradoxical concept, attractive to many because it is associated with the values of democracy and national community, repellent to others because it is also associated with ethno-nationalist fascism and anarchy, it is important to attempt to specify, as closely as possible, its precise meaning in the discourse of the FF.[18]

THE INSTITUTIONAL FORMS OF SELF-DETERMINATION

Not only did the interim and final constitutions of South Africa make provision for the right to self-determination, they also included articles on language and cultural rights (Article 11). However, the FF considered these clauses to be insufficient to provide protection for minorities. Their conception of self-determination thus goes beyond what is captured in these articles. The first important clue to their understanding of the idea of self-determination is to be found in their problematization of 'mere individual rights'. While both the ANC and the NP regard individual rights as sufficient to protect individuals belonging to ethnic communities, the idea of liberal individualism is deeply inimical to the FF. To fulfil their demands for cultural recognition and continued existence, they hold that several institutional mechanisms are necessary, including a *Volkstaat* (a separate territory for 'the Afrikaner people') and, at municipal level, cultural councils.

The cultural councils – elected on an intra-community basis – are designed to deal with community self-determination at a local level. In other words, those functions of local government that affect and determine cultural identity.[19] These local institutions are to be complemented by territorially based institutions. These areas would be created by voluntary movement, and they would facilitate the development of the conditions conducive to large and concentrated settlements of Afrikaners, so avoiding the need for large-scale 'ethnic cleansing' or forced removals, as they have been known in South Africa. These areas could also develop into sub-regions with special, delegated powers of an autonomous nature.

Taken together, these institutions are to ensure language rights; the right to community-oriented, mother-tongue education; the right to autonomy in matters affecting cultural identity, including the right to local self-administration; the right to separate organizations and associations; and the right to territorial autonomy in negotiated areas where majority occupation by Afrikaners could be established. In sum, they aim at establishing some form of special status to secure control over 'own affairs' in such areas. Such a *Volkstaat* would thus act as a base where Afrikaans would be the first language and where universities, other tertiary Afrikaans institutions, and the 'typical Afrikaner lifestyle' could survive.[20] Moreover, they would provide new opportunities for many Afrikaners who stand to lose their jobs in the process of affirmative action.[21] Thus, they argue, the need for a separate territory, in addition to other constitutional guarantees, arises from the fact that Afrikaners now form a numerical minority in South Africa, and are disempowered as a result of 'democratization on the liberal principle of individualism only'.[22]

These arguments, however, do not lead in a secessionist direction. The FF accepts the inviolability of the state: the initial demands for a sovereign *Volkstaat* were scaled down because of the absence of proof of the type of suppression on which a claim for secession (according to international practice) could be based.[23] Moreover, the FF, unlike earlier Afrikaner nationalists such as those in SABRA[24] with whom they share a set of preoccupations, accepts the economic interdependence of the region and holds that growth and development are prerequisites for successful reconstruction. Discrepancies in income, for instance, should be addressed, and any form of self-determination for the Afrikaner must 'not sustain the discrepancies but contribute to their reduction'.[25]

JUSTIFYING SELF-DETERMINATION

How, then, does the FF justify its demands? The arguments provided are fairly typical of the range of justifications deployed in comparable situations and rehearsed in the theoretical literature.[26] They range from claims to traditional links to the land, to arguments that territorial autonomy is important to provide psychological and physical security for the Afrikaner minority, which fears 'cultural over-powerment and eventual extinction'.[27]

On closer inspection, it is important to note the *dual* nature of the FF's justification. There is an appeal both to the international and domestic contexts in legitimating these claims. Internationally, the FF argues, questions concerning minority rights stand at the centre of political debates. In Europe there is an ongoing discussion about how the rights of minorities may be accommodated in pluralistic societies. Events in the former Yugoslavia, in parts of the former Soviet Union, in Rwanda and Burundi, in Nigeria and Somalia, they argue, are all reminders that one cannot avert one's eyes from the 'realities of civilization conflict'.[28] Thus, the FF presents the struggle for self-determination as a universal one, and one in which they partake.

Sketching out the context in which the principle of self-determination emerged, General Viljoen – the leader of the FF – recalls that it was first introduced after the First World War 'in search of a mode for co-existence that would ensure peace in a situation of a society under stress and in a process of restoration'.[29] In the era of decolonization, he argues, it was used to foster 'respectful recognition of the widely divergent cultural and national groups who . . . became interdependent . . . and had to find a way of peaceful coexistence in this one world'.[30] Today, Viljoen argues, the challenge is to find effective ways of coexistence within pluralist societies. And that is indeed, according to the FF, what happens in Europe today, in the dialogue on minority rights. It is important to note, though, that this dialogue is construed by the FF as an attempt to develop an alternative to individualist liberalism that will also cater for the collective value system and expectations of ethnic and cultural groups in one society.[31] This is a crucial dimension of the FF's discourse, and is what ultimately underlies their insistence – *contra* the ANC and NP – that measures falling short of territorial settlements of one sort or another are inadequate; they are suspicious, and indeed, reject liberal individualist forms of argumentation.[32]

Domestically, the FF claims that it has accepted 'the demands and the responsibilities of a common society'. Their claims relate *only* to a 'meaningful form of autonomy for the Afrikaner community within the structures of the State of South Africa, which will allow the community the freedom to have control over matters pertaining to its own community and cultural life, while sharing with other South Africans the responsibility in non-racial structures of Government on all matters of common consent'.[33] However, embedded in this is the FF's conception of the South African people which, upon closer examination, significantly weakens the degree to which *any* possible 'matters of common consent' may be found. In this discursive universe, South Africa consists of a diversity of minority or ethnic groups, some of which may be less visible than others as a result of the 'anti-ethnicist' form which anti-apartheid resistance has taken historically. The demand for self-determination is thus a demand for the recognition of the Afrikaner as one minority group amongst others: '[w]e are not asking for the retention of privileges of the past. We only ask for understanding for the position of a people that through its own history . . . has developed a sense of national and cultural coherence and now feel threatened because of its permanent minority status in a society where the danger of alienation is a very real one.'[34] On this reading, the 'disempowerment' of the Afrikaner led them from 'a position of being a Government in control of what they considered to be their own land', to a position of 'a minority subjected to a majority which is clearly willing to enforce its majority position, without any reference to a legitimate form of group rights that would ease the apprehensions of the minority group'.[35]

Moreover, the different cultures or minority groups making up the South African population are *by nature* potentially in conflict with one another.[36] As Viljoen argues:

> Culture . . . supplies the fibre of a world view and the parameters of a value system. It tends to become a non-negotiable when it is strongly pronounced. And once it has been structured through polarisation and antithesis like that of the Afrikaner vs. the English, it tends to become more rigid and inflexible. It is this fact that accounts for a number of

escalating local and regional conflicts in the world today. From the outside these conflicts seem silly and without foundation. From the inside they are very, very real, uncontrollable and often extremely difficult to resolve. They defy all reason and resent any interference often until it takes carnage and homicide of a shocking degree to bring the feuding parties to a table to come to some degree or mode of self-determination in order to establish both the structures and the willingness to find a way of co-existence.[37]

Thus, the potential for conflict, arising out of cultural identifications, is such that it cannot be ignored.

This view of cultures is, of course, closely tied to a particular view of history. The FF regards Afrikaner history as the history of an embattled group: 'the long and intense struggle the Afrikaner culture as indigenous South African substructure had against the over-imposing dominant imperialistic Anglo-Saxon culture . . . our struggle is well-known and need not be elaborated on'.[38] This echoes deeply problematic nationalist and ethnicist histories, and has the effect of taking the FF right back into the fold of apartheid from which they wish, purportedly at least, to escape.

Viljoen proposes that the argument developed with reference to the *international* context – namely that self-determination was a mechanism to facilitate trust and nation-building, and so by implication, to find modes of co-operation between divergent cultures – is relevant to the domestic situation in post-apartheid South Africa. Just as self-determination internationally was a mechanism to address the 'basic problem of cultural divergence and polarization of contending, cultural systems', it has to function within the South African state.[39]

Self-determination is thus not about 'self-indulgence in exclusivistic withdrawal'; their aim is to engage in co-operation on the basis of self-respect and mutual respect between others. 'It is supposed to be a way . . . of addressing the common problems of the new society in a uniting world. It is an antidote for stress and patented conflict in human society.'[40] It is about security and strategies for peace; to be 'true to its real form it must be conflict solving and promote mutual trust and cultural tolerance'.[41]

REINVENTING AFRIKANERSKAP: BETWEEN NOVELTY AND REPETITION

Much of the possible legitimacy of the foregoing argumentation turns on the question as to whether the FF's argument on identity, and more specifi-

cally cultural or group identities, is sustainable. In this respect it is absolutely crucial to pause for a moment in order to look at their answer to the
question: 'who is an Afrikaner?' Or rather, one might ask: 'who is *the*
Afrikaner?' This is a question which stood at the core of the history of
apartheid, and it has serious and immediate political implications for the
FF, which has to be able to show support from its constituency before a
Volkstaat could be established. Moreover, it is a question that goes to the
heart of theoretical justifications for demands for self-determination. One
only has to think here of the commonly held position, reiterated by
Margalit and Raz, that one can assume that 'things are roughly as they are,
especially that our world is a world of states and of a variety of ethnic, national, tribal, and other groups'[42] and that the pertinent questions to ask in
respect of these groups are quite simply, 'who has the right of self-determination?' and 'under what conditions is it to be exercised?'

I will return to these matters shortly. For the moment, let us look at the
articulation of these ideas in the discourse of the FF. At issue here is the
question as to whether 'the Afrikaner' is a people who may be accorded a
right to national self-determination. Attempting to answer this question,
the FF invokes the distinction between the *objective* and *subjective* features
of community, and both are held to be supportive of the claim: '. . .given
the objective features of the Afrikaner people of language, culture, ethnic
consolidation etc., and given the subjective criteria of a perception of a
common history, a sense of corporate cohesion, and of the will to survive as
a people, there will be [no] serious doubts as to whether the Afrikaners constitute a people or not'.[43]

However, the issue is not quite that simple, for there is no obvious, or
natural, coincidence between persons who claim the appellation 'Afrikaner'
and supporters of the FF. In response to this problem, the FF has two
strategies. The first is to emphasize the importance of the 'subjective'
nature of identification: '[t]he answer to the problem of definition is to
accept the principle of voluntary association, i.e. self-perception of being
an Afrikaner'.[44] While this answer does fit in with general specifications
for the identification of 'groups', since such identification forms an important part of one's identity, and allows one to distinguish socially pertinent
from non-pertinent groups,[45] one should also be aware of the reasons why
one may place so much emphasis on self-identification.[46] In the South
African context, 'race' has traditionally been, and probably remains, an
important factor in the self-identification of groups. But, with good reason,
it is no longer possible to express the desire for racially based forms of identification on a public level. An appeal to 'subjective' forms of delimiting
groups may, under these circumstances, allow the re-entry of racial differ-

entiation into the self-selection of groups. This is most evident in the fact that the FF, for instance, is reluctant to make pronouncements on the position of coloured Afrikaners. When pushed on the issue, they simply argue that self-identified 'Afrikaners' will decide who count as 'Afrikaners'. A discourse of democratic self-identification is thus mobilized to exclude coloured Afrikaners surreptitiously from the fold.

The second strategy is one which has a similarly long and ignoble history, namely, the attempt to define, ever more closely, who may count as 'true' Afrikaners. Here a problem arises, not from the question of race, but from persons who may regard themselves as Afrikaners, and who may identify with 'Afrikaans cultural life', but who do not have any sympathy for the politics of the *Volkstaat*. This has led the FF into the traditional response of purifying the ranks of Afrikaners, expelling those who were less than 'pure Afrikaners' from the inner circles of their definition of the community. Landman of the FF, for instance, argues that the Afrikaans language contains distinctions between *'Boere Afrikaner'*, *'Afrikane'* (analogous to European, referring to the continent of Africa) and *'Afrikaanses'* (all speakers of the Afrikaans language).[47] Constand Viljoen mobilizes a similar set of distinctions, all of which serve to make clear that *not* all those who speak Afrikaans can be considered a part of the *Afrikaner volk*, a concept which does not denote political unity, but which does signify cultural homogeneity.[48]

PROBLEMATIZATIONS

This policing of the boundaries of the *volk* highlights a series of problems which neither liberal nor communitarian commentators have the tools to address in their account of the nature of cultural rights in general and self-determination in particular. I have referred earlier to the statement by Margalit and Raz on dealing with what one 'finds in the world' so to speak. Neither group of theoreticians regard it as of primary importance to inquire into the *processes* through which 'groups' are constituted, the contestations to which the drawing of identitary boundaries may be subjected (except insofar as they are to do with claims of the individual against the group), and the consequences of such investigations.

It is only through giving attention to those processes that intractable problems with the discourse of the FF, such as the exclusivist nature of its focus on cultural and ethnic identity, may be addressed. In the absence of such attention, the focus on 'cultural recognition' alone can all too easily avoid any account of white supremacy. In other words, it could lead to a flattening out of differences between discourses in a manner that makes them appear equal.[49] This does not mean, of course, that one can in an *a priori* fashion argue that all discourses of cultural authenticity necessarily conceal a racist argument; nor is it straightforwardly evident that the FF's position is simply reducible to racism or neo-racism. However, it should be noted that their strategy accords quite closely with a more general contemporary trend to cast race-based arguments in culturalist terms. Commenting upon this trend, Solomos and Back point out that

> what is clear from recent accounts of the growth of new forms of cultural racism is that within the language of contemporary racist movements there is both a certain flexibility about what is meant by race as well as an attempt to reconstitute themselves as movements whose concern is with defending their 'nation' rather than attacking others as such. . . . in this context one finds a combination [of] arguments in favour of cultural difference along with negative images of the 'other' as a threat . . . [50]

This depiction is applicable to the discourse of the FF in many respects: their concentration on an absolute 'cultural difference' is combined with a view of interaction between 'cultures' as doomed to conflict; the 'other' is thus cast in the role of a threat in much the same way as was the case in apartheid discourse.[51] The use of metonymic elaborations[52] such as the emphasis on merely being engaged in 'protecting a way of life', then allows what Solomos and Back regard as 'racist effects' occurring alongside arguments denying the relevance of the issue of colour or phenotype in politics.[53]

Moreover, the emphasis on an identitarian conception of cultural difference or, as Gilroy calls it, 'ethnic absolutism', reinforces the misconception that 'socio-cultural groups' are essentially unchanging and atavistic entities; it ossifies the complex and changing nature of social, cultural and political life.[54] This leads to an excessive focus on cultural identity, at the expense of developing and taking account of competing and/or complementary forms of identification. This means that the FF, despite its rhetorical commitment to the broader democracy within which it functions, at best downplays, and at worst discourages, the development of identifications of subjects *as* South African citizens. In the absence of such an emphasis on the fostering and legitimization of democratic citizenship, the discourse of the FF cannot but fall into the trap of an extreme and exclusionary separatism, making their commitment to non-racial democracy practically redundant.

This emphasis on cultural identity as if it is timeless and ahistorical also has effects on the FF's view of history; sensitivity to context is patently absent in the discourse of the FF. As I have shown earlier, the FF is keen to situate its discourse in the history of our present, the now, in relation to non-racial democracy at home and multicultural struggles abroad. In this enunciative context, they strenuously deny any identification with the past, for the past signifies apartheid racism. This recognition of apartheid racism, however, has not led them to investigate *what* it was in the past that linked together the struggle against colonial control and the repressive history of apartheid. When dealing with Afrikaner history and with the de-velopment of the idea of self-determination, the focus of the FF has been almost exclusively on the 'glorious' history of 'Afrikaner struggles' against imperialist oppression.[55] Selectively ignoring the past has allowed the FF to develop a duplicitous strategy, claiming a certain 'novelty' for the concept of self-determination in South Africa (by ignoring its long history and centrality to the discourse of apartheid), but also arguing that it has always already been part of the Afrikaner's struggle against domination. This was also more than evident in the FF's submission to the Truth and Reconciliation Committee. In it, Constand Viljoen, the leader of the FF repeated and defended actions perpetrated by the apartheid regime by invoking images, such as 'the communist threat', utilised in apartheid dis-course to dehumanize those who were regarded as enemies of the state.

In the absence of a serious scrutiny of the coincidence between claims to *purity* of Afrikaner identity, and racism towards other groups, and in the absence of a sustained engagement *in the present* with those problems, the FF will never be able to legitimize the demands which it so evidently de-sires (and needs, if they are going to be taken seriously). Its claims for the right to self-determination must ring hollow so long as it is incapable of admitting, and taking responsibility for the wrongs of the past. And to base these claims, in large measure, on some purported discrimination which may take place in the future, must appear nothing less than farcical.

CONCLUSION: IDENTITY AND DEMOCRACY

In conclusion, I would like to bring together the more theoretical claims about identity which have informed my argument, and which I have at-tempted to develop throughout this chapter. These issues all concern, in one way or another, the question of the *relation* between claims for cultural recognition (used here as a broad, catch-all term) and democracy. Let me start with the specific claim of the right to self-determination. It has recently been noted that a *democratic* interpretation of this right ascribes it to *citizens* of the state, while the *ethno-nationalist* interpretation ascribes it to *nations* of their own state (recognizing that they may coincide in empirical cases since democratic states may be based on the hegemony of ethnic groups).[56] However, this way of distinguishing between democratic and ethno-nationalist forms of self-determination leaves one potentially impotent before cases where there is an empirical coincidence of which one may, nevertheless, want to be critical. One may even be tempted to argue that, given the fact that it has been agreed to democratically, it is unnecessary to subject it to critical scrutiny.

Now, given my discussion of the FF, I would argue that this response is constitutively inadequate. If one takes into account the *processes* through which groups claiming self-determination come into existence – and I have argued that liberals and communitarians systematically ignore these processes – then it seems to me to be abundantly clear that one cannot be content with the argument for 'democratic' ethno-nationalism. To be able to see what is problematic about such a conception, one only needs to take cognizance of the tendency for such claims to be based upon a purported 'purity' of identity. In the case of the FF, this has led both to a view of cultures as eternally conflictual, and to a systematic 'purging' of the ranks of 'Afrikaners'. Moreover, in so doing they have traded upon, and continue to do so, a conception of identity, an identitary logic, of which apartheid is the exemplary form. They therefore risk racism. My claim is that such purist logics of identification will tend to lead towards ethnocentric, anti-democratic and even racist outcomes since they are informed by what I earlier called a billiard-ball conception of cultures in which cultures are regarded as separate, bounded and internally uniform. This discursive form must necessarily lead to exclusions and the suppression of difference. It is constitutively unable to allow and to foster the sort of relations amongst and within identities that will lead to a democratic negotiation of difference.

Other contemporary examples of the difficulties of this type of 'misdescription' and identification are clearly evident to us today; Rwanda and Bosnia-Herzegovina are signifiers of the abhorrent attempts to bring the overlapping cultural diversity of contemporary societies in line with the norm of one nation one state. Not only do cultures overlap within geographic spaces, they are also densely interdependent in their formation and identity. They exist in complex historical processes of interaction with other cultures. As Tully argues, the modern age is characterized by the interaction and entanglement of cultures: '[c]ultural diversity is not a phenomenon of exotic and incommensurable others in distant lands and at different stages of historical development, as the old concept of culture made it

appear. No. It is here and now in every society.'[57] Cultures are thus not
internally homogeneous. They are continuously contested, imagined,
reimagined, transformed, negotiated, both by their members and by their
interaction with others:[58] '[c]ultural diversity is a tangled labyrinth of in-
tertwining cultural difference *and* similarities, not a panopticon of fixed,
independent and incommensurable worldviews in which we are either prisoners or cosmopolitan spectators in the central tower.'[59] In short, both liberals and communitarians get it wrong, for their focus on the issue of the
primacy of 'the community' or 'the individual', and the relationship between them, misses the crucial point, namely that identity as such is constitutively marked by an impossibility of suture[60] and that, as a result, we are
always already in relations of entanglement with each other.

The deeper question that arises is the following: what are the implications of this for our political practice and institutions? If we *do* view cultures,
and identities more generally, as overlapping, interactive and negotiated,
how would this open the space for a consideration of a range of solutions
not usually contemplated where the focus falls narrowly on political self-
determination within a given territory? There are many possible areas of
contemporary theorizing which are suggestive in this regard. William
Connolly's work on non-territorial forms of democracy, for instance, seeks
solutions outside the boundaries of the nation-state, by questioning those
national boundaries.[61]

There are also important theoretical interventions which deal with processes *within* the state. From this perspective, and for my purposes, James
Tully's recent work on constitutionalism is suggestive in its focus on precisely those questions which arise in the process of drawing up new constitutions. I will only be able to draw a few suggestions from his work, for it
deserves and calls for far more detailed engagement than I can give it
here.[62] In his reworking of modern constitutionalism, which, he claims,
has stifled expressions of difference Tully explores the possibilities of
moving towards a post-imperial conception of constitutionalism that puts
into question the central tenets of modern constitutionalism.[63] For instance,
he argues that constitutional agreements reached in dialogue are seen as
foundational and universal.[64] This Platonic image reinforces the attitude
that agreement must be comprehensive and exclusive. This rules out different, more open conceptions of agreement, where agreement is seen as one
link in an endless chain, which is always open to review and renegotiation
in future dialogue, as well as the hidden diversity of actual constitutional
dialogue.[65]

To come to terms with this *aspectival*, rather than *essentialist* form of
identity – a view of identity which recognizes its own unsutured nature, and

which changes as one moves about, rather than one which portrays one's culture as providing a seamless background or horizon according to which one determines where one stands on fundamental questions[66] – one needs to regard constitutional negotiations as dialogues not monologues, and constitutions as 'chains of continual intercultural negotiations and agreement', not as fixed and unchangeable agreements reached at some foundational moment. Approaching the diversity of forms of demands for cultural recognition in this manner, will affirm diversity as a good, rather than trying to eliminate it, and may offer more flexible, less finalist ways of conceiving of interactions. Moreover, a constitutional association which recognizes and accommodates diversity, can provide a basis for critical reflection on, and dissent from, one's own institutions, for an ethos of critical freedom will be sustained by the public acknowledgement that the constitution is open to review, and that discussion of it is a valuable dimension of citizenship. This dimension, it should be added, remains excluded, for the time being, from the discourse of the FF.

NOTES

1 This chapter was first presented in the Department of Government at the Queen's University of Belfast. I should like to thank the participants in that seminar, as well as others who commented on the written version, most notably, Michael Freeman, David Howarth and Mark Devenney for their comments on this chapter.

2 It is not clear to what extent the appellation 'far right' adequately depicts the political discourse and disposition of the FF. The FF itself rejects this characterization as inadequate. While this may not be a decisive reason to problematize it, the fact that much of the conflicts in our political world no longer correspond to Left/Right divisions could be argued to be. This view, more importantly, conceals the possibility that ideologies may relate to one another on a number of different idea-dimensions. As Freeden argues, in such cases, it may be more appropriate to conceptualize relations among ideologies as multi-dimensional. See M. Freeden, *Ideologies and Political Theory*, Oxford, 1996, pp. 24–5.

3 I am deliberately avoiding the use of the term 'rights' here. Although these demands or claims may be conceptualized in terms of right-based discourses, those conceptualizations do not always aid understanding and possible resolution of conflicts since, as Tully argues, it tends to lead us to dismiss as irrelevant the concrete cases which alone can help to understand how conciliation is actually achieved. J.Tully, *Strange Multiplicity. Constitutionalism in an Age of Diversity*, Cambridge, 1995, p. 173.

4 This view is articulated most forcefully in the works of Derrida. While in the context of South African historiographic debates, Posel has articulated

a position which may on the face of it sound similar, the fact that she does not question the identitary dimensions of each of the positions severely limits the import of her intervention. D. Posel, 'Rethinking the "race-class" debate in South African historiography', *Social Dynamics*, vol. 9, no. 1, 1983, pp. 50–66.

5   Tully, *Strange Multiplicity*, p. 7.

6   This is the case even in the context of contemporary South Africa where the logic of apartheid has made it difficult to deal with the voicing of culturalist demands. The ANC's willingness to engage in debate on the issue bears witness to the fact that a certain wider legitimacy is already granted to those demands. Cf. A. Sachs, *Protecting Human Rights in a New South Africa*, Oxford, 1990; as well as G. Coetzee, 'Human rights – the start of a new culture', *RSA Review*, vol. 8, no. 2, 1995, pp. 31–40.

7   M. Walzer, *Thick and Thin. Moral Argument at Home and Abroad*, Notre Dame, 1994, p. 68 (emphasis added) and p. 72. Walzer holds that once we are confronted with modernity, 'all the human tribes are endangered species; their thick cultures are subject to erosion. . . . We can recognise what might be called a right to resist these effects, to build walls against contemporary culture, and we can give this right more or less scope depending on constitutional structures and local circumstances; we cannot guarantee the success of the resistance.'

8   A. Margalit and J. Raz, 'National self-determination', *Journal of Philosophy*, vol. 87, no. 9, 1990, p. 439.

9   Tully, *Strange Multiplicity*, p. 7.

10 The dominant constitutional norm is that every nation should be recognized as an independent state; the concepts of people, popular sovereignty, citizenship, unity, equality, recognition and democracy all tend to presuppose the uniformity of a nation-state with a centralized and unitary system of legal and political institutions. Tully, *Strange Multiplicity*, p. 9.

11 Tully points out that contemporary demands for cultural recognition constitute a third form of anti-imperialism and constitutionalism, the other two being the development of nation-states, and movements of decolonization.

12 Tully, *Strange Multiplicity*, p. 11.

13 For a detailed discussion of the historical context in which the far right re-emerged, see J. van Rooyen, *Hard Right. The New White Power in South Africa*, London, 1994, pp. 117–55; J. van Rooyen, 'The white right', in A. Reynolds, *Election '94 South Africa*, London, 1994, pp. 89–106; as well as A. J. Norval, *Deconstructing Apartheid Discourse*, Verso, 1996, pp. 75–98. The analysis of the discourse of the FF presented in this chapter is based on extensive reading of press releases, papers and documentation of the FF.

14 For a discussion of the content of these principles, see D. Kotze, 'The new (final) South African constitution', *Journal of Theoretical Politics*, vol. 8, no. 2, 1996, pp. 137–41.

15 A Volkstaat Council was established in terms of Section 184(a)1 of the Interim Constitution, Act 200 of 1993. This Council serves as a constitutional mechanism enabling proponents of the idea of a Volkstaat to constitutionally pursue the establishment of such a Volkstaat. While there is some overlap in mandate and membership of the Volkstaat Council and the FF, this chapter deals primarily with the discourse of the Freedom Front.

16   'Unmandated defining statement on the principle of self-determination',
      appendix to 'Accord on Afrikaner Self-determination between the Free-
      dom Front, the African National Congress and the South African Govern-
      ment/National Party, 23 April 1994'. The FF repeatedly asserts its
      anti-racist character. See also, C. L. Viljoen, 'Self-determination – a re-
      connaissance of the concept: universal need and practice', FF publication,
      21 February 1996.
17   M. Freeman, 'Democracy and dynamite: the peoples' right to self-determin-
      ation', *Political Studies*, vol. 44, no. 4, 1996, pp. 746–7.
18   Freeman argues that there are three important theoretical discourses on
      self-determination which may bring new rigour to the debate on self-deter-
      mination: communitarianism, liberal democracy and liberal realism. Free-
      man, 'Democracy and Dynamite', pp. 754–9.
19   Viljoen also proposes elected Afrikaner Councils on Provincial and Na-
      tional levels.
20   The question of Christian education is a good example of an issue which
      would fall under the rubric of an 'Afrikaner lifestyle'. For a discussion, see
      C. Landman, 'Die Afrikanervolk in die nuwe Suid-Afrika', Speech deliv-
      ered to The Nederlands-Zuid Afrikaanse Vereniging in Utrecht, The Neth-
      erlands, 12 February 1996, pp. 7–9.
21   See, for instance, Landman, 'Die Afrikanervolk in die nuwe Suid-Afrika', p. 3.
22   C. Viljoen, 'Die beginsels van self-beskikking en 'n volkstaat in 'n
      demokratiese samelewing' , 24 August 1995, p. 7.
23   C. L. Viljoen, 'Keynote address', in Volkstaat Council (ed.), *Proceedings
      of the International Conference on Self-determination*, held in Somerset
      West, 6–7 March 1996, pp. 5–20.
24   During the 1950s the South African Bureau for Racial Affairs (SABRA) ar-
      gued for a policy of 'total segregation', a policy which one could argue
      comes quite close to that of the idea of a *Volkstaat*.
25   The FF argues that its engagement in comprehensive agricultural aid
      projects in African states should be seen in this light. See C. Viljoen,
      'Territoriale selfbeskikking en hoe dit gedesentraliseerde ekonomiese
      groei kan stimuleer', 24 January 1996.
26   Freeman argues the right to self-determination can be grounded in various
      widely accepted political principles: the liberal right to resist tyranny, the
      liberal right to freedom of association, the democratic principle of popular
      sovereignty, the nationalist value of cultural community and the realist re-
      quirement of world order. Freeman, 'Democracy and dynamite', p. 759.
27   C. L. Viljoen, 'Self-determination – a reconnaissance'.
28   C. Viloen, 'Die beginsels van selfbeskikking en 'n volkstaat in 'n
      demokratiese samelewing', Press Club of South Africa, 24 August 1995,
      p. 2. (All translations from the Afrikaans are mine.) These references ap-
      pear over and over again in the discourse of the FF.
29   Viljoen, 'Die beginsels van self-beskikking', p. 5.
30   C. Viljoen, 'Die Vryheidsfront en die politiek vandag', Address delivered
      at Pretoria City Hall, 26 Oktober 1995, p. 5.
31   Viljoen, 'Die Vryheidsfront en die politiek vandag', p. 5.
32   This rules out as illegitimate a series of important checks and balances
      which a liberal approach may incorporate to, for instance, protect the indi-

vidual against pressures to conformity to the group. It is also crucial to emphasize this if one is to counter the argument that there is a commonality of purpose and politics between the far right and 'multicultural' demands world-wide (the latter having developed out of and as a deepening of already instituted forms of liberal democracy).

33 AV /12.3.96, 'Opening statement', Wednesday 13 March 1996.
34 C. Viljoen, 'Parameters for self-determination in the South African context', 28 November 1995, p. 4.
35 Viljoen, 'Parameters for self-determination', p. 4.
36 In both of these cases, the FF's discourse repeats central tenets of apartheid discourse.
37 Viljoen, 'Parameters for self-determination', p. 3.
38 Ibid., p. 2.
39 Ibid.
40 Viljoen, 'Die beginsels van selfbeskikking', p. 6.
41 Ibid., p. 6.
42 Margalit and Raz, 'National self-determination', p. 440.
43 Viljoen, 'Parameters for self-determination', p. 5.
44 Viljoen, 'Keynote address', p. 16.
45 Margalit and Raz argue, for instance, that a fiction-reading public is not one which has a strong element of self-identification and thus of social salience.
46 Margalit and Raz, 'National self-determination', p. 446. Margalit and Raz are typical in this respect of both liberal and communitarian approaches to questions of identity. Since they start from identity as given, they do not inquire into the processes through which identities are brought into being, and so miss several of the more important politically salient features of the issue of self-determination.
47 C. Landman, 'Die Afrikanervolk in die nuwe Suid-Afrika', p. 1.
48 C. Viljoen, 'Die Afrikaner en die Afrikanerkultuur vorentoe', Speech delivered to the Federation of Afrikaans Cultural Organizations Congress, Bloemfontein, 15 July 1994. These distinctions were also widely mobilized in the discourse of members of the *Volkstaatraad*, whose membership does not simply overlap with that of the FF.
49 Linda Martin Alcoff, 'Philosophy and racial identity', *Radical Philosophy*, no. 75, Jan/Feb 1996, p. 10.
50 J. Solomos and L. Back, *Racism and Society*, London, 1996, p. 208.
51 I have analysed the manner in which blacks were constructed as a 'threat' in NP discourse at length in my book *Deconstructing Apartheid Discourse*, London, 1996.
52 This means that racism may be expressed through a variety of what Solomos and Back call 'coded signifiers', such as the protection of 'a way of life'. Solomos and Back, *Racism and Society*, p. 27.
53 Ibid.
54 Gilroy in Solomos and Back, *Racism and Society*, p. 132.
55 This is particularly apparent in the unreconstructed nationalist history of the idea of self-determination in the literature of the Volkstaat Council. See, for instance, H. C. G. Robbertze, 'Selfbeskikking. Die Geskiedenis van die selfbeskikkingsgedagte by die Afrikaner', unpublished mimeo.

56   Freeman, 'Democracy and dynamite', p. 749.
57   Tully, *Strange Multiplicity*, p. 11.
58   Ibid.
59   Ibid.
60   The Lacanian term 'suture' refers to the process through which closure is instituted in an ideological discourse. Here it is used to designate the final impossibility of closure of any identity.
61   W. E. Connolly, *Identity/Difference*, New York, 1991, p. 218. Connolly argues that the contemporary need is to supplement and challenge structures of territorial democracy with a politics of non-territorial democratization of global issues.
62   I am investigating the process of constitution-making in contemporary South Africa from this perspective.
63   Tully argues that modern constitutionalism has the following seven central characteristics, all of which serve to exclude or assimilate cultural diversity. The first draws together three concepts of popular sovereignty, all of which eliminate cultural diversity as a constitutive aspect of politics; the second is that it is defined in opposition to ancient constitutions (both premodern European and non-European), as superseding those stages of development; the third is the contrast between regularity and unevenness in modern and ancient constitutions; the fourth is the recognition of culture within the theory of progress; the fifth is the identification between modern constitutionalism and a specific set of European institutions; the sixth, the idea that a constitutional state possesses an individual identity as a 'nation'; and the seventh, that the modern constitution is a founding act which stands behind democracy. For a full discussion of these features, see Tully, *Strange Multiplicity*, chapter 3.
64   Ibid., p. 135.
65   This view is clearly critical of Habermas' idea that participants in a dialogue aim to reach agreement on universal principles. Rather, Tully argues, the aim of negotiations over cultural recognition is to bring negotiators to recognize their differences and similarities so that they can reach agreement on a form of association that accommodates their differences in appropriate institutions, and their similarities in shared institutions. Ibid., p. 131.
66   Ibid., p. 183.

6 Identity and the Changing Politics of Gender in South Africa

Debby Bonnin, Roger Deacon, Robert Morrell and Jenny Robinson

The democratic election in South Africa in April 1994 signalled the end of the four-year transition from white minority rule and the birth of a non-racial Government of National Unity. However, the accession of Nelson Mandela to the presidency of South Africa marks the end of transition in one sense only. At the level of government, voteless and powerless blacks have been enfranchised and empowered. At many other levels, particularly the terrain of gender politics, the process of transition is incomplete and struggles continue. In this chapter, we argue that the politics of gender during the period of transition reflects both an engagement with international debates and a response to the specific dynamics of the transition. Paradoxically, the possibilities for advancing feminist causes have multiplied even as the categories of 'women' and 'men', as well as the project of feminism itself, have been called into question. In the present period of rapid social change various gender identities are being fragmented and challenged. This presents opportunities for a more productive politics of gender at one moment even as it seems to close off possibilities at another. As far as gender is concerned, the transformation of South African society is still very much underway. Indeed, the nature of the changes in political identities – including gender identities – during this period of transition raises important questions about apartheid-era interpretations of South African politics, which theorists have been slow to abandon. New ways of imagining politics and transformation need to replace the dualistic political imaginary which underpinned both apartheid and anti-apartheid politics and analysis.

Since 1990, women and men from across the political spectrum have begun to assert their rights in ways which both produce and reinforce and yet also fragment and subvert their gendered identities. A Women's National Coalition has emerged to demand that the process and the product of negotiating a new constitution and Bill of Rights provide effective equality for women. At the same time black women have begun to protest strongly at their exclusion from white feminists' political and theoretical projects, raising issues of gender difference, the fragmentation of the subject and of the category 'woman' by race, class and culture. Thus a feminist politics of identity is being asserted against phallogocentric hegemony[1] while itself being challenged on grounds of its racial exclusivity. At the same time, the politics of masculinity has emerged as an important new contributor to the transformation of the dominant gender order, with something of a crisis of masculinity identifiable during the phase of transition. Some men have organized themselves either to violently reaffirm heterosexual masculine hegemony or to undermine and contest it. These contestations of the character of masculinity and femininity make us aware of the need to rethink the foundations and direction of gender politics.

Many recent challenges to the feminist project have come from that very broad movement more or less easily captured under the rubric of 'post-modernism'. Our first section engages with the implications of the extensive theoretical debates between feminists and 'postmodernism', and thereafter we explore in detail the politics of gender during the transition in South Africa; the second section charts the emergence of the Women's National Coalition, showing how local feminist politics has worked creatively with the tensions between identity and difference; while dominant and embryonic counter-hegemonic constructions of masculinity are surveyed in the third section, both at the level of organization and in the various broader contexts where gender identity is constantly enacted. This leads finally into an examination of the politics of representation as played out within academic feminist circles, with specific attention being paid to the powerful cross-cutting effect of race in the construction of gender identities. As the conclusion will suggest, important aspects of general feminist dilemmas are exemplified in the South African case, and these might instruct feminists elsewhere even as our interpretation has been informed by their thinking and experiences.

FEMINISM AND THE POSTMODERN CRITIQUE OF IDENTITY

Postmodern challenges to feminism, traditionally premised upon essentialist conceptions of identity, are profound. Rather than understanding identity as a pre-given attribute of a self-present and already sexed human agent, a postmodern critique suggests that identity can be more fruitfully conceptualized as a 'borderline self [which] is . . . a bricolage of broken images and assorted idioms, other people's narratives and mannerisms, loosely assembled into a fragile crust or pastiche with nothing but void at its centre'.[2] Whereas feminism has depended upon the category 'women' as the natural constituency of their political project, debates concerning the social construction of gender have fed into a general account of identity as inherently unstable, and performative. The notion of the subject as self-presence is seen as derived: a product or effect of ongoing (as well as accumulated) everyday practices, which are *post facto* presumed to represent this self-presence – 'woman' and 'man' are only stable, unified subjects to the extent that they are performatively constituted as such out of a plurality of discursive domains.[3] 'Sex', 'gender' and 'woman' only form part of a multiplicity of overdeterminations – race, class, ethnicity, place, sexuality – and identity is thus never fully formed but always (at least minimally) contested, often contradictory, and hence both questionable and mutable.

The transformation of gender relations also becomes much more difficult to understand than a conventional invocation of challenges to a (singular) patriarchal order might imply. For different experiences of gender might lead to very different sorts of demands for change. And if the possibilities for the transformation of gender relations lie in the instability of a performed gender identity,[4] then the direction of changes in the gender order(s) also becomes unpredictable. However, and perhaps paradoxically, it is likely that this set of theoretical positions will make it more possible to recognize and celebrate a proliferation of challenges to dominant gender identities and relations. Rather than being a site of the unremitting reinforcement of dominant gender relations, everyday performances of gender become the stage for the constant possibility of disrupting and challenging these relations.

Some feminist scholars have reacted aggressively to these postmodern trends, even suggesting that the fragmentation of identity is a male plot designed to undermine the cohesion of the women's movement:[5] 'just at the moment when [feminists] are achieving "identity" and articulating "interests", these fundamental categories are being rejected by a group of predominantly male theorists'.[6] However, the postmodern challenge, and especially the post-colonial turn, has seen feminism take on board a critique which calls into question its own, previously unexplored, class and racial biases.[7] Nonetheless, there is an emerging body of literature which insists that despite these advances, a number of theorists, especially those within French deconstruction and psychoanalytical traditions, have continued to subordinate the feminine, and to assert an (albeit castrated) superordinate masculinity.[8] For our purposes two important themes emerge from the broader feminist engagement with postmodernism: firstly, the images of transformation which feminist theorists are mobilizing; and secondly, the implications of contemporary accounts of identity for the way in which we understand political relationships and organization. Before we explain why we feel that it is possible to reconstruct a feminist project out of the fragments of political identities and revolutions, we would like to ground our analysis in the contemporary politics of gender in South Africa.

Our arguments run against the grain of many South African feminists who often dismiss as irrelevant postmodern debates over the fragmentation and construction of identity.[9] It is thought that the esoteric theoretical debates of Western feminists, unconcerned with the real material struggles of ordinary poor women, will not be helpful in understanding feminist concerns in this context. On the contrary, we feel that Western and Third World women frequently contest – albeit in different arenas – aspects of the same political, intellectual and economic heritage, and that there is much to be learned from an engagement between feminists in different places.[10] But to use an Irigarayan image, this engagement needs to be like a 'lovers' embrace', reciprocal and mutually enriching: Western feminist theorists might learn from our interpretations of the politics of gender in South Africa as much as our interrogation of the categories used to build feminist politics and our hopes for change will benefit from the sustained critiques of those whose battles are different.

In the following sections, we investigate how local gender politics is responding to the disruption of once-essential categories, and argue that attempts to subvert and dismantle dominant gender relations must necessarily go beyond binary oppositions towards a form of coalition politics, even if this remains only one possible option. This kind of politics can contingently unite those who contest, in all sorts of arenas, dominant forms of gender relations even as differences and divisions are creatively mobilized to ensure a feminist politics whose character and direction reflect the complexity of the wider social order and the gender identities which emerge in this particular place.

IDENTITY AND DIFFERENCE IN THE WOMEN'S NATIONAL COALITION

The Women's National Coalition, launched in April 1992, brought together a wide range of women's organizations across racial, political, religious, welfare and other divides. Such an organization of women, with a membership of over 60 national organizations and 13 regional coalitions, was previously unthinkable. Prior to 1990 feminism was almost a dirty word – national liberation came first and women's liberation second (or even third).[11] In earlier periods many women's organizations existed as the wings of political parties.[12] In the late 1970s some overtly feminist groups were formed: made up predominantly of white women, and constituted primarily around issues of domestic violence (like Rape Crisis) and abortion reform, they operated mostly outside of mainstream parliamentary and extra-parliamentary politics. Many of the women involved in these groups were also involved in other political organizations (the African National Congress (ANC), the United Democratic Front (UDF), and various housing groups) and in the re-emerging grassroots women's movements of the 1980s (the United Women's Congress, the Federation of South African Women, the Federation of Transvaal Women and the Natal Organization of Women). At the same time as these feminist influences were patterning the internal anti-apartheid movement, women in exile, inspired by the International Decade of Women, were trying to develop 'their own thinking on women's issues and constantly struggling to get women's concerns and the whole question of gender onto the agenda of the National Liberation Movement'.[13]

The unbanning of the liberation movements in 1990 made it politically more acceptable to organize specifically around women's issues. However, questions of race and location also intervened to ensure that the emerging feminist discourse took difference as its starting point. As both a product and one of the producers of this new discourse, the Women's National Coalition aimed to achieve equality for women under the new constitution. It had long been recognized that the removal of white minority rule would not correct sexist practices which were well entrenched within the structures of both the Congress of South African Trade Unions (Cosatu) and the ANC.[14] This realization, borne out in South Africa with the appointment of a new Cabinet which is predominantly male in composition and style, strengthened the impetus to develop a broad coalition, with 'women', not 'the struggle' or 'the poor and needy', as its essential starting point.

The main purpose of the Coalition was to draw up a Women's Charter, concentrating on five key areas: women's legal status; access to land; violence against women; women's health; and women's work. A multipronged research strategy – a survey, focus groups, workshops and chain letters – was utilized in order to gather the data which would determine the final Charter, which was finely tuned to both the similarity and the diversity of issues which affect South African women: 'as much as respondents speak "with one voice" in censuring the roles and treatment they are subjected to, there is a keen awareness of the complexities of this oppression – especially when culture and tradition enter the frame'.[15] On the one hand,

then, the campaign and the Charter reinforced the unitary identity of
'women' and their oppression. But it also actively provided space for the
differences between women, notably in terms of location, race, religion
and class, to emerge (for example through constituting particular focus
groups). Through involvement in the campaign women became more
aware of their gender identity, of what, despite political differences, they
have in common with other women. As one participant commented: 'I
would hate to see the Coalition stop. . . . When I first attended, I did so simply as an NP [National Party] delegate. But now I believe it is doing good
things in bringing together women from all walks of life. It's made me realize how much we have in common. I, myself, got close to women from
the ANC and IFP [Inkatha Freedom Party]. Politics wasn't an issue.
There's little difference in our aspirations.'[16] This realization of common
interests, both as a condition and an effect of the Coalition, is also evident
in the way in which the Women's Lobby at the multi-party talks often managed to forge common ground on issues regardless of party differences and
sometimes in spite of party opposition.

However, the Coalition's attempts to work creatively with difference
and diversity led some women and organizations to express dissatisfaction.
At one point, the National Party threatened to withdraw on the basis that the
Coalition was dominated by ANC women; other women felt that the
diversity of the Coalition had compromised its ability to come out with a
clear position on abortion.[17] As a political lobby group concerned with 'attempts to achieve women's equality . . . and . . . decisive interventions to
alter the low status of women',[18] the Coalition tended to focus on representing women's interests, rather than on 'the processes whereby they are constituted', which would imply a concern with 'the discursive fields in which
social reality and individual and group identities and interests are constituted'.[19] However, this bold statement needs to be tempered with an understanding of the research process which established these interests: the
outcome of the group discussions was a focus on women's interests, but the
process of getting there required women to discuss how their lives and conditions were constituted.

The establishment of a Gender Advisory Committee at the Conference
for a Democratic South Africa (CODESA) (in 1992) was the result of
intense lobbying. CODESA was short-lived, however, and at the next round
of negotiations, the Multi-Party Negotiating Process, the Coalition went
on to demand that at least one member of a party's team had to be female
and present at all sessions.[20] At the time this decision created great controversy, and was slated as tokenism by the media and by many men at the
talks (who referred to the female representatives as the 'Broomstick Bri-

gade'). However, subsequent research[21] has shown that this decision made a very positive contribution: men's attitudes changed, female negotiators felt increasingly capable and confident, and a women's lobby was created with the ability to mobilize around issues which women wanted addressed. In addition, the Coalition managed to secure a Transitional Executive Council sub-council on 'The Status of Women', with powers to 'scrutinise and advise on existing and proposed legislation and executive acts, develop a national strategy and liaise with all role players affecting the status of women and ensure free and independent voting rights'.[22] The multi-party talks thus constituted the first national forum where the level of women's participation has been so high (50 per cent of the negotiators) and where a quota has been enforced, although similar gains have been made in other arenas (such as some trade unions) where there has been a conscious attempt to get more women to participate.

Central to the negotiation of the Interim Constitution was Chapter Three of the Charter of Fundamental Rights, in short the Bill of Rights. Two issues related to the Bill of Rights produced conflict: firstly, 'the demand that an equality clause should enjoy priority in the Bill of Rights in order to pave the way for gender equal affirmative action'; and secondly, that traditional and customary law be democratized.[23] Initially women were divided on these issues, with many feeling that custom and culture should take priority. There was also a lobby for a moratorium on issues of traditional law before they are subjected to the Bill of Rights. The Coalition argued that 'unless the women unite and formulate a clear position setting out their views on every aspect, and debate it as a united front, the matter is likely to be decided in favour of the traditional leaders'.[24] The traditional leaders formed a strong lobby at the multi-party talks, arguing that 'customary law should be entrenched as a "right" not subject to any other section of the Bill of Rights and without taking "freedom of association" into account'.[25] They also argued that the position taken by the women's lobby represented Western women's interests. This, however, was countered by the strong role played by the Rural Women's Movement and, in particular, one of its members, MamLydia Kompe, who opposed the imposition of customary and traditional laws which disadvantage women. Through membership of the Coalition, rural women were able to identify their interests and represent them at the talks, and it was very difficult for traditional leaders to argue that these were the ideas of Western women when they were being faced by representatives of the Rural Women's Movement themselves. These events problematize the idea that interests can be read off location. 'Rural' or any other group of women do not have preconstituted interests. The interests of any group of women are a result of any number of intersect-

ing factors which constitute identity. 'Experience' is crucial to these constructions. For rural women their experiences of customary and traditional
law have not been empowering.[26] Similarly the idea of 'Western women's
interests' is problematic and homogenizing.

It was finally agreed to remove the clause on customary law, even
though demands for an explicit gender equality trump clause could not be
won. Women were assured, however, that the equality clause has a special
position in the Bill of Rights and would generally override discrimination
based on custom and culture. Even so, this can only be applied vertically
(between individuals and the state or written law) and not horizontally (in
terms of private relationships or contracts).[27] The implication is that custom, culture and equality can be challenged in the public sphere but the
private domain is still private and beyond the reach of the Bill of Rights.

At various points, for sometimes obscure reasons, women who were at
other times at loggerheads within the Coalition (for example, over abortion) came together and presented a united front in the negotiations. Operating with a nuanced and differentiated view of women's interests and
needs, the Coalition seems to have built its campaign around the slogan of
'unity in diversity'. It was not arguing that women are a homogeneous
group, with similar interests; rather, it attempted to unite women with different interests and across party lines around specific issues. The drawing
up of the Bill of Rights was a process of different and competing interest
groups (political parties, traditional leaders, women and others) demanding to have their needs met. Without strong representation at the negotiations it is likely that many parties would have ignored the demands of
women in order to obtain the support of the traditional leaders. The price
paid for this representation has been a tendency, however, for differences
to be subordinated to overlapping identities, to entrench the male/female
dichotomy and to deny the possibility of a broader and more nuanced critique and displacement of hegemonic social forms.

CHANGING DISCOURSES OF MASCULINITY

The mobilization of women against the dominant gender order in South
Africa has provoked both violent and sympathetic reactions from a range of
unequal, unstable and competing masculinist discourses. In many cases
these discourses share common assumptions about women and operate as
part of gender regimes of male governance; occasionally they develop new
forms of masculinity which challenge and expose the limits of these
regimes.

The militarization of South African society, particularly in the last two decades, had profound implications for local readings of masculinity. Conscription forced young white males to serve in the armed forces, while political oppression, educational disadvantage and the absence of employment opportunities produced amongst urbanized black youth an enthusiastic adherence for the armed struggle as well as less politically correct but equally violent forms of anti-establishment behaviour. Regardless of whether one was a teenage comrade, an elderly member of the local amabutho, a white Afrikaans-speaking right-winger or a young white conscript, a man's job was to do the fighting. This militarization of an already profoundly macho society has analogies in the world of sport. The members of the new South African soccer team, nicknamed 'Bafana Bafana' (Boys Boys) by adoring fans,[28] offer a performative reading of masculinity in its most naked form; they are considered prime examples of virile manliness, and are worshipped and lionized for succeeding in a white-dominated society where many African men are deeply alienated by unemployment and challenges to their traditional authority. This powerful, athletic and independent identity stands alongside the more stately and orderly view, personified by Nelson Mandela, where education and intellect, political power and position are marks of true masculinity.

It is a measure of the acceptance of masculinity as given that the role of men in the low-intensity civil war that preceded, accompanied and has followed the transition has not been problematized. Even the socially conscious and explicitly radical journal, *Work in Progress*, analysing white, right-wing, primarily Afrikaner, militancy, resorts to masculinist stereotypes like 'boys will be boys' in order to explain the apparently primordial willingness of men to resort to violence. At the same time the journal attempts to distance itself from any suggestion of gender-prejudice by describing these same right-wing militants as 'main manne' (literally 'main men', those who consciously set themselves up as epitomes of manhood), implying that the strutting, arrogant and intolerant subjects under discussion are 'other', Neanderthal and obsolete, while the alternative masculinity implicitly claimed by the journal is of a modern, critical, self-aware and sensitive kind.[29]

There have been moments when the dominant gender order has been called into question. Women have often been (self) represented as peacemakers and nurturers yet in some instances they have disrupted that easy reading. Women, black and white, have challenged the male monopolization of coercion. Institutionally they, but particularly white women, have begun to claim places hitherto denied them – in 1995 the South African Air Force gained its first female combat pilot and the new-look Defence Force contains a number of female generals. In the townships, the trend, already evident in the late 1980s, of women taking up weapons to have their demands noted, continues to shake comfortable orthodoxies about the woman's place being (passively) at home. And horrifyingly, young black schoolgirls have become much more involved in violence (often leading to murder) particularly in the politically unsettled period before 1990.[30] Similarly, black youth, in particular the 'young lions' or the 'foot soldiers of the revolution', grew in stature and significance during the 1980s, invading the domain of the elders and becoming a voice that could not be silenced. It was the youth who defended townships from the South African Defence Force, and who, in KwaZulu-Natal, challenged the political leadership of Inkatha, taking over the role of 'useless' adults as they did so. In instances of radical social change it can happen that gender relations alter. In this case, however, the rights of the male elders were arrogated by the youth: women were not allowed to fight or to express opinions, and were not elected on to civic and other organizations.[31]

In this, the otherwise radical youth were implicated in the conservative vision of society held out by their IFP opponents, which represents an attempt by the beleaguered elders and tribal chiefs of the region to re-establish control over the youth and women, a control that has been shaken by recent political upheaval and protracted recession. The fact that their programme has attracted the support of significant numbers of rural whites suggests that an alliance based on gender and generation is being developed, not unlike that in colonial Zimbabwe and South Africa, where African patriarchs in the early twentieth century used a particular moment of rupture in social relations to ally with male colonial administrators and reassert their rule over their wives and daughters.[32]

Hegemonic masculinities may be changing, but only 'in slow motion'.[33] Damon Galgut, described as the first author to seriously examine masculinity in South African literature,[34] presents in his 'The beautiful screaming of pigs' (1992) different formulations of masculinity – of homosexuality, of political dissidence, of a rejection of societal norms. Neither an anti-hero of the James Dean variety who can easily be accommodated into mainstream boerewors and rugby masculinity,[35] nor an other who can simply be dismissed as having no relevance to or purchase on South African realities, Galgut's character erodes from within, with enough in him for us all to recognize, but too much for us to ignore. Nevertheless, despite efforts such as these to displace 'those naturalised and reified notions of gender that support masculine hegemony and heterosexist power',[36] the South African Left has neither politically nor culturally yet succeeded in generating a discourse that challenges heterosexual hegemony and offers a different vision of a man's role(s). Despite the existence of a gay movement, 'the homosexual' remains alienated, an other, something to point to and at but not to assimilate into one's person or into the body politic. The case of Koos Prinsloo, Afrikaans writer and cultural dissident, is instructive. Described as 'the most brilliant and promising young writer in the Afrikaans community', as brutally honest, as somebody who sacrificed public acceptance so as not to compromise his anti-establishment political position, terminally ill Prinsloo refused to acknowledge until his death that he was dying of AIDS.[37] He wrote about gay society and gay issues, but would not confront his own sexual politics publicly. While Prinsloo could defy political constraints and cultural taboos and voice his contempt of and opposition to the society in which he lived, he could not 'come out'. The major reason for this was the oppressive homophobia within South African society. More personally for Prinsloo, he had to deal with the perceptions and reactions of his own colleagues and cultural crusaders, one of whom, Johannes Kerkorrel, also a vocal dissident and critic, assaulted Prinsloo because he felt that one of the latter's books had portrayed him as gay. For Kerkorrel being a cultural dissident was fine, being a 'moffie' (homosexual) was not.

The development of 'Men's Studies' and a Men's Movement in the industrialized West is now a decade and more old,[38] but the latter has no unity and little coherence. Locally, the most well-organized strand is the South African Association of Men (SAAM), launched in February 1994. Its goal is to fight discrimination against men in order to 'restore the tattered remains of the male image'.[39] Headed by a Johannesburg businessman (John Loftus) and a University of South Africa political science lecturer (Kieran O'Malley), it explicitly dedicates itself to challenging modern feminism whose core is said to contain 'an often-vicious loathing of traditional masculinity'.[40] Seemingly an exclusively white, middle-class and heterosexist organization, it is oriented towards the mythopoetic American men's movement inspired by the work of Robert Bly. Bly believes that the male quality of assertiveness has been suppressed by two decades of feminist activism, and needs to be rediscovered for the psychic well-being of men to be restored. This movement calls for men to rediscover the 'wild man' within themselves and resist feminist-inspired domestication.

A second strand can be seen emerging among some well-educated, politically progressive and gender-sensitive white professionals. Supportive of international campaigns for gender tolerance and equality, they have begun responding to the discomfort of being a man within the parameters of South Africa's hegemonic masculinity by entering therapy or men's groups. Disconcertingly, however, this strand has also adopted some of Bly's essentialist ideas on manhood, in the form of men's weekends devoted to investigating male

angst and men's trips to the mountains. A third strand is the increasingly asser-
tive gay movement. Gay bars, film festivals and marches have all brought gay
issues forcibly to public awareness in the last few years. A 1994 court decision
has paved the way for gays to be allowed to adopt children, and the movement
has also been actively testing whether the new constitution's Bill of Rights
protects individuals from discrimination against sexual orientation. The political position of the various strands of the men's movement nevertheless
remains unclear. The ANC's male-dominated hierarchy is not renowned for
its progressive gender politics, yet when a gay and lesbian parade was held in
Johannesburg in October 1994, ANC Vice-President, Thabo Mbeki, and ANC
Regional Chair, Tokyo Sexwale, both sent messages of support.[41] The men's
movement thus appears to be open to articulation by both 'reactionary' and
'progressive' political positions.

The onset of AIDS has forced masculinist discourses to confront the subjects of sex and sexuality, and has provoked a number of regulatory re-
sponses. Initially, the disease was treated by the media (and some members of
the medical profession) as a divine judgement inflicted on errant white
homosexuals. As the disease spread to the heterosexual (predominantly
African) population public reception also shifted. AIDS was now considered a God-given, Malthus-inspired solution to South Africa's overpopula-
tion 'problem'. The scale of the problem and the gradual erosion of racial
barriers has now generated a new, medically emphatic discourse focused
on prevention and the wearing of condoms. One effect has been to rupture
the comfortable assumption of unencumbered male entitlement to the
female body. Women are urged to insist on their rights to decline sex if their
partner will not wear a condom. It is difficult to know whether this message
has significantly affected patterns of sexual intercourse, though AIDS
workers find that there is strong male resistance to using a condom. To cope
with such institutional challenges to their masculinity, some men are
emphasizing their sexual prowess,[42] and are thus as likely to insist on their
'right' to sex, violently if necessary, as to accept the new preconditions for
sex and respect the wishes of their partner. In this situation, men are no
longer supported by female complicity or with social codes which bound
and confer legitimacy upon their demands of women,[43] and cases of rape
and sexual harassment have become numerous as the assertion of masculinity becomes more forceful: 'jackrolling' (routinized rape) in Soweto; the
'modelling' of female informers (forcing them to walk naked through the
streets); and the invasion of female dormitories by boys to assault, gang
rape and otherwise 'teach girls a lesson'; while in KwaZulu-Natal political
violence itself has been related to a crisis of masculinity among black
males, youth and adult alike.[44]

The field of masculinity displays other tensions and signs of transition. In an escalator at the University of Natal, amongst the standard political, homophobic and sexist graffiti was scratched the following: 'Say No to AIDS, Say Yes to Ukusoma'. Ukusoma, a form of consensual sex which does not involve penetration, was practised as a form of birth control before the onset of colonial rule and was a way of obtaining sexual release when full sexual intercourse was prohibited for political rather than demographic reasons. This accentuation of a historical practice, located as it is in images of pre-colonial freedom, adds a new dimension to the discursive struggles generated by the killer disease. It mingles ambiguously with the Inkatha Freedom Party's invocation of a patriarchal and nationalist 'traditional culture' as well as with the claims of forward-looking traditionalists to preserve institutions like the chiefship and to accept the status and role of herbalists and other traditional healers. Elsewhere, similar challenges to conventional gender identities are becoming public. In Pietermaritzburg, the Reverend Dennis Dlamini has publicly announced his homosexuality and claimed his calling to be the counselling of homosexuals within his parishes. Even in the staid world of academic writings, matters are less predictable and stable than they used to be: Zackie Achmat,[45] political and gender activist, recently became the first scholar in South Africa, to our knowledge, who has responded to the gay challenge, 'I'll show you mine, if you show me yours',[46] by writing of his own homosexual experiences in a Cape prison.

The politics of gender is naturally much more complex and contradictory than it has thus far been rendered, artificially split into feminist and masculinist discourses. Take the case of Winnie Mandela, erstwhile partner of Nelson Mandela and candle of militant politics in the country. Despite many reverses, she remains a figure with a large following and credibility. Her roles have included hero(ine), spokesperson for the youth, leader of militant extremists within the liberation movements, mother, social worker, sympathiser of the poor and sick, and articulate and independent politician. At one moment, camouflaged, bellicose, unyielding, brutal and sexual; at another, attractive, poised, a victim of apartheid. While some of these roles are no longer viable, even in the wake of the Seipei murder case,[47] rumours of her sexual infidelity, the conduct of her Football Club and her personal extravagance she remains a powerful figure. Her durability has rested on the way she has presented herself as a new type of woman, often drawing upon masculinist images. This multi-dimensional identity is potent for a range of groups including those already disillusioned with the slow pace or absence of change. For the youth she is the warrior who is prepared to continue the fight, even when the grey-heads urge moderation; for many women she is the embodiment of liberation – from male containment and confinement, from domestic subjugation and economic exploitation. Not surprisingly, few gender activists have smiled upon the image of Winnie – presented through the media as arrogant murderer, intolerant child-beater and cuckolding demagogue. Her disregard for political discipline has not, thus far, ended her career, for, quite against all expectations, she has recovered from each reverse to capture important positions. Her popularity, we argue, can only be understood in terms of the gendered representations her activities allow. She has challenged and reinforced, undermined and upheld both hegemonic and oppositional, feminist and masculinist, discourses of gender.

RACE, REPRESENTATION AND THE POLITICS OF GENDER

Alongside the experiences of women's and men's organizations during this period of transition, the terrain of academic feminism in South Africa has had to confront significant challenges. The problems of differences amongst women and of the representation of some women by others in academic writing emerged at the centre of controversy at a conference in January 1991.[48] The Women and Gender in Southern Africa Conference held at the University of Natal had been organized by a group of mostly white academic women, and most of those who attended and gave papers were also white academic feminists.[49] Although activist and grassroots women's organizations had been invited to participate in all aspects of the programming and presentations, in practice the conference, in both its content and its form, excluded and marginalized women without an intellectual background, especially black women. The conference logo (Figure 6.1) was criticized as 'a tiny-headed, naked and burdened Other, "present" only as object for scrutiny by the self-defining, theorising subject'[50] – and black women were seen to be objectified in this way more generally by white women writing (about) black women. Conference organizers noted that the logo was chosen for its local and historical significance, being the only surviving San painting of a woman, portrayed in her role as 'breadwinner', heading off to gather food with her digging implement and container.

The debate over the logo in many ways symbolized the contrasting and emotionally charged positions taken by an 'old guard' of (mostly white) committed feminist academics and a new wave of articulate and critical black writers. We argue that neither of the essentialist positions which have since been adopted in this debate – white feminists defending the essential unity of the feminist project on political grounds, black feminists seeking to ground their authenticity in a racial unity and in the privileged realm of experience – are tenable in the light of postmodern debates around identity and the subject.[51] For just as racial identity disrupts a too easy assumption of 'sisterhood' even in an environment where a non-racial politics was paramount in resisting apartheid, so divisions across education, location, language and class all potentially disrupt any appeal to race (let alone experience) as a primary foundation for the right to appropriately represent others. The recognition of identities as multiple and fragmented means that we need new models for representing others and for building political relationships around gender concerns.

Figure 6.1   Logo, 'Women and Gender in South Africa' Conference, January 1991

A first step is to think differently about opposing identities, to seek out alternative ways of conceptualizing disabling modernist dichotomies (self/ other; male/female; heterosexual/homosexual; white/black; researcher/researched). In political practice, exemplified by the Women's Coalition discussed above, this might sometimes entail mobilizing categories such as 'women' or 'black' in a strategic sense while ensuring an ongoing examination and critique of the silencing effects of this 'strategic essentialism'.[52]

While such a creative mobilization and deconstruction of political categories is one avenue worth exploring, it is also helpful to reconsider the nature of the relationship between 'competing' political subjects. Given the hybridity of most subjects, their always incomplete constitution on the basis of many different and unstable discourses, the image of opposing, self-contained and mutually exclusive (racially defined) subjects which has informed the debates about representation and epistemic violence amongst South African feminists seems misguided. Similar images of political subjects have informed the analysis of political change in South Africa more generally, with a power bloc of apartheid enforcers seen as mobilized against the non-racial anti-apartheid alliance. The post-apartheid era has exposed these binary oppositions as far more fragile, intertwined and prone to fragmentation than previously allowed for.

Homi Bhabha has argued that competing political subjects are necessarily involved in a process of mutual constitution and transformation, and that possibilities for political change exist in the subtle disruptions which emerge in everyday engagements. Rather than assuming the necessary effacement of one political identity by another (whether dominant or subordinate), he has called for 'a more dialogic process that attempts to track the processes of displacement and realignment that *are already* at work, constructing something different and hybrid from the encounter: a third space that does not simply revise or invert the dualities, but revalues the ideological bases of division and difference'.[53]

This 'third space' which Bhabha refers to is being surveyed, in different ways, by an influential triad of French feminist writers – Luce Irigaray, Julia Kristeva and Hélène Cixous – as they search for ways of symbolizing and imagining the possibility of alternative gender arrangements even while acknowledging our necessary, inescapable location within a phallogocentric social order. In their quest to avoid the dilemmas of representation, these writers draw upon images of subjects and spaces which take into paradoxical account both the sameness and the otherness of those one is relating to: the mother–daughter relationship, for example, or the relationship of woman to woman (between people of both sexes) written about by Cixous, and the mother–child relationship – capturing the image of the 'other within' – characterized by Kristeva in her discussions of maternity. These offer us images of the kinds of relations which could dislocate phallogocentric repressions and dualities and which could underpin new understandings of interactions and strategies for transformation within gender politics.

While these post-colonial and feminist accounts do stress their inevitable implicatedness in the present social order, they all have a vision of transformation which centres around strategies of disruption, based on the experiences of hybridity signposted by gendered and post-colonial identities. Bhabha suggests that a subversive strategy is potentially present in the disruptive in-between of the colonial encounter, which produces always mediated, always ambivalent subjectivities on the part of both colonizer and colonized:

> In occupying two places at once ... the depersonalised, dislocated colonial subject can become an incalculable object, quite literally, difficult to place. The demand of authority cannot unify its message nor simply identify its subjects. For the strategy of colonial desire is to stage the drama of identity at the point at which the black mask slips to reveal the white skin. At that edge, in between the black body and the white body, there is a tension of meaning and being, or some would say demand and desire. ... It is from that tension – both psychic and political – that a strategy of subversion emerges. It is a mode of negation that seeks not to unveil the fullness of Man but to manipulate his representation. It is a form of power that is manipulated at the very limits of identity and authority, in the mocking spirit of mask and image.[54]

In colonial as in gender encounters, then, and in their multiple interactions, we observe the impossibility of asserting an originary subjectivity and the revolutionary potential inherent in this recognition. It follows that racial and gender regimes can be, and are, routinely challenged by processes of exposure, disruption, mimicry and mutual transformation. These subversive strategies precisely demonstrate the constructed or performative nature of identities and their necessary transformation as a consequence of all sorts of colonial, sexual and political engagements. Thus we identify the potential for a new kind of gender politics aimed at manipulating representations, subverting identities and inventing subjectivities, both at the level of the wider social order and at the level of the everyday.[55] A non-essentialist reading of the politics of Irigaray, Kristeva and Cixous also offers strategies for disruption and transformation through a re-reading of the excluded 'feminine' and the assertion of the possibility of a 'third space' beyond the dichotomies of male/female, masculine/feminine, patriarchal present/ utopian feminist future.

The corollary of this analysis, though, and one which these theorists have been a little reticent to emphasize, is that the nature and direction of transformation is difficult to predict. The utopian visions of earlier feminist theorists have been replaced by an acute awareness that any alternative imaginaries are going to be shaped by their origins in the present order. But if we consider that the social order is fragmented, varying according to both physical and social location, then the uncertainty of the process of transformation becomes an appropriate recognition of difference. Abandoning teleology, then, does not mean abandoning the hope of transformation. It means embarking upon a struggle to make and read history transformatively, even as we accept that that process can only ever be both uncertain and contested.

CONCLUSION

Although our account of recent events in South Africa may indicate that the dominant gender order may be enduring and resistant to rapid and radical reformulation, we hope that we have also demonstrated, both empirically and theoretically, that it is also perpetually being subverted and displaced. The new democratic government remains dominated by men and challenges from either a unified women's movement or disparate masculinist discourses have proved organizationally and conceptually difficult. Where women have come together (in the Coalition) they have not been able to deny or escape from the political mobilization of conventional categories, nor have oppositional images of masculinity made much headway against hegemonic norms. Thus resistance often does not disrupt the binary of men and women and may even endorse some forms of masculine power (such as forms of state) as a necessary requirement for defending women's immediate perceived interests. What resistance has done, however, is to expose the limits of gender regimes and to demonstrate their incompleteness, instability and fragility. In acknowledging our necessary, inescapable location within a gendered social order, we need to find ways of imagining and inventing possibilities of alternative identities. A recognition that the borders of phallogocentrism are internal makes it possible to conceive of a politics which is both implicated and transgressive. This politics of the 'in-between', a place of mediation between the self and the other, offers us new ways of discursively producing and potentially transforming gendered identities.

NOTES

1   A term derived from Lacan which suggests the pre-existence of a symbolic order dominated by the phallus. This term can either replace or supplement the structuralist concept of patriarchy.
2   G. Ivey, 'Life among the remnants: postmodern consciousness and the borderline self', *Theoria* , no. 81/82, 1993, p. 145.

3   J. Butler, *Gender Trouble: Feminism and the Subversion of Identity*, London, 1990.
4   Ibid.
5   Bordo, 'Feminism, postmodernism and gender-scepticism', in L. Nicholson (ed.), *Feminism/Postmodernism*, London, 1990, pp. 133–56; S. Moore, 'Getting a bit of the other – the pimps of postmodernism', in R. Chapman and J. Rutherford (eds.), *Male Order: Unwrapping Masculinity*, London, 1988, pp. 165–92.
6   R. Pringle and S. Watson, ' "Women's interests" and the post-structuralist state', in M. Barrett and A. Philips (eds.), *Destabilizing Theory: Contemporary Feminist Debates*, Cambridge, 1992, p. 54.
7   P. Parmar, 'Other kinds of dreams', *Feminist Review*, vol. 31, 1989.
8   A. Jardine, *Gynesis: Configurations of Women and Modernity*, Ithaca, 1985.
9   A. Levett, 'Childhood sexual abuse and problems in conceptualisation', *Agenda*, no. 7, 1990, pp. 38–47; D. Russell, 'The damaging effects of discounting the damaging effects: a response to Ann Levett's theories on child abuse', *Agenda*, no. 11, 1991, pp. 47–56; E. van Niekerk, 'Towards a South African feminism', paper presented at the Women and Gender in Southern Africa conference, University of Natal, Durban, 1991; but see D. Lewis, 'Feminisms in South Africa', *Women's Studies International Forum*, vol. 16, no. 5, 1993, pp. 535–42.
10 See G. C. Spivak, 'The politics of translation', in Barrett and Philips, *Destabilizing Theory*, pp. 177–200.
11 S. Hassim, J. Metelerkamp and A. Todes, ' "A bit on the side": gender struggles in the politics of transformation', *Transformation*, no. 5, 1987, pp. 3–32.
12 See C. Walker, *Women and Resistance in South Africa*, Cape Town, 1991.
13 Conference transcript: Frene Ginwala at the conference on Women and Gender in Southern Africa held at the University of Natal in January 1991. See D. Bonnin *et al.*, 'Report of the conference on women and gender in Southern Africa', Gender Research Group, University of Natal, Durban, 1991, pp. 1–28.
14 P. Horn, 'Post apartheid South Africa – what about women's emancipation?', *Transformation*, no. 15, 1991, pp. 26–39; P. Horn, 'ANC women's quota: the debate continues', *Work in Progress*, no. 77, 1991, p. 37; P. Horn, 'Marxism and feminism: uneasy bedfellows?', *African Communist*, vol. 126, 1991, pp. 10–20.
15 *Work in Progress Supplement*, 'Great expectations – women's rights and the 1994 election', *Work in Progress*, no. 96, 1994, p. 18.
16 E. Randall, 'Making friends in a war-zone', in *Work in Progress Supplement*, 'Great expectations', p. 17.
17 A. Kemp *et al.*, 'Draft report on women's organisations in South Africa', Ford Foundation 1994, unpublished mimeo, not paginated.
18 *Work in Progress Supplement*, 'Great expectations', p. 18.
19 Pringle and Watson, ' "Women's interests" ', pp. 63–4.
20 C. Albertyn, 'Women and the transition to democracy in South Africa', in C. Murry (ed.), *Gender and the New South African Legal Order*, Cape Town, 1994, pp. 39–63.

21 M. Finnemore, 'Negotiating power', *Agenda*, no. 20, 1994, pp. 16–21.

22 *Women's National Coalition News*, Third Issue, July/August, 1993, p. 3.

23 Women's National Coalition, 'Multi-party negotiating process monitoring report to the Women's National Coalition', *Ninth Report*, 19 November 1993.

24 Women's National Coalition, *Sixth Report*, 1 October 1993.

25 Women's National Coalition, *Seventh Report*, 22 October 1993.

26 M. Kompe and J. Small, 'Demanding a place under the kgotla tree: rural women's access to land and power', paper presented at the Women and Gender in Southern Africa conference, University of Natal, Durban, 1991.

27 Women's National Coalition, *Ninth Report*, 19 November 1993.

28 *Daily News*, 9 June 1994.

29 *Work in Progress*, no. 96, 1994, pp. 15–16.

30 *Daily News*, 10 February 1990 and 19 May 1990.

31 Hassim *et al.*, ' "A bit on the side" '; J. Seekings, 'Gender ideology and township politics in the 1980s', *Agenda*, no. 10, 1991, pp. 77–88.

32 E. Schmidt, 'Negotiated spaces and contested terrain: men, women, and the law in colonial Zimbabwe, 1890–1939', *Journal of Southern African Studies*, vol. 16, no. 4, 1990, pp. 622–48; C. Walker (ed.), *Women and Gender in Southern Africa to 1945*, Cape Town, 1990.

33 L. Segal, *Slow Motion: Changing Masculinities Changing Men*, New Brunswick, 1990.

34 E. Boehmer, 'Dark jokes and desert light', *Southern African Review of Books*, vol. 5, no. 1, 1993, pp. 8–9.

35 Boerewors (literally, farmer's sausage) is a symbol of rugged outdoor life – a meal prepared over an open fire by men usually in the exclusive company of other males. Rugby, South Africa's national sport (at least for most red-blooded white males), is synonymous with rugged masculinity.

36 Butler, *Gender Trouble*, p. 34.

37 *Sunday Times*, 13 March 1994.

38 H. Brod (ed.), *The Making of Masculinities: The New Men's Studies*, Boston, 1987; J. Hearn and D. Morgan (eds.), *Men, Masculinities and Social Theory*, London, 1990; R. W. Connell, *Masculinities*, Cambridge, 1995.

39 Quoted in J. Lemon, 'Masculinity in crisis?', *Agenda*, no. 24, 1995, p. 61.

40 K. O'Malley, 'The rape of the male', *The Liberator*, November 1994, p. 26.

41 *Sunday Tribune*, 2 October 1994.

42 S. Westwood, 'Racism, black masculinity and the politics of space', in Hearn and Morgan, *Men, Masculinities and Social Theory*, pp. 55–71.

43 A. Giddens, *The Transformation of Intimacy: Sexuality, Love and Eroticism in Modern Societies*, Cambridge 1992.

44 C. Campbell, 'Learning to kill: masculinity, the family and violence in Natal', *Journal of Southern African Studies*, vol. 18, no. 3, 1992, pp. 614–28.

45 Z. Achmat, ' "Apostles of civilised vice": "immoral practices" and "unnatural vice" in South African prisons and compounds, 1890–1920', *Social Dynamics*, vol. 19, no. 2, 1994, pp. 92–110.

46 G. W. Dowsett, 'I'll show you mine, if you'll show me yours: gay men, masculinity research, men's studies, and sex', *Theory and Society*, no. 22, 1993, pp. 697–709.

47   Stompie Seipei, a fourteen-year-old boy, was an activist in Tumahole township in the Orange Free State. Hounded out of his home town by security forces, he found short-lived refuge with Winnie Mandela and her football team. Accused of being an informer and of homosexual activity, he was assaulted and killed in 1989.
48   Lewis, 'Feminisms in South Africa'; S. Hassim and C. Walker, 'Women's studies and the women's movement in South Africa: defining a relationship', *Women's Studies International Forum*, vol. 16, no. 5, 1993, pp. 523–34; J. Robinson, 'White women researching/representing others: from anti-apartheid to postcolonialism?', in G. Rose and A. Blunt (eds.), *Writing Women and Space*, London, 1996, pp. 197–226.
49   K. Letlaka-Rennert, in 'Impressions: conference on "Women and Gender in Southern Africa" ', *Agenda*, no. 9, 1991, p. 22; F. Lund, in 'Impressions: Conference on "Women and Gender in Southern Africa" ', *Agenda*, no. 9, 1991, pp. 20–3.
50   D. Lewis, 'Theorizing about gender in South Africa', paper presented at the African Association of Political Science/Southern African Political Economy Series conference, Cape Town, 1992, p. 16.
51   G. C. Spivak, *The Post-Colonial Critic: Interviews, Strategies, Dialogues*, New York, 1990.
52   G. C. Spivak, 'The politics of translation'.
53   H. Bhabha, 'Postcolonial authority and postmodern guilt', in L. Grossberg (ed.), *Cultural Studies*, London, 1992, p. 58 (emphasis added).
54   H. Bhabha, 'Foreword: remembering Fanon. Self, psyche and the colonial condition', in F. Fanon, *Black Skin, White Masks*, London, 1986, p. xxii.
55   Butler, *Gender Trouble*.

7 Education, Development and Democracy in South Africa
Roger Deacon and Ben Parker

The Government of National Unity in South Africa has proclaimed that the new system of education, as a key element within the overall Reconstruction and Development Programme, will aim to nurture as well as reflect democracy and development, and build a new nation by laying the basis both for popular participation in local government and public service provision, and for the expansion in skills and infrastructure necessary for economic development. Examining the assumptions which underpin this education-for-democracy-and-development project, the portrayal of which is taking on the fairy-tale if pragmatic proportions of a dialectical realization of popular hopes and dreams, this chapter argues that the undertaking shares the same Enlightenment values that informed its colonial and apartheid predecessors. Simultaneously identical to and different from what came before, it bears with it both positive and negative consequences for social and educational change in South Africa. On the one hand, the rupture of the central racially defined dichotomy of the apartheid era has opened up previously unheard-of opportunities for the majority of the population; on the other hand, diverse new oppositions have emerged, old tensions have resurfaced and multiple realignments have been set in motion. In particular, the evolution and context of implementation of the diverse and often competing education policy formulations at the root of the project suggests not only that democracy has been subordinated to development, but that educational transformation will be influenced as much by its entanglement in political (central/periphery), spatial (rural/urban) and temporal (modern/traditional) tensions as by policy directives.

FROM CONFRONTATION TO NEGOTIATION

From a certain point of view, there is a beguiling dialectical narrative to the political events of South Africa's recent past. The apartheid regime, one of the twentieth century's most authoritarian examples of institutionalized racism, was confronted ostensibly by its negation, a national liberation movement premised upon non-racialism and inclusivity. After struggles which arguably can be traced back over 300 years, the antagonists fought each other almost to a standstill before beginning to negotiate a transition to a mutually acceptable new order; and half a decade later, a broad-based and synthetic set of values and an embryonic governance system had been collectively constructed, culminating in the ratification of an interim constitution and the extraordinarily peaceful election of a new government at the end of April 1994.

The history of education in South Africa also appears to support a dialectical narrative characterized by contradiction and transcendence. The absolutist values of apartheid's Christian National Education underpinned a conscious attempt to simultaneously segregate populations on the basis of race and cater for the needs of a capitalist economy. In direct opposition to the resulting stark inequalities (a massive shortage of classrooms, a lack of basic infrastructure, few textbooks, uneducated and untrained teachers and huge student–teacher ratios), spontaneous student revolts from the mid-1970s together with oppositional discourses such as People's Education transformed education into a key space in which to wage the liberation struggle, contrasting the evils of apartheid education against a vision of free and compulsory education based on non-racialism, non-sexism, a unitary state, democracy and redress.[1] The numerous education policy investigations over the past several years, emanating from both the National Party and the African National Congress (ANC), could thus be seen as negotiated compromises intended to both permit identity and accommodate diversity, and strike a balance between centralized and decentralized school governance, learner- and teacher-centred pedagogies, and vocational and academic skills.

The dialectical narrative is a hallmark of the dominant discourses of the apartheid era. The new conditions pertaining in the 1990s have made possible, even necessitated, a radical rethinking of the nature of political and particularly educational struggle and change and of the relations between education, development and democracy. It is important to recognize that the educational analyses and visions of the apartheid state and the liberation movement, as well as the new Government of National Unity, are grounded upon Enlightenment values. The main thrust of the Enlightenment was that human reason is capable of objectively describing and explaining the nature of reality, both natural and social, thus providing humanity with the knowledge required to transform the world and construct a better society.[2] In the context of the emergence of a secular, materialist and rationalist world order of expansionist, industrialist and capitalist nation-states and large-scale administrative and bureaucratic systems of social regulation,[3] the modern epoch to which the Enlightenment gave birth has centred itself around the sovereign subject of Western humanism, 'man', 'atomistic and autonomous, disengaged and disembodied, potentially and ideally self-transparent'.[4] Current attempts to resolve the problems of South African education, in the form of a state-managed process of modernization aimed at improving and making more effective and efficient material and human resources, clearly manifest these values of autonomy, identity, reason, liberty, progress and justice.

In Africa as in Europe, schooling developed initially under the auspices of the Christian churches but was soon brought within the purview of the state. Colonialism and its attendant missionaries wove the institutions and values of both Christianity and Enlightenment firmly into the fabric of African education. In the case of apartheid education, a particular brand of Calvinism merged with a form of scientific reasoning to produce a mass schooling system in which racism could be justified on religious and scientific grounds. One key assumption that apartheid inherited from the Enlightenment was the centrality of identity to any logical or social project. The peculiar history of Western thought has made it all but impossible to reason or govern without discriminating between the true and the false and the same and the different. Apartheid took the worship of identity to an extreme, and attempted to suppress its dependence on difference. To assert an identity or an equivalence, to apply criteria of consistency, and to rule out what is different or contradictory is to exercise power through the creation of boundaries between categories. Thus the production of social identities (individual subjects, populations, institutions and states) sets up a dynamic of inclusion and exclusion which has both positive and negative consequences. Ethnicity and nationalism were used to construct nation-states which played a vital role in developing democratic governance, civil society and a global economy; they are also at the heart of twentieth-century genocide. Similarly, the dual origins of (South) African schooling in Christianity and Enlightenment not only promoted scientific advances and productive successes but in doing so, contributed to the domination of local peoples and the devastation of indigenous cultures.

The concept of social identity assumes a discrete, identifiable and conscious subject. In so doing, it sets up a contradiction against 'the other', that which is different and excluded. Identity and difference are reflected in the centrality of exchange to modern consumerism: it is our ability to say of two different things that they are equivalent in monetary value that enables us to enter into exchanges.[5] It follows that even people living in remote rural areas are ensnared by a growing web of equivalences, as things that were previously unconnected to the economy are given exchange values and thereby connected into global economic relations. The implications of this are two-fold: that which is called modernity does not stand opposed to but already saturates that which modernity itself denigrates as traditional or premodern even as it seeks their dialectical overcoming; and that which is called postmodernity, and its associated theories, far from being esoteric and inapplicable are exceptionally relevant for understanding a globalizing modernity within which education, development and democracy figure prominently.

A postmodern sensitivity facilitates a reconceptualization of South Africa's recent political and educational history which does not hold itself aloof from the paradoxes of identity and difference. The strategic opposition between the apartheid state and the liberation movement, far from being resolved or transcended in a dialectical synthesis, was instead ruptured as policy imperatives shifted from confrontation to negotiation. Out of this rupture other dichotomies have come to the fore: between equity and growth, democracy and development, centre and periphery, rural and urban and tradition and modernity. 'February 2nd [1990] made us witness to the rupture of the oppositional symbolic order. The state refused its "historically assigned" role and assumed another, returned in fact to the buried and displaced terms of liberal pragmatism'.[6] To speak of a rupture is to take account not only of the different local and global circumstances pertaining since the beginning of the 1990s, but also its close continuities with that which preceded it. In addition, it alerts one to the fact that change is often the unpredictable effect of multiple and even apparently insignificant determinations. Nevertheless, the unbanning of the liberation movements by the state on 2 February 1990 conveniently if crudely marks the moment when South Africa's owl of Minerva belatedly took account of the changes in the strategic situation: of the political and military impasse; of impending economic ruin and social disintegration; as well as of sudden and unexpected transformations, the dimensions of which were both global (as Eastern European socialism was swept away) and, less momentously perhaps but equally significantly, all too human (in the incapacitation of the Chief Jailer and the astute diplomacy of his Prisoner).

The rupture of the dominant political order was both a condition for and an effect of events in other sectors of society, not least on the educational terrain. The subjection of whites to a mass formal schooling system in South Africa had begun over a hundred years ago, in the manner characteristic of modernity in which dominant groups were historically the first targets for governance,[7] and these technologies were only extended to Africans in the 1950s. The proliferation of theories and even a science of education (in the form of Fundamental Pedagogics) was made possible by this progressive extension of power relations to invest a wider population, which in turn was facilitated by the knowledge educed through the scrutinization of learners and the professionalization of teachers. But the collapse during the 1980s of the culture of teaching and learning called into question the viability and even the possibility of modernization in South Africa, at least in terms of the Enlightenment blueprint. The stones and petrol-bombs of the 'young lions' had succeeded not only in making apartheid education ungovernable but in their *danse macabre* with the automatic weapons of the state also made it impossible for any alternative to be implemented. Oppositional educational discourses were hamstrung by an irresolvable tension between the necessity for confrontation and the contingency of planning for reconstruction in the future. The rupture broke this deadlock, making educational transformation infinitely more ambivalent and uncertain even as it became eminently possible: the opposition between racial domination and non-racial liberation was not replaced by a new unitary identity, as a dialectical narrative would have it, but instead supplanted by a flux of new oppositions and multiple realignments. The sphere of education policy research and the context of its practical implementation offer prime examples of the persistence rather than transcendence of conflict, the shifting of boundaries and the enduring presence of our Enlightenment-inherited paradoxes of identity and difference.

EDUCATION POLICY RESEARCH IN SOUTH AFRICA, 1991–94

Since negotiations began in 1990, a plethora of policy research has been conducted in almost all areas of South African civic life from the economy, education, housing, land and development to security, health and welfare. Six major policy investigations have been undertaken within the field of education and training alone, proposing changes either to specific aspects of the existing system or to the system as a whole. The 'Education Renewal Strategy' (ERS)[8] represented the policy discourse of the reforming apartheid bureaucracy, politically aligned with the National Party; the 'Policy Framework for Education and Training'[9] represented the policy discourse of the African National Congress. The Policy Framework itself drew on the work of four earlier initiatives: the National Education Policy Investigation (NEPI);[10] the Congress of South African Trade Unions' (Cosatu)[11] proposals for training and adult basic education; and, to a lesser extent, issues of distance education, lifelong learning and tertiary education being addressed by the South African Institute for Distance Education (SAIDE)[12] and the Union of Democratic University Staff Associations (UDUSA).[13]

By the end of the apartheid era the South African education system consumed approximately 22 per cent of the state budget, employed about

350 000 people and provided schooling for 12 million students, divided into 18 separate racially defined departments. The ERS proposed that a restructured system should provide freedom of choice, equal opportunities and a balance between commonality and diversity.[14] Balancing administrative centralization, and national standards, against the decentralization of power to local communities or individual institutions would enable schools to be differentiated according to particular values, locale, religion, language and culture – in fact, any criteria except race. The ERS's advocacy of decentralization was a significant shift from the emphasis under high apartheid where multiple, separate and unequal educational institutions constituting different racial identities were imposed from the centre. Broadly, the ERS was an attempt to rescue what it could of apartheid education by promoting a kind of 'apartheid from below', to maintain identities (and inequalities of power) established on the basis of 'free association' by relying on the geographical distribution of population and institutions to provide a significant number of predominantly white and semi-privatized local schools with control over the collection and distribution of their own financial and other resources.

It is ironic, then, that the central question that confronted the ERS – 'how to accommodate diversity in an educationally acceptable manner, without prejudice?'[15] – was indirectly echoed in the research conducted by the liberation movement, and notably in NEPI. The ERS was searching for a way to justify differences and even inequalities in a single education system; NEPI faced the same dilemma, but approached it in the name not of freedom of association but of development. Though inheriting the values of People's Education, NEPI differed considerably from its 1980s' predecessor in that it treated the state and its policies no longer as the enemy but 'as themselves representing the views of a powerful set of interests'.[16] Most importantly, whereas People's Education simply demanded democratic education and did not pay much attention to the need for development, NEPI recognized in addition that a restructuring of education to support a high-skill development path is likely to be constrained by shortages of well-trained teachers and systemic inertia.[17] In a new context of pragmatic negotiation, NEPI constituted itself around the tension between the demand for equity, signifying the importance of redressing historical inequalities, and the need for development, understood as economic growth and modernization through reintegration into the world economy:[18] development is necessary if South Africa is to increase its national collective wealth but has the consequence of requiring the differential allocation of scarce resources to groups already privileged by their existing (class, racial, gender and geographical) positions in relation to the economy.[19]

The distance between the confrontational politics within which People's Education emerged and the politics of negotiation which framed the first education policy investigations, particularly NEPI, is also the distance between their stress upon democracy and development, respectively. NEPI's tendency to assume that these concepts are in conflict is a vestige of the earlier dichotomy between state and liberation movement and indicative of NEPI's location, like that of the ERS, in the space between the old and the new;[20] its additional tendency to make the former concept secondary to the latter was what took it beyond apartheid and the ERS. For NEPI the choice was seen to lie between the two poles of a means–end continuum: 'Means-based models will emphasize equity, while ends-based models will stress development. Some kind of trade-off is inevitable.'[21] Equity here represents the needs-based popular and democratic demands of People's Education and development signifies the actual means for satisfying them in a negotiated restructuring of apartheid education under restrictive economic and political conditions.[22] The democratic redress of historical inequalities is thus made dependent upon development, itself narrowly understood in terms of economic growth, and it is this skewed relationship between the two major concepts underpinning education change that begins to influence all subsequent policy formulations.

The Policy Framework for Education and Training[23] – a discussion document which has since closely informed the first Education White Paper – not only fails to resolve the tension between democracy and development but goes so far as to describe education and training almost exclusively in terms of the latter concept. Asserting that all individuals should have access to these basic human rights irrespective of race, class, gender, creed or age, it takes lifelong education to mean the development of human potential, so that every person is able to contribute freely to society, advance common values, and increase socially useful wealth. This developmental conception of lifelong education is in turn seen as contributing to the realization of democracy, so that independent, responsible and productive citizens will be enabled to participate fully in all facets of life in their communities and the nation at large; to the reconciliation of liberty, equality and justice, so that citizens' freedom of choice will be exercised within a social and national context of equality of opportunity and the redress of imbalances; and finally to the pursuit of national reconstruction and development, transforming the institutions of society in the interests of all, and enabling the social, cultural, economic and political empowerment of all citizens.[24]

The Policy Framework's near reduction of democracy to development is intelligible in the light of the key role that education is to play in terms of the Reconstruction and Development Programme (RDP).[25] The responsibility of the state to provide ten years' free and compulsory general education is only a dimension, if one of the most important, of 'a coherent and comprehensive national social and economic reconstruction and development programme' in which special emphasis will be placed on 'the redress of educational inequalities among historically disadvantaged groups such as youth, the disabled, adults, women, the unemployed and rural communities'.[26] The primary aim of education, notwithstanding government rhetoric suggesting that there is no contradiction between 'growth and development, or growth and redistribution',[27] is thus development first and foremost, for not only is development to make possible the 'special' redress of inequalities but it is also to foster national identity. Democracy and the need to accommodate diversity are not discounted, but they are subordinated to the priority of development, regardless of whether the dichotomy is treated as a full-blown contradiction (as when it is argued that equity and the satisfaction of basic needs requires the allocation of resources away from stronger or more competitive sectors which could facilitate development by expanding the amount of resources available for allocation)[28] or as a precarious balance (in which 'the strategic problem is to construct policies aimed at both goals, although it must be recognized that this will have the effect of limiting what can be achieved in respect of each at any particular stage').[29]

Earlier policy research, notably NEPI's inability to choose between representative and participatory democracy and its predilection for development over democracy, is also reflected in the different and competing conceptions of democracy found in the Policy Framework and the RDP. On the one hand, NEPI understood representative democracy as the requirement that a unitary democratic state and education system represent the aspirations of the majority; this is also the position taken in the Policy Framework. On the other hand, the RDP takes up NEPI's idea of participatory democracy as consisting of direct participation at local and institutional levels operating through regional and national civil associations, as well as through a general obligation on the state to consult and inform people.[30] While NEPI accepted that education governance must promote a balanced distribution of powers and functions between different levels of the system,[31] it refused to make a clear choice between a systemic perspective in which policy formulation takes place in consultation with interest groups, and a school governance perspective in which key social forces (such as parent–teacher–student associations and trade unions) participate at each level of governance and are responsible for both policy formulation and implementation.[32]

Similarly, while the RDP does not hesitate to insist that development can only work if there is strong democratic participation in policy formulation and implementation, it too seems unable to choose unambiguously between differing conceptions of democracy, proposing instead that in order to ensure that 'the people shall govern. . . an institutional network fostering representative, participatory and direct democracy'[33] will be required. At the same time it appears that no known form of democracy will be able to displace development from its central position, for the RDP continues to treat economic growth as 'a basic goal', and only thereafter considers the location, sustainability, distribution, impact on the environment and contribution to productive capacity and human resource development of that growth.[34]

Paradoxically, it seems that now that South Africa has a democratically elected government, development can and must be emphasized even if this is at the unfortunate expense of democracy. Certainly, the priority given to development in political and educational discourse, the absence as yet of any social movement in civil society with no links to the new Government of National Unity, the existence of a large bureaucracy and the 'structural history' of the system suggest that the principal characteristics of South African education will persist for at least another decade. The greatest pressures for change are likely to come neither from within the system (from organized teachers and students), nor even from 'the people', but from those most versed in the intricacies of the development discourse: business, weighing in on the side of economic growth, and labour, championing democracy.[35] Development requires a stable and functioning system of education; it does not need it to be democratic. The urban middle and working classes may have the power to more or less ensure their own educational development, regardless of the pace of educational change; but as new oppositions begin to replace that of race, apartheid's legacies persist in that many of those who benefited least even from Bantu Education – the rural, the migrant, the destitute – will continue to find themselves marginal to processes of governance and development planning in which they may even be encouraged to participate.

ON THE MARGINS: RURAL EDUCATION

Despite all the education policy research since 1990, there remains a profound silence over rural issues, and to a lesser extent, women, the unemployed and youth, precisely those strata of the population recognized to be the most historically disadvantaged. The following exploration of the context of rural education in the province of KwaZulu-Natal will attempt to show how these silences are indicative of new or renewed exclusions which additionally are entangled in tensions between political parties, national and provincial governments, government and community funding, and modern and traditional cultures.

Over the past few years spatio-temporal boundaries, which already during the 1980s were becoming more elastic as a result of the suspension of the pass laws controlling movement between town and countryside, have blurred and shifted: whereas the primary geographic division under apartheid was between white farmlands and black homelands, now it lies between those living in, or near, urban agglomerations and the 46 per cent of the population living in the rural areas.[36] This geographic fault-line reflects multiple overlapping inequalities based on different forms of land tenure and political authority, unequal access to resources, wealth and power, and varying combinations of modern, Western and urban, and traditional, African and rural cultures. In 1993, there were approximately 17 million South Africans living in poverty, 11 million of whom were living in the rural areas and approximately 1.5 million of whom were utterly destitute.[37]

In this context, where a third of all children under the age of 14 are estimated to be malnourished and underweight, and where the illiteracy rate is over 50 per cent, the importance of schooling is highlighted by the 1991 African matriculation statistics: out of a total of 281 000 candidates, 200 000 (71 per cent) were enrolled in the erstwhile homelands, mostly at community and farm schools. This rural/urban dichotomy is at its starkest in the province of KwaZulu-Natal, where the Department of Education and Culture, currently the second largest but most underfunded in the country, had in 1991 a student enrollment of 1.6 million in 3000 schools, of which 82 per cent were in rural and peri-urban areas and 98 per cent built out of community funds. The dichotomy is also intertwined with tensions between centre and periphery: in 1992, the per student expenditure in KwaZulu-Natal was R428 compared to R1248 per student in the Department of Education and Training (which administered non-homeland African education under apartheid), far greater even than the gap between the latter Department and white education. In addition, the student-to-teacher ratio in KwaZulu-Natal was 53:1 at primary level and 42:1 at secondary level, compared to a national average in African schooling of 29:1 for primary schooling and 27:1 for secondary schooling.[38]

Given, on the one hand, these vast disparities in educational provision between rural and urban areas, which are exacerbated by tensions between the national and the provincial and between government and community funding, and, on the other hand, the new government's emphasis upon the redress of educational inequalities among historically disadvantaged groups, one might legitimately expect that such disparities would figure prominently if not enjoy priority in educational policy-making. But such is the dominance of development over democracy that these same tensions structure education policy proposals for rural areas. Both the ERS and NEPI were thoroughly urban-centred, and produced next to nothing dealing with the particularities of providing education in rural areas. The Cosatu, UDUSA and SAIDE proposals were hardly more vocal, though taken in the abstract adult and distance education are indispensable in a rural context. Only the Policy Framework made explicit policy proposals for rural education – all in the space of two pages out of a 119-page document.[39]

On the one hand, education policy researchers appear to assume that rural and farm schools, which are responsible for the education of the majority of students in South Africa and are the most deprived in terms of both quantity of schools and quality of education, simply require more of the urban same, to be brought 'into the mainstream',[40] and that this entails largely technical and quantitative considerations about increasing access, improving infrastructure and democratizing governance without much attention needing to be paid to the specificities of the rural context. Even the Centre for Education Policy Development's policy implementation plan, which produced the most comprehensive and extensive proposals thus far for democratizing rural educational governance and improving access and quality, allocated only one out of over 20 national Task Teams to this project. On the other hand, rural education is conceived of as a 'special issue',[41] raising the spectre of reduced but persistent and now legitimated if not concealed inequalities between urban and rural education once any additional resource-allocation for rural redress runs dry. This tension within education policy locates rural education uneasily in a no-man's land between forces which simultaneously stress its difference from and its similarity with mainstream education: it is identical but special; it is different but equal.[42]

Competing conceptions of the role that tradition is to play within modernity also map directly on to the rural/urban opposition. In the context of KwaZulu-Natal, these are entangled in tensions between the major political parties, particularly the ANC and the Inkatha Freedom Party (IFP), groupings which to a significant extent, particularly at a leadership level, also represent modernizing and traditionally oriented forces, respectively. Over a decade of political violence between these parties did not end with the April 1994 election, in which the IFP's 50 per cent share of the votes made KwaZulu-Natal the only province in which a homeland governing party came to power. Led by Chief Mangosuthu Buthelezi, who also acted as the traditional prime minister for King Goodwill Zwelithini and is now Minister of Home Affairs in the new Cabinet, the primary support base for the IFP's ethnic Zulu nationalism is located in KwaZulu-Natal's strong traditional authority structures, which preside over 10 million people (almost one-quarter of the country's entire population).

At stake, however, is not a simple choice between the modern and the traditional. On the one hand, to allow such a huge (and predominantly rural) section of the population to remain under the political and economic power of traditional authorities would threaten the unity and cohesion of the entire society. On the other hand, to attempt summarily to dismantle traditional structures and to drag both chiefs and their subjects unprepared and unwilling further into the unfamiliar light of the new and untested democratic dispensation would be to encourage a political backlash and strengthen authoritarian tendencies. Nevertheless, although the identity and role of traditional authorities have become a source of conflict, it is not necessary for a modernizing society to reject all traditional institutions, beliefs and practices: it must be borne in mind that traditions are always alive and practised in the present, while modernity is itself a tradition in perpetual motion. Instead, the social atomization, privatization of interests and subjectivization of the individual intrinsic to Western Enlightenment, in which being has identity, autonomy and freedom only when privatized, must be forced into a confrontational but productive interface with the communal orientation of traditional and local cultures in which people have identity only as part of a community and freedom only as a result of the concrete privileges, responsibilities and immunities which arise from communal life.[43] The reality, if not the desirability, of tradition and ethnicity in South African education is undeniable, but the identity of that reality is not yet fixed.

To attempt to play off the powerful influence of traditional authorities over rural education and development in KwaZulu-Natal against the more violent modernization tendencies of the Government of National Unity by reciprocally confronting modernity with tradition, development with democracy, the urban with the rural and the centre with its margins, is to both delimit (or reinforce) current fixations with identity and de-limit (or subvert) them. Far more important than the terms of any of these oppositions is the tension between them: democracy and development, for example, ought not to be taken as objectives in themselves but merely as means to more particular ends. Just as it would be a mistake to limit development to growth and democracy to enfranchisement and equal rights,[44] so too it would be a mistake to believe that democracy is secured once local citizens are participating in governance. Democracy is a process of struggle which is never secure, regardless of the number of formally enshrined rights or the degree of substantial involvement in decision-making. Democracy must not be allowed to put itself forward as an harmonious transcendental medium overcoming the apartheid-era divide of 'socialism or capitalism'; instead, it must be seen for what it is, an affective and constitutive matrix of power relations which need to be persistently defended and extended even in spite of themselves. So too development, no matter how benevolent, must be understood as a project which brings with it new forms of exclusion and relations of inequality.

Similarly, rural education, constituted simultaneously as different from and identical to the educational mainstream, displays a tension which, though irresolvable, is potentially productive and may, paradoxically, even augur well for the future of South African education as a whole. On the one hand, the dominance of development amidst the nebulousness that is post-apartheid education policy presupposes and simultaneously reinforces rural lack: paraphrasing Latouche, it can be argued that 'the devaluation of [rural] societies . . . is actually the price and pre-condition of their entry onto the path of economic development'.[45] Nevertheless, while rural education may continue to find itself marginalized, its persistent peripheral presence will serve to blunt efforts to declare educational transformation complete. On the other hand, the dominance of development cannot simply be condemned, for not only does it have substantial positive effects, but the extent to which rural education is brought into the urban mainstream will be an indication of the degree to which the entire system has reconceptualized itself beyond the rural/urban dichotomy. Beyond education, development and democracy, yet within modernity, lies the potential for the persistent questioning of identities and the constant recognition, foregrounding and harvesting of the productive tensions between them.

CONCLUSION

Post-apartheid South Africa has set in motion a comprehensive and wide-ranging programme aimed at social and economic reconciliation and advancement. This nation-building programme, within which education features prominently as the means by which democratization and development can be fostered, is another in a series of attempts throughout the history of South Africa to achieve social coherence through comprehensive social engineering. Apartheid's attempt to construct a pure Afrikaner identity in a context of racial capitalism gave rise to a swollen, arrogant and interventionist state which excluded and exploited the majority of the population and prohibited or controlled everything from access to jobs and education to social and sexual miscegenation. The new Government of National Unity seeks to construct a far more open and democratic but arguably no less exclusive and dirigiste order, in which identity will be framed in terms of national development amidst the intensifying and increasing regulation of social life and where inequalities will be spatio-temporally rather than racially determined.

Just as the opposing forces called into being under the sign of apartheid constituted different, though symbiotically intertwined and dependent, versions of a developing modernity, the new tensions which have emerged from the rupture of the racial dichotomy also take their cue from the Enlightenment will to knowledge and power and assume discrete, identifiable and unitary subjects, an ultimate goal of unity and discoverable laws of social development. Indeed, the possibility, process and completion of negotiations about a post-apartheid South Africa depended in very large part on a prior, unspoken agreement among all concerned to fashion a new national order premised on democracy and development (even as the definition and scope of these values were being contested). The paradox of social transformation in which South Africa has always been entangled is that it is precisely those values and practices that foster democratic participation and economic growth which also promote elite hegemonies, suppress difference and exclude whole populations. While such broad consensus may have rendered the old politics of confrontation obsolete, it must not blind us to the fact that few rural people were involved in the politics of negotiation; indeed, even their self-styled representatives, both traditional and non-governmental, were largely sidelined throughout the process, and rural education policy, such as it is, is being made by urbanites.

No doubt the increasing salience of spatio-temporal divisions is partly a consequence of the fact that most rural people have little or no access to or experience of democratic structures; on top of this, their lack of economic resources makes developmental intervention from the outside probable, even unavoidable. South African transformation – necessary and yet inadequate – is clearly dominated by powerful modernizing and development-oriented forces amongst which the main tendency is towards a de-racialized post-capitalist political economy, characterized by limited growth and dependent development but nevertheless bolstered by new-found state legitimacy with solid intellectual backing, an urbanized, integrating middle class, strong unions, liberation euphoria, affirmative action and steady reincorporation into the gradually expanding global economy. The cacophony of these forces often drowns out rural voices along with those of women, youth, traditional authorities, the non-unionized and the unemployed – but they are unable to render them mute. Hence the acid test for the new urban-centred, post-apartheid hegemony will be the extent to which it can accommodate the absent presence of the margins at the centre, conceal persistent inequalities within the new democracy, tolerate radical differences which emerge within the new unity and justify the unevenness of national development. From this perspective, the struggle for democracy and development in South African education has only just begun.

NOTES

1   G. Mashamba, 'A conceptual critique of the People's Education discourse', *Education Policy Unit Research Report No. 3*, University of the Witwatersrand, 1992; H. Perry, 'Education demands and the principles of the progressive education movement', paper produced for the National Education Policy Investigation's (NEPI's) Principles and Frameworks Committee, Braamfontein, 1991.

2   R. Deacon, 'Education for liberation? Reflections on critical theory', *Working Papers*, no. 6, Media Resource Centre, University of Natal, Durban, 1990, p. 1.

3   S. Hall, D. Held and L. McLennan, 'Introduction', in S. Hall, D. Held and T. McGrew (eds.), *Modernity and its Futures*, Cambridge, 1992, p. 3.

4   T. McCarthy, 'Introduction', in J. Habermas, *The Philosophical Discourse of Modernity*, Cambridge, 1987, p. ix.

5   F. Jameson, *Late Marxism: Adorno, or, The Persistence of the Dialectic*, London, 1990, p. 23.

6   T. Morphet, 'Brushing history against the grain: oppositional discourse in South Africa', *Theoria*, no. 76, 1990, p. 98.

7   M. Foucault, *The History of Sexuality: An Introduction*, Harmondsworth, 1981, pp. 120–7.

8   Committee of Heads of Education Departments (CHED), 'A Curriculum Model for Education in South Africa: Discussion Document', Pretoria, 1993; Committee of Heads of Education Departments (CHED), 'Educational Renewal Strategy: Discussion Document', Pretoria, 1991.

9   African National Congress, 'A Policy Framework for Education and Training: Discussion Document', Braamfontein, 1994.

10   National Education Policy Investigation (NEPI), 'The Framework Report and Final Report Summaries', Cape Town, 1993.

11   Congress of South African Trade Unions, 'Report: Lifelong Learning – Policy Proposals', Braamfontein, 1993.

12   D. Swift, 'Open learning and distance education', Braamfontein, 1993.

13   Union of Democratic University Staff Associations, 'Framework Document and Proposals for Post-Secondary Education', Braamfontein, 1993.

14 CHED, 'Educational Renewal Strategy', pp. 20–1.
15 J. G. Garbers, Presentation to the National Education Policy Investigation Workshop, Johannesburg, 1992.
16 NEPI, 'The Framework Report', p. 8.
17 Ibid., pp. 24–5.
18 Ibid., p. 24.
19 B. Parker, 'Intellectuals and education system change', *Perspectives in Education*, vol. 14, no. 2, 1993, p. 224.
20 J. Muller and N. Cloete, 'To outwit modernity; intellectuals and politics in transition', *Transformation*, no. 14, 1991, p. 38.
21 NEPI, 'The Framework Report', p. 37.
22 Ibid., p. 11.
23 ANC, 'A Policy Framework for Education and Training'.
24 Ibid., p. 3.
25 African National Congress, 'The Reconstruction and Development Programme: A Policy Framework', Johannesburg, 1994.
26 ANC, 'A Policy Framework for Education and Training', pp. 3–4; ANC, 'The Reconstruction and Development Programme', p. 84.
27 ANC, 'The Reconstruction and Development Programme', p. 6.
28 H. Wolpe, 'Towards a Short-Term Negotiating Policy on Education and Training', NEPI working paper, Braamfontein, 1991.
29 H. Wolpe, 'A New Post-Secondary Education System', DSA in Depth: Reconstructing Education, *Die Suid-Afrikaan*, Cape Town, 1994, p. 64.
30 NEPI, 'The Framework Report', p. 15.
31 Ibid., p. 154.
32 Ibid., p. 163.
33 ANC, 'The Reconstruction and Development Programme', pp. 119–20.
34 Ibid., p. 6.
35 J. Muller, 'Development, reconstruction and education: a review for the Urban Foundation', Johannesburg, 1993.
36 F. Wilson and M. Ramphele, *Uprooting Poverty: The South African Challenge*, Cape Town, 1989, p. 17.
37 ANC, 'The Reconstruction and Development Programme', p. 14; Institute for Local Governance and Development (INLOGOV), 'Rural Local Government in South Africa', Johannesburg, 1993, p. 2.
38 J. Moulder, *Facing the Education Crisis: A Practical Approach*, Johannesburg, 1991.
39 ANC, 'A Policy Framework for Education and Training'.
40 Centre For Education Policy Development (CEPD), 'Policy Proposals Regarding Rural Education: Proceedings of the Workshop on Rural/Farm Schools', Broederstroom, 1993, p. 4.
41 CEPD, 'Policy Proposals Regarding Rural Education', p. 2; ANC, 'A Policy Framework for Education and Training', p. 102.
42 R. Deacon and B. Parker, 'Development, democracy and rural education', *Matlhasedi*, vol. 13, no. 2, 1994.
43 C. Ake, 'What is the problem of ethnicity in Africa?', *Transformation*, no. 22, 1993, p. 10.
44 ANC, 'The Reconstruction and Development Programme', p. 120; M. Mamdani, 'Contradictory class perspectives on the question of democ-

racy: the case of Uganda', in P. A. Nyong'o (ed.), *Popular Struggles for Democracy in Africa*, London, 1987, p. 93.

45   S. Latouche, *In the Wake of the Affluent Society: An Exploration of Post-Development*, London, 1993, p. 10.

8 The Fruits of Modernity: Law, Power and Paternalism in the Rural Western Cape[1]

Andries du Toit

Why coloured farm dwellers? This is a question with which sceptics often confront those of us who concern ourselves with agrarian problems in the Western Cape. The questions facing the new polity born at the end of April 1994 are momentous: the end of white political rule, the formation of a new state, the institutionalization of democracy, the reconstruction of the economy, the construction of a national identity. As the poorest, the most exploited, and the most marginal of South Africa's black workers, farm dwellers might deserve our sympathy – but surely there are other, more pressing South African problems that demand our attention?

There are reasons to think that a look at the white farmlands can help us understand the complexities of the transition from apartheid. Consider, for example, the potency of the imagery still associated with the notion of the white-owned South African farm. In popular conceptions, the plight of farm dwellers has over the years become a kind of metaphor for the worst aspects of apartheid rule. It is often the white farmstead, where the white *baas* (master) rules with the whip, that still symbolizes the essence of apartheid society. Witness the recent popularity among militant black township youth of the slogan 'kill the *boer*, kill the farmer': by the 1990s the word 'boer' no longer referred simply to white Afrikaans-speaking farmers, but came to epitomize the essence of white racism in the society as a whole.

These stereotypes have a seductive power if we turn our gaze to the white farmlands. Formally, white rule has ended, but in many ways the world of the farm has been left almost untouched by the politics of a country in transition. Low wages, dangerous working conditions, poor housing, the absence of the most basic human rights, eviction and physical violence are still prevalent. It is a grim reality that racial domination and poverty are still a fundamental part of rural life on the commercial farmlands. In this context, a nuanced understanding of the subtleties of racial inequality in one rural corner of South Africa can help us go beyond stereotypes to understand the limits and possibilities of change.

UNDERSTANDING RURAL CHANGE IN THE WESTERN CAPE

Not too long ago, the equitable resolution of rural power struggles was held by some to involve the revolutionary transformation of capitalist social relations, and the key problem on the farmlands was held to be the absence of a revolutionary agricultural proletariat and the backwardness of agrarian capitalism.[2] Today, this fantasy is in some quarters being replaced by another – one in which 'socio-economic forces' sweep aside the cobwebs of the past, and farmers jettison 'old fashioned' racist paternalism in favour of commonsensical and presumably non-racial 'businesslike relationships'.[3] The challenge to students of the transformation of the South African countryside today is to come to a more nuanced understanding of modernization, 'progress' and their implications.

My own case studies of labour relations in transformation in the Western Cape in the early 1990s have been directed at this aim. These studies have involved detailed attention to the particular ways in which identities and political claims are discursively articulated, and to what Foucault called the micro-technologies of power. In the pages that follow, space does not permit a blow-by-blow account of particular case studies. Instead I have tried to construct a more panoramic view of the discourses of rural transformation. In doing this, I have tried to 'supplement' existing analyses of the political economy of the rural Western Cape.[4] My aim has been, not to displace these powerful analyses, but to emphasize the *politics* in the 'political economy' – to emphasize, in other words, the extent to which these changes are not to be understood reductively in terms of any teleology of modernization, but rather in terms of disjuncture, discontinuity, repetition, contingency and struggle.

These contests are being played out in a complex context – one shaped, not only by the transformation of the political horizon of the South African polity as a whole, but also by the particular discursive formations and apparatuses whereby the social and labour relations of the rural Western Cape are regulated. For the sake of simplicity, we can isolate four of these frameworks and sites of struggle. The first is the white moral economy of racial paternalism. The second is constituted by the subaltern spaces and networks of the white farmlands' 'black underground'. Thirdly there are the changing disciplines and technologies of production and human resources management. And finally, there is the regulatory machinery of the law, and a discourse of rights and entitlement centred on the new constitution.

PATERNALISM

Any attempt to understand the complex terrain of struggle constituted by the intersection, integration and mutual interruption of these different apparatuses of regulation must begin with the cultures, forms of life and modes of practice which are constituted by paternalism, and their deep roots in colonial history.

Over the course of the 1970s and 1980s, a generation of scholars loosely grouped under the label of 'social historians' have explored the genesis of these exploitative and servile relationships.[5] Though for most of the 1980s these historians have remained broadly within the bounds of historical materialist orthodoxy, the sensitivity they have shown to the discourses and institutions that have shaped agrarian change provides a valuable foundation for a student of the hegemonic forms of white supremacy and racialized domination on the farmlands. These social forms have been intricately connected to the ideological and political legacy of eighteenth-century Atlantic colonialism in general, and the legal and racial order of colonial slavery in particular.[6] Their expectations shaped by these traditions, colonial farmers came to conceive their relations to their workers in terms of a discourse of paternalism which described the farm as a family-like community, and which emphasized the master's despotic power over the 'child', his servant.[7] In the rural hinterlands of the Cape Colony, this relationship was elaborately concretized in the institutions and rituals of farm life itself.[8]

These forms of practice did not simply vanish after emancipation, nor were they swept aside by 150 years of capitalist development and modernization. This is a fact with which optimistic prophets of economic rationality have failed to grapple. The Western Cape is a region that has known capitalist relations of production longer than any other in South Africa, while fruit and wine farming are among its most 'modernized' sectors. But even in the heartland of the fruit and wine industry research has shown the stubborn persistence of the discourses and practices of racialized paternalism. The history of paternalism is a history, not of its disappearance, but of its ceaseless return, in re-invented, reconstituted forms, to the white farmlands of the rural Western Cape. Even in the mid-1990s one could find still in place on farm after farm, the discourses and practices that constructed the farm as an organic family-like community, presided over by a patriarchal master, and bound together by ties more intimate and obligations more inclusive than those found in urban industry. To work on a farm is not merely to be in an employer–employee relationship; but to become part of a community, indeed, *deel van die plaas* (part of the farm).[9]

Two crucial points need to be made about this fact. Firstly, it is important to realize the deep roots of this notion in the lives of those who live and work on wine, fruit and wheat farms. The notion of being 'part of a family' is often still an integral and genuine part of the world-views, not only of white farmers, but also of the coloured farm dwellers they exploit. The social relationships on South Africa's farms are indeed highly exploitative and unequal, but we cannot explain their persistence simply in terms of farmers' *control*, or the exercise of naked coercion or violence. It also rests, in some measure, on the maintenance of *hegemony*, on farm dwellers' consent.[10]

Secondly, this hegemony should not simply be understood as a 'myth' or an ideology. It is not a lie, obscuring the 'real' social relations of farm life; rather, it is constitutive of the very identities involved in the contestation of power relations on the farm.[11] We should remember the crucial point that a discursive totality is not merely a linguistic phenomenon, but is formed out of the articulation, at the level of social practice, of both linguistic and non-linguistic elements. It is a thoroughly material ensemble of practices, institutions, arrangements and discourses – what Foucault would call a *dispositif* or 'apparatus'.[12]

Thirdly, though paternalism is constitutive of these identities, this does not mean that its logic utterly determines them, nor that the meanings it constructs are exhaustive of the reality of farm life. Inherent in a materialist, Foucauldian conception of discursive unity is a Derridean recognition of its inherently heterogeneous nature, and the extent to which the field of identities it constructs never manages to be fully fixed.[13] Paternalism is not characterized by a single essential or unitary character. It exists nowhere but in its particular articulations, and the 'family resemblances' and historical connections between them; and its component practices, discourses and institutions are subject to constant re-invention, mutation and re-articulation. In addition, it also needs to be recognized that paternalist discourses and practices are not the only ones to be found on the farms. This is a point I shall return to below.

But even though other, competing conceptions of identity do exist on the farm, paternalism plays a role of particular structural importance. To use a term coined by James C. Scott in his analysis of rural society in Malaysia, paternalist discourse shapes the 'public transcript' of farm life.[14] It lays down the privileged framework of legitimation within which claims and counter-claims are made and negotiated. As such, paternalism provides the rituals, institutional forms and vocabularies of power on the farm.

In this way paternalist discourses have instituted racial domination in the form of local 'micro-technologies of power'. The power relations between farmer and farm dweller are set up in racially coded practices that are woven into the very fabric of farm life, that structure its spatial organization and which shape the most elementary features of labour process. All these conspire to make the farmer, in Foucauldian terms, the sole 'speaking subject' on the farm: the only person whose words could count as judgements, and whose judgements carried institutional weight.[15] To be a coloured farm dweller, conversely, is to be continually defined in terms of one's lack of power, one's childlike status, one's dependence on the 'master' of the farm for almost every single resource needed for survival.

This has had profound consequences for farm dwellers in the Western Cape. Their security in the context of the farm has depended in the last instance on nothing more than the farmer's performative judgement, on the question of whether or not they were '*in die bass se oë*' (in the masters' gaze). Linda Waldman has shown the repercussions of this disempowerment in the deeply sedimented culture of violence on farms – a violence not only exercised by the farmer on the workers, but also between farmworkers themselves. It is female farm dwellers, who typically do hard manual labour for flat rates less than even the most unskilled male worker, and who shoulder the burden of household labour, who bear the brunt of the daily violence of battery and rape.[16]

FARMWORKERS' 'BLACK UNDERGROUND'

Thus far my argument has focused on discursive formations and bodies of practice that have lain, to some extent, outside farm dwellers' direct control. If it is not to reduce farm dwellers to stereotyped victims, any account of change on the white farmlands of the Western Cape must also consider their own survival strategies and institutions

This is a complex issue, since it is clearly bound up with the broader political and cultural questions surrounding the construction of coloured identity in South Africa. The debates and discussions that have arisen on this topic cannot be treated in detail here. Suffice it to say that these debates have pivoted on the implications of the history of slavery, genocide and colonial dispossession in the aftermath of which various versions of coloured identity came to be articulated. The destruction of Khoi and San society, culture and language, the denial of slave identities and their differential incorporation into eighteenth-century colonial society meant that, for those now reduced to labour on colonists' farms, any attempt to constitute a new cultural identity had to take place under the conditions described by Edouard Glissant in his discussions of the politics of creolization and forced poetics.[17] Conceptions of colouredness, in other words, had to be constructed from the bricolage of a cultural apparatus that ultimately denied and excluded from its dominant institutions those it defined as non-white.

The keyword here is 'ultimately'. The construction of a coloured identity involved the *contestation* and *appropriation* of elements of settler culture, not a passive acceptance of them on settlers' terms. As in the context of Caribbean slavery of which Glissant wrote, farm dwellers have been able to create and sustain sites and spaces of relative autonomy. Characterizations of farmworkers as deferential or passive therefore miss the point. Besides the public performances of deference and obeisance to white supremacy, there also exists what James C. Scott has called a 'hidden transcript' – the off-stage, behind-the-scenes traditions of disrespect and self-respect, of quiet rebellion, insubordination, evasion, petty sabotage and pilfering which make survival and sometimes even dignity a possibility in the life of subordinated people.[18] These are the traditions and spaces of what we could call the Western Cape's 'black underground'.[19]

What the notion of the 'underground' highlights is that workers' resistance to paternalist hegemony happens in an off-stage, surreptitious way. The consensual surface of farm life is only half the picture. Public conformity with the paternalist orthodoxy exists side by side with numerous forms of covert resistance or simple non-cooperation. Besides the 'public' acquiescence with the farmer's command, there are the things farm dwellers do not say in front of the holders of power. Any description of Western Cape farms therefore needs to take into account their 'hidden side' – a rich world of submerged traditions that include not only the jokes, riddles and stories of farm dweller folklore, but also the illicit world of the *smokkelhuis* (shebeen), the fraternities of the *rokers* (smokers of marijuana) and the links with gang and prison life.[20]

The metaphor of the 'underground' should not be seen as an attempt to reinvoke a unitary, homogeneous, proletarian 'subject'. Neither should we see it simplistically or romantically as the site of some authentic or irreducible resistance, a space where the 'truth' of farm dwellers' experience is articulated. The moral codes of the paternalist 'contract' are a source of protection as well as oppression, and do have real legitimacy on the farm; and the discourses of dissent are discontinuous, fragmented and internally contested. They are characterized by conflict, violence and competition as much as by co-operation. They are not stable and exhibit no clear internal unity. In some ways the 'black underground' is a residual category: it is comprised out of those elements and experiences that cannot be integrated into the organic framework of paternalist narrative, or that lie in some way beyond the white master's gaze. The ties of kinship, religious affiliation and prison life are not necessarily in opposition to white farmers' power – but in times of need they give shape and backbone to hidden and subversive networks of solidarity, mutual support and shared knowledge.

This brings me to crucial aspects of the 'black underground'. The first is that it is a *black* world, in the wider sense of the word. Farm paternalism, we must never forget, is a racialized paternalism, one which links the hierarchical inequalities of labour relations to very particular racial categories. The same goes for its submerged counter-cultures. The forms of knowledge and perception that are transmitted along its circuits have much in common with the forms of highly coded, indirect circulation of knowledge known as 'signifyin' that the African-American scholar Henry Louis Gates has studied in black American counterculture.[21] Its 'speaking subjects' and its 'implicit listeners' are constructed in terms of racialized categories; its messages are not intended for white ears.

This had implications for my research. While the well-worn paternalist clichés about the 'special relationship' were time and again articulated, in various forms, by farmers and workers almost without prompting, workers' dissenting voices were far more difficult to access. Like the dark side of the moon, the 'other side' of the harmonious farm community does not present itself simply to the gaze of outsiders such as myself. For me, confrontation with this more unspoken world involved sidestepping the public transcript and focusing on those aspects of life it tried to repress or pass over. It involved leaving the 'white spaces' of official discourse on the farm – the field, the toolshed, the office – and entering into the more private and secret spaces of coloured workers.

This raises a second issue. As should be obvious by now, the 'black underground', of course, is an 'underground' particularly from a *white* perspective! It is a field of cultural resources defined in part by the extent to which it is closed off to white ears and eyes. In my own research, I have been able to win farm dwellers' tolerance, if not trust, and they have shared some of their more disenchanted, critical perspectives with me. But even when I have been invited into workers' own homes, my white skin has marked me as an interloper from the world of the masters, and linked me to the structures of white domination. This raises important methodological and identity questions for researchers – particularly for those committed to a respectful encounter with the cultures and traditions that have sustained coloured farm dwellers through years of oppression and exploitation. I will return to this at the end of this chapter.

MODERNIZATION AND CHANGE

The institutions of rural paternalism are undergoing profound changes. The deep crisis of South African agriculture has not threatened grape and fruit farming to the extent it has other sectors; to some extent fruit and wine farmers have been well placed to take advantage of the opportunities presented by the increasing globalization of the fruit industry. But in this export-oriented sector growth and survival have depended on innovation. To some extent this has involved increasing degrees of casualization and feminization of the workforce (particularly in the fruit sector). It has driven many farmers to explore new methods of management geared at promoting worker productivity. It also led to a growing consensus on the need to extend basic workers' rights to farm dwellers. Farming practice in the Western Cape has been characterized by the rapid proliferation, diversification and spread of discourses and practices of farm and human resources management.[22]

These reforms cannot simply be dismissed as mere cosmetic change. They involved a rearticulation of basic aspects of paternalist practice. Above all, they involved a reconstitution of the basis of farmers' authority. The farmer could no longer exercise authority as the sovereign 'master'. What the new discourses of management institutionalized on the farm was the supreme authority of the impersonal 'principles of farming', which stood in impartial judgement over the decisions of farmers as well as workers. The new discourses and practices of management functioned to de-centre farmers' authority, and created limited but real opportunities for the empowerment of coloured workers who were appointed to supervisory positions and drawn in to participate in management decisions.

This has created a complex and unstable situation. Management change has neither 'rescued' nor 'replaced' traditional paternalism; rather it has resulted in a profound crisis characterized by the increasing instability, 'slippage' and ambiguity to which the identities and relations between white farmers and coloured workers are prone. The most characteristic trend of the discourses that shape labour relations on the wine and fruit farms of the Western Cape is the increasing *dislocation* of previously stable and settled discursive identities in a context where a new hegemonic order could not unequivocally establish itself.

This ambiguity has provided a context for political challenge and the contestation of key elements of paternalist practice. No one – not the farmers, nor even the gurus (such as they are) of modern farm management – has been able to predict the direction and the rhythm of changes. Management change was originally conceived in terms of the replacement of the 'backward attitudes' embodied in paternalism with the technocratic rationalism of modernity. In reality the course of transformation has been rather more hybrid and uneven. Originally intended to pre-empt 'labour unrest' and conflict on the wine and fruit farms, they have at times created situations of increased conflict and uncertainty.

It has also brought to light the flexibility and adaptability of the paternalist imaginary. The most salient lesson of the changes of the 1990s has been the substantial space and opportunity for the *internal* contestation of paternalism. In many cases, workers' struggles have not been directed against the entire edifice of paternalist practice itself, but on the renegotiation of its terms. The notion of the 'farm as family' has been used in arguments in which workers claim recognition for their contribution to the farm as a whole, and in which they have rejected the institutionalized disrespect and racial subordination implicit in traditional paternalism. The same is true of the increasingly popular models of farmworker equity share schemes being touted in some sectors of the fruit industry.[23]

LAW

It is in this context that the impact of broader political and constitutional transformation must be understood. In many ways it is still too early to assess the impact on the rural Western Cape of the ANC's ascent into power and the winning of the popular franchise. The new decision-making spaces, organizations and institutions that have mushroomed all over South Africa with the ascendancy of the development industry have also had very limited effects. At the moment the most concrete ways in which the broader transformation of the South African polity are being felt is in the field of legal reform. Current political changes have done little for the rural poor, but they have, however, held one promise: they entailed a radical broadening of the scope of *legal* contestation.[24]

Parallel to the negotiated transfer of power there has been another change: the dawn of a new legal dispensation on the farmlands. In 1990, after the successful campaign of the Congress of South African Trade Unions (Cosatu) against the amended Labour Relations Act, the Minister of Manpower announced in parliament that the Basic Conditions of Employment Act (BCEA) and the Unemployment Insurance Act (UIA) would be amended to include farmworkers. After a long series of standoffs and wrangles, all parties agreed on a single piece of legislation, the Agricultural Labour Relations Act (ALRA). This Act, besides conferring basic rights on farmworkers, also made, for the first time, provision for collective bargaining in agriculture. This Act came into effect on 17 January 1994. With this, the centuries-old exclusion of farm labour relations from regulation by state authority came to a close.

These developments should not be seen simply in terms of the extension to the farmlands of the practices and politics of urban industrial labour relations. They have a far more fundamental political importance. As I have argued elsewhere, the re-articulation of labour relations was one of the most important ways in which the *politics* of the new South Africa arrived on the farm.[25] In the Western Cape, it signalled a distant but decisive shift in the balance of power. The state was insisting that farmworkers should be juridical subjects. No longer could farmers insist that no one had the right to interfere in the 'special relationship' between them and their workers. Farm dwellers' legal struggles, in other words, are also struggles about the extent and depth of the reach of state power and state authority in the white farmlands.

This is true, not only of the Agricultural Labour Relations Act, but also of other Acts, like the Restitution of Land Rights Act, which allows for the making of claims for the restitution of land appropriated after 1913 in the pursuit of racial segregation and apartheid. They do not, by themselves, bring about any real change, but what they do is to *create a framework in which the basic relationships of paternalist power can be contested*. For farm dwellers engaged in collective bargaining, lawsuits against unfair labour practice, and claims for expropriated land, far more is involved than the precise details of the case at issue. Farm dwellers negotiating about basic demands are, by doing that, doing something else as well. They are subverting the regional and local bulwarks of white supremacy in the farmlands, and undermining white farmers' claim to sole authority. They bring new ways for farm dwellers to understand themselves. They render concrete the abstract notion that they, too, are bearers of rights. New institutions, new practices, new circuits of power are created. Each round of negotiations questions coloured farm dwellers' marginality and asserts their right to speak and be heard.

CONCLUSION

The rural Western Cape is a landscape in transition. The direction of this transition defies easy characterization. Upbeat predictions of innovation and progress and trade unionist narratives of proletarian struggle oversimplify the picture just as much as do the bucolic images of rural tranquillity manufactured and disseminated by the tourist industry. Farmworker villages, share equity schemes, Patterson scales, quality circles – all are part of the picture, as are the processes of feminization and casualization, labour conflict, evictions, violence and mechanization. One of the only tendencies that is clear is that the forces that impact on the white farmlands open the way for a proliferation of *diverse* struggles, negotiations and contests.

These contests are far from equal. If the mid-1990s hold promise for farm dwellers insofar as they are presented with opportunities for political contestation, we should also bear in mind that they are being waged on uneven terrain. This is another reality optimistic prophets of economic progress would perhaps prefer us to forget: though the language of rights has won an important set of spaces, this does not mean that farm dwellers' interests are best served by the political agendas of liberalism. Perhaps one of the more ironic lessons of the mid-1990s is the effective ways in which formally non-racial discourses of administration can serve to perpetuate and excuse from challenge the racialized and gendered hierarchies of power and privilege bequeathed by apartheid.

Consider, for example, the complex set of questions facing those involved in implementing the Government of National Unity's programmes of reconstruction and development in the rural areas. They face the particular problems and challenges attendant upon the *distance* I have described between the formal, official spaces of power and decision-making, and the informal networks of black rural survival and solidarity. The relatively autonomous cultural spaces in which farm dweller 'knowledges' have circulated exist particularly far away from the apparatuses of official power, such as those of the law, and the technologies of power and knowledge instituted by development practice. The persistent legacies of subalternity, and the enduring and subtle enforcement of unwritten rules of exclusion of what Barnor Hesse, writing in a different context, has called 'white governmentality'[26] mean that we cannot simply assume that the decision-making forums and spaces instituted by the new state are unproblematically available for those who have been silenced so long.

Nowhere is the complexity, the intractability and the painfulness of these problems more evident than in what Colleen Crawford-Cousins has named 'apartheid's last frontier' – the *gendered* allocation of resources among poor black rural communities in general.[27] If white farmers are the privileged speaking subjects of farm paternalism, female farm dwellers are doubly marginalized: overtly and covertly, practices of silencing and the general devaluation of women's words exclude them even from the new spaces of decision-making and contestation opened by current reforms.

In this context, much depends on the ambiguous promise of government support for models of 'participatory development'. The emphasis on capacity building and 'people-centred development' in key policy statements on the RDP and land reform are a reflection of the hegemony of approaches like PRA (Participatory Rural Appraisal) in South African land policy circles. PRA has been widely criticized, and rightly, for its naive and unthinking populism.[28] Less obvious, but as relevant, is its availability for reduction to a set of 'methods' that can be readily incorporated into 'development discourse' and its micro-technologies of power/knowledge.[29]

But, white governmentality or not, we should not overstate the 'systematicity of the system'. The procedures and institutions of administration and development, like those of law, are potentially a site of contestation. The limitations mentioned here should not allow us to lose sight of the powerful potential of a participatory approach, and its part in 'holding a space' in which marginalized and silenced voices can be heard. This work can help construct creative relationships between institutions of rural local government and the informal networks of subalternity. This will require going beyond 'populism' and 'technicism' to a *political* understanding of participatory work with poor black rural communities. Such work entails a confrontation with the powerful, creative, conflictual and antagonistic energies bound up with racial, gender and class identities. They pose the challenge of embracing change and pain as part of the process of rural transition.[30]

This is an important lesson to bear in mind even for those who are not concerned with the messy realities of development implementation and transition 'on the ground', and whose labours are focused on the broader processes of rural transformation of which these processes are but a part. In the corridors of power and knowledge where policy is designed, it is widely accepted that the legacy of apartheid and its racial and gender inequalities are not easily left behind. It seems to be less widely understood that this does not mean the new South Africa is simply a place where pre-given and unchanged 'racial' or cultural identities confront each other, in the context merely of a different legal framework and policy environment. What change 'on the ground' teaches us is true elsewhere as well: the assertion of the primacy of an egalitarian South African identity draws the political frontiers of a new terrain upon which the content and significance of racial, class and gender identities must be renegotiated and reinvented. This is a political process. No one looks down on it from Olympian heights of objective neutrality. The process of transition is always a process that entails conflicts in which we confront the burdens and riches of the particular identities *we ourselves* have inherited from the past. If these contentious issues are plastered over with the bland language of 'governance', the machinery of the state is likely to remain unresponsive to the poor black rural people it professes to serve.

NOTES

1   This paper presents some of the results of my current PhD research (A. du Toit, 'Paternalism and modernity on South African wine and fruit farms: an analysis of paternalist constructions of community and authority in the discourse of coloured farmworkers in the Stellenbosch region', unpublished PhD dissertation, University of Essex, 1995). Some of the earlier sections of this paper have been presented under the same title at the Seminar on the Institute for Commonwealth Studies' Societies of Southern Africa in the nineteenth and twentieth centuries in December 1994, and in A. du Toit, 'Farmworkers and the "agrarian question"', *Review of African Political Economy*, no. 61, September 1994, pp. 375–88. I also draw on arguments developed more fully in Andries du Toit and Steven Robins, 'Legal literacy and the functioning of advice offices in the defence of farmworkers' rights', unpublished document, University of Cape Town, 1995. The arguments set out here have benefited from the criticism and commentary of many people – including Ben Cousins, Colleen Crawford-Cousins, Bill Freund, Zimitri Erasmus, Barnor Hesse, Jeremy Krikler, Ernesto Laclau, Colin Murray, Aletta Norval, Steven Robins and Gavin Williams.

2   See, e.g. Tessa Marcus, *Modernising Super-exploitation: Restructuring South African Agriculture*, London, 1987; Jeremy Krikler, 'Reflections on the transition to socialism in South African agriculture', *Africa Perspective*, vol. 1, no. 5/6, December 1987, pp. 95–120.

3   Merle Lipton, 'Restructuring South African agriculture', in Merle Lipton and Charles Simkins (eds.), *State and Market in Post-Apartheid South Africa*, Oxford, 1993, pp. 373, 383.

4   Johann Hamman, 'Farmworkers and labour policy: the impact of labour legislation on rural livelihoods on Western Cape wine and fruit farms', paper presented at the Workshop on Creating Sustainable Rural Livelihoods in South Africa, Stellenbosch, 11–13 March 1995; Joachim Ewert and Johann Hamman, 'Labour organization in Western Cape agriculture: an ethnic corporatism?', *Journal of Peasant Studies*, vol. 23, no. 2, 1996, pp. 146–65; Michael de Klerk, *Prospects for Commercial Agriculture in the Western Cape*, Cape Town, 1992.

5   See, to mention only some of the more important book-length studies, Colin Bundy, *The Rise and Fall of the South African Peasantry*, London, 1979; Timothy Keegan, *Rural Transformations in Industrialising South Africa*, Johannesburg, 1986; Helen Bradford, *A Taste of Freedom: the ICU in Rural South Africa*, London, 1987; William Beinart and Colin Bundy, *Hidden Struggles in Rural South Africa*, Johannesburg, 1986; Colin Murray, *Black Mountain: Land Class and Power in the Eastern Orange Free State, 1880s to 1980s*, London, 1992; Jeremy Krikler, *Revolution from Above, Rebellion from Below*, Oxford, 1993.

6   Stanley Trapido, 'The Cape Dutch and problems of colonial identity', paper presented at the Institute of Commonwealth Studies, 25 February 1994, p. 7. See also D. van Arkel, G. C. Quispel and R. J. Ross, *'De Wijngaard des Heeren?' Een onderzoek naar de wortels van 'die blanke baaskap' in Zuid Afrika*, Leiden, 1983, p. 52; Robert Carl-Heinz Shell, 'Slavery at the Cape of

Good Hope, 1680–1731', Yale University, unpublished PhD dissertation, 1986; Clifton Crais, *White Supremacy and Black Resistance in Pre-industrial South Africa: The Making of the Colonial Order in the Eastern Cape, 1770–1865,* Cambridge, 1992; Richard Elphick, *Kraal and Castle: Khoikhoi and the Founding of White South Africa,* New Haven, 1977, pp. 217–39; Richard Elphick and Hermann Giliomee, 'The origins and entrenchment of European dominance at the Cape, 1652–c.1840', in R. Elphick and H. Giliomee (eds.), *The Shaping of South African Society, 1652–1840* (2nd edn.), Cape Town, 1989, p. 522; Nigel Worden, *Slavery in Dutch South Africa,* Cambridge, 1985, pp. 6–16; James C. Armstrong and Nigel A. Worden, 'The slaves, 1652–1834', in Elphick and Giliomee *The Shaping of South African Society,* pp. 136–43.

7   Here, it is important to avoid misunderstandings over terminology. Many historians have implicitly associated *paternalism* with the notion of *benevolence*; they have assumed some kind of contradiction between the use of violence and coercion and the existence of paternalist relations, which they saw as an ameliorating force. Historians like Worden have therefore tended to avoid the term altogether when describing early slave society at the Cape, and, with James Armstrong, Worden has questioned the emphasis on paternalist relationships in slave society, insisting that slave society at the Cape was far from 'mild' (Armstrong and Warden, 'The slaves' , p. 150). Crais has similarly eschewed the term, preferring to use the term *patriarchy.* As I shall show later (and as Van Onselen argued recently) this opposition is not at all necessary: to characterize labour relations as paternalist does not deny the centrality of violence. Armstrong and Worden are nearer the mark when they point out that 'the essence of paternalism was an underlying subordination of the slave to his or her owner' (Armstrong and Warden, 'The slaves', p. 150). Crais makes the same point in the case of patriarchy, pointing out that violence in master/slave relations was not antithetical to the idea of the 'family'; '. . . . of all institutions in Western society,' Crais reminds us, 'the family has been among the most brutal, and "domestic" violence was very much part of slave life at the Cape' (Crais, *White Supremacy,* p. 35).

8   Pam Scully, 'Liquor and labour in the Stellenbosch district, 1870–1900', paper presented at the 'Cape: Slavery and After' conference held at the University of Cape Town, 10–11 August 1989, pp. 2–3; Clifton Crais, *White Supremacy,* p. 5.

9   Andries du Toit 'The micro-politics of paternalism: discourses of management and resistance on South African fruit and wine farms', *Journal of Southern African Studies,* vol. 19, no. 2, June 1993, pp. 314–36.

10   See Andries du Toit, 'The micro-politics of paternalism'; and 'Paternalism and modernity on South African wine and fruit farms' for a survey of the literature and historiography on this question.

11   See A. du Toit, 'Paternalism and modernity' for a detailed exploration of these identities.

12   Michel Foucault, 'Confessions of the flesh', in Colin Gordon (ed.), *Power/ Knowledge: Selected Interviews and Other Writings 1972–1977,* Brighton, 1980, p. 194; see also Hubert Dreyfus and Paul Rabinow, *Michel Foucault: Beyond Structuralism and Hermeneutics,* Sussex, 1982, p. 121.

13 Ernesto Laclau and Chantal Mouffe, *Hegemony and Socialist Strategy: Towards a Radical Democratic Politics*, London, 1985, pp. 110–11.

14 James C. Scott, *Weapons of the Weak: Everyday Forms of Peasant Resistance*, New Haven, 1985, pp. 40–1, 184–9.

15 Michel Foucault, *The Archaeology of Knowledge*, London, 1972, p. 224; Dreyfus and Rabinow, *Michel Foucault*, p. 45.

16 Pearl Linda Waldman, 'Here you will remain: adolescent experience on farms in the Western Cape', unpublished MA dissertation, University of Cape Town, 1993.

17 Edouard Glissant, *Caribbean Discourse: Selected Essays*, Charlottesville, 1989, tr. Michael J. Dash, pp. 14–17, 103–4.

18 Scott, *Weapons of the Weak*, pp. 28–37.

19 I thank Steven Robins for these insights. These ideas are explored more fully in A. du Toit and Robins, 'Legal literacy'.

20 Some of these are hinted at in Wilfried Schärf, 'The impact of liquor on the working class (with particular focus on the Western Cape): the implications of the structure of the liquor industry and the role of the state in this regard', unpublished MA dissertation, University of Cape Town, 1984. See, for example, p. 156.

21 See Henry Louis Gates, *The Signifying Monkey: A Theory of African-American Literary Criticism*, London, 1988.

22 See Derrick Purdue, 'Farm labour in the Western Cape: a study of one farm', University of Cape Town, unpublished BA Honours dissertation; David Mayson, 'The rural foundation, management and change', University of Cape Town, unpublished MA dissertation, 1992; Andrew Murray, 'Restructuring paternalism', University of Cape Town, unpublished MA dissertation, 1993; De Klerk, *Prospects for Commercial Agriculture*; Johann Hamman, 'Farmworkers and labour policy'.

23 Ewert and Hamman, 'Labour relations in Western Cape agriculture'.

24 A. du Toit, 'Farmworkers and the agrarian question'.

25 Ibid.

26 B. Hesse, 'White governmentality: urbanism, racism, nationalism', in S. Westwood and J. Williams (eds.), *Imagining Cities: Signs, Scripts, Memories*, London, 1996.

27 Programme for Land and Agrarian Studies, 'Problems in the participation of women in LRPP community structures in the Western Cape: diagnostic evaluation study', Land Reform Provincial Steering Committee, unpublished typescript, 1996; Colleen Crawford-Cousins and Andries du Toit, 'Women, land reform and power/knowledge: participatory method and gender in the Southern Cape land reform pilot project', unpublished typescript, 1996.

28 Ian Scoones and John Thompson, 'Knowledge, power and agriculture – towards a theoretical understanding' in Ian Scoones and John Thompson (eds.), *Beyond Farmer First: Rural People's Knowledge, Agricultural Research and Extension Practice*, London, 1994, p. 19.

29 Thus the techniques and truisms of PRA are nowadays no longer disseminated by radical critics of northern development orthodoxy, but have been assimilated and incorporated into the methodologies of development agencies such as USAID and the World Bank.

30   These insights and these words I owe to Colleen Crawford-Cousins. They are explored in an important but unpublished paper by Colleen Crawford-Cousins and Michelle Freedman, entitled, 'Holding the space: class, race and gender in training', unpublished typescript, 1994.

9 South African Literature, Beyond Apartheid

Mark Devenney

At a crucial juncture in Mandla Langa's 1996 short story, 'The Naked Song', Richard, a returned South African exile 'realise[s] that he has no country'.[1] Richard's story echoes that of many others, and Langa retraces in fiction an experience which those living in the country, under apartheid, were prohibited from knowing. But Richard's story is also about the difficulty of return, and of living in a South Africa where 'those whose lives had depended upon the continuation of the struggle'[2] are thrust back into an alien world, without the protective umbrella of moral protest, after the introduction of a democratic political system. Richard writes his story for Leonard Gama, a psychologist, himself a returned exile, offering therapy to those bruised and damaged by a long history of division and oppression. He writes because he is incapable of speaking. His words have been cut off as a consequence of his participation in the struggle to transform South Africa. Paradoxically, Richard's musical creativity is thwarted with the inauguration of the new democracy. I will return to the detail of Richard's story further on. What interests me here is Richard's claim that he has no country. He recollects reaching this conclusion in Lagos while participating in an international festival of the arts, and writes it down at the beginning of his therapy with Leonard Gama. Here the therapist, himself 'undergoing a therapy session that all South Africans, the guilty and the innocent, should undergo',[3] acts as an uncertain prophet, guiding the injured back to health. But how does one interpret this claim 'I have no country'. This question goes to the nub of the problem which concerns me: the difficult relationship between nationalism, politics and literature. There are two obvious answers. The first is to view this as a claim that art (in this case Richard's music) has no homeland, that an aesthetic validity transcends context. In this case literature has no business propagating politics, or a particular politics, but obeys only its own laws, which distinguish it from other discourses. A second interpretation suggests that Richard has no homeland, as of yet. The South Africa in which he could be at home does not yet exist. Thus music, here read literature, should contribute to the building of that future homeland, through active participation in the struggle. This may mean the sacrifice of art, or even in Richard's words the realization that 'as of then, his life didn't belong to him'.[4] The alternative

165

I trace towards the end of this article, suggests that matters are more complex.

Both of these interpretations had much currency during the 1980s and early 1990s. Moreover, the ghosts of the clash between aestheticism and politics still haunt writing in the new South Africa. Taking these questions seriously demands an interrogation of what the new South Africa *is*, what we understand by literature, and the extent to which it is even appropriate to speak of a South African literature, a literature defined in the last instance in relation to its place of origin, and context of utterance. In what follows I: (1) outline the premises and the challenge posed by the demand that literature is defined in terms of its politics; (2) suggest an alternative approach to the relationship between the discourse of politics and nationhood, and the discourse of literature; and (3) discuss Langa's recent short stories in more detail. In each instance I will refer, where appropriate, to novels and short stories published since the election of a new Government of National Unity.

THE ARTICULATION OF LITERATURE TO NATIONHOOD

Let me briefly analyse the consequences of the articulation of literature to the machinations of political struggle, a response to the claim that in an abnormal society there cannot be a normal literature.[5] This articulation became hegemonic in the national democratic movement, which demanded that politically committed writers in organizations such as COSAW (the Congress of South African Writers) subject their writing to the demands of political struggle, and resist developing a space for individual expression outside of this formation.[6] Certain key features unified these writers:

(1) Literature participated in what amounts to a theological discourse. Commonly it relied upon the idealization of a traditional African past (before colonization), and the projection of a utopian future.
(2) The poetry, especially, relies upon context for its effect. It is a poetry of performance, formulaic, repetitive, and mnemonic. 'Functionally like much of the emergent culture it serve[d] to mobilise and unite large groups of people.'[7]
(3) Literature's function is to raise consciousness. Novels employ a documentary realism, in which political challenge occurs at the level of content, whilst the form conforms to the classic model of the European *Bildungsroman*.
(4) The hero of this literature is not the individual but the collective struggle of the people. Resistance literature finds its theory in its pol-

itics, participating in a process where the people regain their historical personality, and projecting itself as the collective expression and reclamation of the culture of the oppressed.[8]

While this stance was not universal it developed strong institutional conditions of enunciation – in universities, in resistance literary magazines, and through the various organons of the resistance movement which occupied civil society during the 1980s and early 1990s. Benita Parry appositely summarizes its implications:

> Because such an agenda asks of writers that they wear their politics on their sleeves, and insinuates formulae to predetermine the materials of scripts and their performance, it acts to exercise a constraint on literary production . . . the ghost of discredited left tendencies hovers over the concept of cultural agenda . . . [9]

The danger here is that South African nationalism is presented as if it were a presence without a history, a Being whose seeds planted in the forgotten past may finally be harvested with the development of an authentic national democracy. The present, or a version thereof, is read into the past; time is localized and spatialized, its disruptive effects sedimented. The political ego forgets that nations too are complex historical articulations; indeed it actively contributes to that forgetting. Nationalism persists in the present continuous tense, a tense which resists history, a petrified reality which will always remain the same, which could not but be otherwise. This perhaps seems ironic, given that the discourse of liberation insisted on a close analysis of the often contingent conditions of struggle. Yet it is this contingency which is excluded in the alignment of literature to the people, more specifically to the politics of the ANC. To speak of *South African* literature, in this strong sense, is to reduce it to this present continuous tense, to assume that the nation will organically develop its own literature, a literature which emerges from, and expresses in words the truth of nationhood.

Nadine Gordimer's novel *A Sport of Nature*[10] accepted many of these imperatives. The result is a strange text in which the picaresque heroine, Hillela, finally sacrifices her attractive individuality in the interests of the politics of the national democratic movement. I quote the closing passage of the novel. The scene is Gordimer's projection into the future of a resolved South African conflict and the inauguration of a new nation. Hillela Capran has married Reuel, the revolutionary leader of an unnamed African state. As president of the Organization of African Unity he facilitates the peace process in South Africa, and Hillela returns to her homeland on his petards, so to speak. She, born in 1944, has lived during the years of high apartheid and attends this ceremony of conception as 'the President's wife'.

> When the band in gold, green and black leads in the military escort and motorcade with the first black President and Prime Minister of the country, his wife and his cabinet . . . the swell rises to a roar that strikes the mountain, and jets above it to the domain of eagles, ululating shrills of ecstasy. The mountain may crack like a great dark glass shattered by a giant's note never sung before. [Hillela now meets the wife of the President of the new South Africa.] She is embraced by and embraces the wife of the first black President of the country, whom she has never met; a real beauty that one once was, and the distinction is still to be discerned despite and perhaps because of the suffering that has aged her to fulfil a different title . . . the wife [Hillela] of the President of the OAU has slowly risen alongside her husband, beside the first black President and Prime Minister, his wife and other leaders. . . . She takes a breath, perhaps to ease her shoulders in the robe, and her hands hang at her side a moment and then are lightly enlaced in front of her thighs in the correct position. . . . If it is always true that the voice of life is always addressing someone – for the religiously devout it is a God, for the politically devout it is a human mass – there is a stage in middle life, if that life is fully engaged with the world and the present, when there is no need for space or reflection. The past is not a haunting, but was a preparation put into use . . . [11]

Gordimer here becomes one of those ululating in the crowds. But let us ignore for a moment the bombast. Instead we might note any number of features: the introduction of Hillela in her formal capacity, the introduction of women as wives of prominent men, all that secures their presence on the platform. We might focus on the claim that in middle age Hillela has found a space in which she is at one with the world, the space of the politically devout. Yet there is one phrase which encapsulates all of these concerns and more, a phrase which, intentionally or not, captures all of the dilemmas of a revolutionary movement new to power: 'her hands hang at her side a moment and then are lightly enlaced in front of her thighs in the correct position'. Overt sexual connotations are overlaced, not so lightly, with political connotations. Her hands, in the correct position, cover her thighs. Sexual energy is 'smoothed taut by the fist of the wind'. The body is written, and domesticated, its energy utilized productively in a public position of affordable power. The 'sport of nature', Hillela, has evolved to a point of non-contradiction, of transparency, of easy access to the real and opacity is removed from the space of her self. Hillela, since her birth, a wanderer without homeland is at peace with herself, her husband, her sexuality, and her nation. Gordimer, too, finds a home in this novel, resolving the problematic question of the relationship between fiction and reality, by domesticating fiction in the same way that she domesticates sexuality. Reduced to the machination of the nationalist political struggle, and the men who control it, women and fiction are but the clothing in which identity covers itself.

Yet what has that national culture become, since the 1994 elections? This is perhaps the most difficult question to answer for those committed to the Left, and to the building of a left-wing political project: a government, once socialist in orientation, committed to increased privatization, and the reality of a flourishing capitalism which puts paid to any faith in the idea that capitalism could not survive without apartheid, one of the more foolish ideals propounded by theorists of national democratic revolution. What has come to dominate, however, is an ideology of mass consumerism, easy entertainment, and the continued prevalence of a culture industry which simply expands its market, and its marketing strategies, with the extension of political rights to the majority of the population: the culture industry once incisively deconstructed by Adorno and Horkheimer in their *Dialectic of Enlightenment,* which many thought would be avoided in South Africa.[12] Once the national democratic movement achieves the lofty heights of power it no longer needs the marginal institution of literature to support reconstruction of the nation. Instead, far more powerful cultural institutions, once integral to the continued power of the apartheid state are brought on board, or strategically jump on board. Examples are legion: sports, television, mass consumerism and all of the institutions of capitalist democracy stand to the attention of the new nationalism. One need only recall the contribution of sports to the building of the mystique of the rainbow nation, to realize the extent to which national democratic literature is at best irrelevant. The freedom gained by once-committed writers is inevitably bitter, bitter because they are at last free to express imaginatively all possible worlds, but free too because the powers that be are no longer particularly interested in their support or criticism. Yet it is precisely this irrelevance which Adorno had argued, with regard to modernist literature, that gives to literature a special place. From this perspective literature is one of the few discourses which manages to resist reduction to utility, in a world where all language serves some interest.

RETHINKING LITERATURE AND POLITICS

Let me expand upon this idea, drawing somewhat critically on the work of Roman Jakobson.[13] His idea is in essence very simple, and by now widely familiar. After identifying six aspects of communication – the expressive function, in which the addresser predominates; the referential function, in which context predominates; the metalinguistic function, in which the code dominates; the connative function, in which the addressee dominates; the phatic function, in which the means of establishing contact dominates; and lastly the poetic function, in which the message predominates – Jakobson suggests that the specificity of literature has to do with the self-referential facility of language. Literature is (sometimes painfully) aware of the materiality of its medium, unlike language in which the referential function dominates. In simplistic terms it might be argued that resistance literary practice insisted upon the predominance of the referential function, resisted tropological transformations of language, and demanded that language serve the struggle. Again Jakobson is helpful. He writes:

> The poetic function is not the sole function of verbal art but only its dominant, determining function, whereas in all other verbal activities it acts as a subsidiary accessory constituent.[14]

Of greatest interest here is Jakobson's suggestive idea that the hierarchy of functions differs between literary forms. Epic, for example, relies heavily on the referential function, while in lyric poetry first-person expression is emphasized. Most important though is the poetic function, which imparts to the text – of whatever nature – a certain opacity resisting easy interpretation. At its most extreme literature points towards the *ultimate* failure of all language to enclose fully its speaking subject, towards the performative capacity of language which resists final closure and sedimentation. We may extend Jakobson's idea in this respect, and argue that literariness is introduced in a text whenever any one of the six features of the communicative act become problematic, introducing undecidability. It matters not if we argue that this is a function of the poetic, asserting its centrality over other domains, or if we suggest that in fact these domains themselves entail this radical possibility.[15] More important is the usefulness of these ideas for our current topic.

It suggests another way in which to read the debate between so-called aesthetes and the demands of the politically correct. This is not simply a clash between a predetermined reality and the opacity of a lyrical individualist user of language. Reference is firstly a function of the linguistic act itself. The anti-apartheid struggle attempted to establish the universal validity of a particular set of referential assumptions, claims which are contestable, precisely because language escapes this final determination. Equally, other elements of language enter into a debate which has been cast in terms of a battle between self-referential form, and content or reference. For example, in asserting the ultimate truth of a particular perspective, the speaker of language (collective or otherwise) implicitly excludes the third person, the receiver of the message, predetermining that the third person cannot but communicate in terms of a first-person perspective. The constitutive undecidability of the linguistic act is closed down with the presence of an omnipresent narrative function which forecloses the possibility of dissent. There is in other terms no reciprocity in the relation between first and third person. With reference to Gordimer's novel discussed above, it becomes clear that she excludes the possibility of response, and undecidability from the place of the political ego. All antagonisms are resolved with the achievement of nationhood, and rewritten as part of a seamless story of necessary struggle. Ironically too the coding of the novel is not questioned. This is ironic because it is the claim of resistance literature that it contests the idea that there is some aesthetic essence independent of context. There is little recognition that the novel is not a neutral medium, that the conventions of the novel are themselves historical and political. There is in the dominance of social realism no politics of form.

This raises a number of difficulties: if literature is a proscenium for a more real world, what precisely is the relationship between literary forms of representation and that reality? If it simply reflects, without any attention to its own internal laws, where lies its specificity, what laws determine that one text is literary, another not? This position is untenable, and probably only of historical interest now. If, however, literature does not simply reveal itself naked to the eye of the political, what terms help explain a literary culture, and literary texts conferred with the authority of South African literature? The prefix South African, expressing all of the questionable motifs of a nation which exists at ease with itself, exists in tension with any answer to the question 'what is literature?', a question which immediately recoils upon itself, if one accepts modernist dogma, namely that literature is in some manner defined by its self-referential nature, a self-reference which puts into question the possibility of an 'is' existing in the present continuous. If this is the case, how then do these two narratives – one of nation, the other somewhat more polyglot, but at the very least defined by a resistance to easy categorization and spatialization – relate to one another? What is the 'role', if indeed such utilitarian considerations are of relevance, of a literature spatialized, and retemporalized in the new South

Africa, once the antagonisms of old no longer neatly divide the social along a bipolarity which admits of no other? Is there a necessity linking these two denominations?

A positivist answer, some would say materialist, partially answers this question. Literature cannot be deemed to have an essence independent of its historical conditions of production, and is conferred legitimacy in a complex process of production. This includes the power of publishing houses, universities, critics, the reading public, and all of the other institutions which participate in the production of literature as a consumable object. Every text carries these marks which are inseparable from features deemed 'literary'. Thus in South Africa we might be tempted to enter into an analysis of various hegemonic literary formations which in articulating these institutions confer authority on different authors, novels and forms of writing. This demands a detailed analysis of the manner in which resistance critics gradually gained access to these institutions, and challenged long-standing versions of liberal aestheticism. Yet none of these factors explains the materiality of the language, of the text itself. That production, which before entering the processes which confer a certain authority upon it, undergoes the solitary labour of the writer, a romantic symbolism too long associated with a neutral aestheticism. As I have suggested above I prefer to understand this resistance of literature to full understanding in terms of the always latent potential of language to resist easy interpretation.

A brief analysis of J. M. Coetzee's *Age of Iron*, will perhaps clarify these points. *Age of Iron* addresses the life of a white South African woman, Elizabeth Curren, living in Cape Town. Unlike Hillela, Gordimer's sport of nature, she is elderly, and dying of cancer. The novel takes the form of four letters written by Elizabeth to her absent daughter, now living in Canada. At the same time as Curren confronts the cancer within her, the cancer which has become her new child, she is forced to confront the brutal cancer of apartheid society, the grim reality of a community torn apart by years of racism. In this polarized world there appears to be no choice than that literature support the forces of revolution, and of justice. Most important for my purposes is the manner in which the novel thematizes the relation between writing (in this case Curren's writing, her elegy, her letters to her daughter entrusted to the hobo Vercueil whom she meets on the day that she is told of her cancer), and the demands of political struggle.[16]

In experiencing these dual crises, and their consequences, Elizabeth confronts her own marginality, a marginality which has no authority. Her crisis alludes to that of literature in a society which is rent by conflict, and in which the voice of justice demands that the writer take a position in support of the forces of liberation. But liberation demands discipline, and with this discipline arises the possibility of sacrificing literature.

When entrusting the letters to Vercueil, Elizabeth is uncertain that he will fulfil the one task she requests, that he post them to her daughter. As readers we are placed in the position of the daughter, the receiver of the letter. But there is no guarantee that we will receive the letter or the message which it imparts. This uncertainty is thematized in the closing scene of the novel:

> For the first time I smelled nothing. He took me in his arms and held me with mighty force, so that the breath went out of me in a rush. From that embrace there was no warmth to be had.[17]

Various critics have read this ending as redemptive: Elizabeth dies having realized (in the dual sense of achievement and recognition) a possible recuperation of a community made impossible by apartheid. Yet this recuperation is both her death and an embrace with death, or alternatively with Vercueil, a man who has no obligation, who is indebted to no one, who lives on the margins of all society. How is it possible to view this moment, in which the self is lost, as simultaneously an achievement?

This narrative equivocation regarding the resolution of the novel is counterposed to another solution, one with which many authors of fiction were confronted. In order to achieve the redemption she so desires Elizabeth contemplates one final act of sacrifice against the madness of her society. She concludes that this is a false gesture. Why?

> Was my test whether I had the courage to incinerate myself in front of the house of lies. I have gone over that moment a thousand times in my mind, the moment of striking the match when my ears are softly buffeted and I sit astonished and even pleased in the midst of the flames, untouched, my clothes burning without singeing, the flames a cool blue. How easy to give meaning to one's life, I think with surprise, thinking very fast in the last instant before the eyelashes catch, and the eyebrows and one no longer sees. Then after that no thought anymore, only pain . . . The truth is there was always something false about that impulse, deeply false no matter to what rage or despair it answered . . . A juggler, a clown, an entertainer, Florence would think; not a serious person. And stride on.[18]

If Elizabeth is no longer capable of finding fulfilment in a lotus leaf languor, which like art for art's sake implies disengagement from the world, she also rejects the sacrifice of that writing on the pyre of political truth. In-stead she acknowledges that her opinions touch no one, that she speaks in a voice which is no voice, and that being a good person is insufficient under the circumstances. Instead of making herself a spectacle, and instead of making Coetzee's writing a decoration on the lapels of the struggle, the novel embraces marginality as an ethic, an ethical act which 'obeys a duty that must owe nothing', a duty that is 'not the mere technical application of a concept'.[19]

The difference between this closing, and that proposed by the liberation movement should immediately be obvious. Instead of a self-certainty, the political realization of Descartes' *cogito*, Coetzee posits a literary practice which thematizes a loss of authority, a loss which begets marginality and takes this marginality seriously. He acknowledges that working within the 'literary' must incur a certain price, yet he accounts for this price seriously, and seriously engages with what is ultimately the false gesture of sacrifice. Coetzee's novels point beyond those questions to interrogate the very idea of national authority, writerly authority and political authority. If literature termed 'national democratic' is a literature at home with itself, comfortable in its certainties *Age of Iron* undermines the careful domesticity which allows simplistic political choices. What is more, Coetzee questions the code in which he writes. Recognizing that the novel is not a neutral medium, that the tradition of novel writing which he both extends and inherits is itself pol-itical, he questions the very conventions upon which he must necessarily draw. Coetzee is very obviously aware that whatever position one adopts on the checkerboard of aestheticism versus politics, a post-colonial context poses serious questions for any consideration of what literature is. The object to which the word literature refers is itself problematized, and what to some may appear as an unproblematic reference is restored to its essential uncer-tainty. Indeed it is at this point, not when literature is reduced to the machina-tions of a particular political project, but in questioning its own essence, that literature challenges those discourses which attempt to colonize the by no means neutral space in which it has been carved out. It is then that Jakobson's poetic function may be deemed political, without necessarily being reduced to a particular politics.

Let me summarize a few crucial points: I have suggested that in spite of claims to the contrary the politics of literature in South Africa is not only about an attempt to represent, and offer critical support to a political struggle. Here the critic or the writer focuses on only one aspect of the rela-tion between a world and a text, namely the propositional content of asser-tions. If we turn instead to the relation between the addressee and the addressed we see that resistance literature all too quickly refuses the addressed a position from which they can speak. In these cases the content of aesthetic representations may have changed, but the form remains the same, allowing the continued dominance of a master narrative.[20] The ironic long-term consequence of such an uncritical appropriation is that literature which adheres to these constraints finds itself confirming the continuation of an uncritical mass culture, dominated by the totalizing logic of the entertainment and sports industry. If the new South Africa is simply about democratizing access to these mediums then it would seem that all of the hopes of resistance culture, indeed the very idea of a proletarian or mass culture is always already perverted by the power which it attempts to overthrow. Once resistance culture becomes dominant, once it takes on board all that it once disclaimed, what happens to those critics and writers who invested their egos and sacrificed their artifice in the interest of true representation?

The result is a crisis, on at least two counts. First of all a crisis of authority for both the critic who allied himself to the movement, and the writer who believed that his product would generate a new culture arising from the phoenix of the old. Indeed these were the two complementary functions accorded the oppositional writer: destruction and reconstruction. Reconstruction required the articulation of a subject unified and certain of its political imperatives, a subject capable of challenging the old culture. No longer. Secondly, a crisis of position, or attachment. No longer is the writer guaranteed his moment in the glorious revolution, performing poetry after the leaders have made their points; no longer does the lyricist sing the collective subject into existence as it assumes its place in history. Indeed the writer no longer has a place in a larger story of the nation: mass culture has occupied the place he once prized; indeed mass culture is far more accessible to the majority than the products he once deemed it their privilege to access, and his to produce. A crisis of position then is also a crisis of the narrative of national democracy to which committed writers once adhered. With these concerns in mind let me return to Mandla Langa's account of the returned exile, Richard.

THE 'NAKED SONG' OF NATIONAL LIBERATION

It will be recalled that Langa's character Richard is a returned exile, and musician. He once played the saxophone for Amandla, a group of musicians aligned to the liberation movement in exile. Yet in the new South Africa Richard no longer plays music, no longer speaks. How did this come about? While in exile Richard meets a woman Nozi, a cadre in Umkhontho

we Sizwe. For a time they live together, though their relationship is tenu-
ous, given that Nozi frequently enters South Africa on missions. In spite of
this uncertainty they marry. Langa writes:

> By Richard's own admission, Nozi was a woman brought by the gods to
> save him from himself. Small and sinewy, Nozi challenged him when
> he was slack, encouraged him when he began to falter. She would laugh
> at him when he hummed for her snatches of tunes he had composed, her
> face transformed by her joy.[21]

Richard's happiness is cruelly cut short when Nozi does not return from a
mission. Before departing, she senses that suspicion has fallen upon her,
after a failed mission in which a number of comrades are killed. Now she
simply does not return. Nobody in the liberation movement can tell Richard
anything. On his return to South Africa, after the unbanning of the liberation
movement Richard seeks Nozi out, 'scouring township after township,
knocking on doors'.[22] He does not find her. Gradually he reintegrates
into South African society, working for the ANC by day, and playing music
in clubs by night. He celebrates the ANC's victory wishing that Nozi was
with him, and wakes up alone with a large hangover. But the past returns
at a moment which should be his happiest. On the morning after the celebrations two members of the ANC visit him, and announce: 'She's dead,
Com. We were with her in Special Ops. This was the time when we were
in Natal. She was caught up in an ambush.'[23] The two admit that Nozi may
have been set up by an infiltrator, and leave:

> [Richard] was in a daze for the whole day. In the afternoon, he ventured
> out of his Berea flat into scenes of jubilation. Thousands of people on
> the street, even foreigners, all exulting in one of the greatest victories of
> the century.[24]

Richard returns to his flat, and finds a letter written by Nozi to him, in the
papers returned by his visitors. He reads its impassioned declaration of
love, collapses, and loses the power of speech. On reading this testimony
Leonard Gama, Richard's psychologist, becomes depressed. Towards the
end of the story he resolves that he will counsel Richard, that:

> the sessions will be painful, as when he would let Richard re-experience
> the trauma, but he, Gama, would make him feel safe. We will play
> music together, he said to himself, and improvise. At the end, we'll let
> ourselves go.[25]

Langa's world is a post-apartheid South Africa haunted by the ghosts of the past, trying painfully to come to terms with that past. He is not afraid to confront that world head on, and many of the stories in this collection comment laconically on the strengths and weaknesses of those participating in the new South Africa. I am most interested though in the implications of the above story for literature. It is clear that Langa's writing is neither protest, nor simple social realism. Richard's pain is a direct consequence of his participation in the liberation struggle, and the withholding of information from him by the liberation movement over a period of four years. Indeed it is this participation which kills Richard's ability to express. While the story, and others in the collection, retains a critical stance, Langa does not, however, revert to cynicism. Indeed he is passionately committed to the aims of national liberation, the alleviation of poverty and the ending of violence. We are now in a better position to assess Richard's claim that he has no country, with which I opened this article. Richard has not found a country with the achievement of national liberation. It is at that moment that he loses the hope he had of finding a homeland in which his anguished personal past is redeemed. Instead the hope which Langa holds out is found in a painful process of working through the causes of his pain. Part of this process involves Richard learning to play music in which he lets himself go, a music which is not simply a herald for the new nation. While Richard's loss of language is attributable in part to the sacrifices which had to be made for the struggle, Langa suggests a painful process of retrieval, a process in which Richard reclaims his music, and is able to let himself go. This suggests too the emergence of an art which is not reducible to national reconstruction, but which can only fully express itself in the context of that liberation. It was often noted under the apartheid regime that writing in South Africa would inevitably be fractured by the social conditions of its production. The consequence of national liberation for these narratives is not, however, that the fractures are overcome, that the ego finally exercises control over those uncanny experiences which interrupt its meditations. A music set free may travel in any direction, and address any number of themes. Perhaps Langa himself would disagree, but I would like to interpret the claim 'I have no country' not simply as a consequence of Richard's exile, but also as a condition for the production of his art. A literature neurotically concerned with nationhood loses its ability to perform as language, to exercise the 'violence of language [which] consists in its effort to capture the ineffable'.[26] I will conclude where I began: if any of the above analysis is valid what are the implications for the relationship between politics and literature in the context of South African nationhood?

There is, firstly, the possibility of cynicism, a response in which the writer takes distance from the dream now unrealized or unrealizable. The utopia becomes a dystopia, and literature revokes the utilitarian impulses of a literature committed to building the nation. Related to, but with an older heritage in South Africa, is the critical survey of the consequences of a reduction of literature to a certain politics. Perhaps the best recent exemplar is Peter Wilhelm's recent novel, *The Mask of Freedom*. Wilhelm presents a dystopian future, in which social cohesion is maintained only by an authoritarian state, and the exclusion of 'shades', AIDS sufferers, from society. At one point the narrative voice describes a scrap of paper kicked by one of the characters, Greta, a political activist opposed to the new totalitarianism:

> There was a dry scrap of newspaper in the path, yellow and caked with filth. Fading words in the last light shone at her, a speech someone had made at a graduation ceremony: 'The continued problem of the "bourgeois artist", alienated from the humanistic principles of democratic social formations, worries me. This insistence on standards and solitary endeavour without constant reference to the people's vigilant and ongoing guidance. . .'[27]

In this future dystopia all the records of South African literature are destroyed; the consequences of an articulation of literature to politics is the sacrifice of literature. Wilhelm's main character, Jason, a potter, attempts to fashion a life free of political interference. Inevitably this dream is interrupted by political affairs, but participation in these results in a loss of freedom. Wilhelm represents a world in which freedom is not attainable through the machinations of politics, but depends on the development of a space which is free of political intervention

A second form of interrogation of the past revisits the simplistic alternatives which we have come to know. Instead of bad government officials and good revolutionaries we are more likely to see a revaluation, and revaluation of the resistance movement, as well as an attempt to understand the logic which allowed a system such as apartheid to exist. Mark Behr's *The Smell of Apples*[28] registers strong antipathy to the system into which the characters were born, but this antipathy is coupled with an attempt to understand the forces to which white South African children were subject, the discourses which created the comfortable cocoon of their worlds until the balloon is pricked by unexpected or inexplicable events. Thus the child/narrator, Marnus, in Behr's *The Smell of Apples* can find no salve when his father betrays the world in which he taught his son to live. Not knowing where to turn Marnus, ironically, pursues a career in the military as had his father. The novel pulls the reader between the two narratives, in different times, revealing the betrayal of Marnus as a young child, and his later realization that the war in Namibia is not his war. Yet the narrative is fractured and uncertain, avoiding easy judgement, and cautious about the future.

There is lastly the possibility that writing produced in South Africa will cease to be South African, in the strong sense which this denotation connoted. One could imagine in this respect the development of genres relatively unexplored: fantasy writing, the deepening of fabulistic traditions already strongly ingrained in the different strands of South African history; crime writing, an almost unknown genre in South Africa, except in the anti-hero stories of James McClure, hardly mentioned in the critical interrogation of literature by South African critics. In this case the very idea of a responsible writing is displaced by an interrogation of the authority possessed by the detective/narrator. In other cases, such as Coetzee's *The Master of Petersburg*, the novel has no recognizable relation to South Africa, yet still engages in a critical interrogation of generational authority, as well as the authority of the writer, the father, to control the history and actions of his progeny. The authority of the paternal nation was always notional; perhaps one of the measures of the nation's maturity will be the extent to which literature is no longer measured in terms of that paternity.

NOTES

1   M. Langa, *The Naked Song and Other Stories*, Johannesburg, 1996, p. 77.
2   Ibid., p. 81.
3   Ibid., p. 91.
4   Ibid., p. 78.
5   It is of course unclear what a normal literature is. Indeed it may be suggested that literature resists normality, a claim found in numerous versions of literary modernism, ever since Breton's Surrealist Manifesto.
6   This process may be analysed in terms of the history of a process of articulation of literary production to resistance politics. In 1982 in Gabarone for example the Culture and Resistance Festival resolved that the term 'artist' should be replaced with that of 'cultural worker', and that the arts should be assessed in terms of their contribution to the creation of a democratic South Africa. Henceforth many resistance critics associated open textual practice with an aesthetic of the private, and believed that art should seek to unveil the interests of the ruling classes. This view was of course not new and had its origin in post-Second World War French literary culture (Sartre's arguments for a *littérateur engagée*), as well as in disputes regarding realism and modernism within German Marxism from the 1930s to the 1950s. The apo-

gee of demands for committed writing was found in the Soviet Union, however, where literary production was for a long time strictly controlled, and had to contribute to the building of the new Soviet Man. Different critics within the resistance movement drew upon different elements of these traditions in order to develop their arguments, but despite variance in terms of different relevant elements the argument generally resorts to the same metaphor: literature reflects, but does not transform the reality with which it engages.

7   J. Cronin, 'Even under the rine of terror' in M. Trump (ed.), *Rendering Things Visible*, Cape Town, 1990.

8   I have written about this discursive formation elsewhere, most comprehensively in a Master's thesis entitled 'The fictions of radical democracy', University of the Witwatersrand, 1994.

9   B. Parry, 'On the critique of resistance literature', in E. Boehmer, C. Chrisman and K. Parker (eds.), *Altered State? Writing and South Africa*, Sydney, 1994.

10 N. Gordimer, *A Sport of Nature*, London, 1987.

11 Ibid., pp. 394–6.

12 T. Adorno and M. Horkheimer, *Dialectic of Enlightenment*, London, 1979.

13 R. Jakobson, 'Closing statement: linguistics and poetics', in T. A. Sebeouk (ed.), *Style in Language*, Cambridge, Mass., pp. 350–77.

14 R. Jakobson, 'Closing statement', p. 356

15 R. Scholes, 'Towards a semiotics of literature', in D. Walder (ed.), *Literature in the Modern World*, Oxford, 1990.

16 Curren experiences a number of interlinked crises. Most obviously she has to address her own death, her own loss of any form of identity. But at the same time she is forced to address the sedimentations of her identity. Her life, delineated by the spatial organization of apartheid, has ranged from the university to her comfortable home in the suburbs of Cape Town. Her political awakening coincides with a spatial reorientation of her world. As Elizabeth's frames shift, as she begins to see what had always been occulted, realizing that she participated in its abhorrent logic, she experiences a crisis of personal identity. 'Awakened' she struggles to fashion a meaningful existence before the cancer she bears consumes her life. But this very crisis of personal identity, while it encourages her to find a meaningful existence also results in a crisis of authorial judgement. She begins to question whether the very attempt to be the author of her own existence, and the author of these letters, is not in itself a betrayal, a betrayal of political obligations and demands, demands which she is forced to address as the struggle for political democracy invades her home. The South African police kill the son of her domestic worker, Florence, as well as his friend. In both cases she is powerless to help them. Her gestures are hopeless. Curren addresses the letters to her absent daughter, and in doing so experiences a crisis of love, of a love which cannot be returned. In a contested society children revolt against their mothers, and the unsolicited love of mother and child is thrown into doubt, as the children become parents of a new and terrible reality, heirs to a world ruined by their parents.

17 J. M. Coetzee, *Age of Iron*, p. 181.

18 Ibid., pp. 128–9.

19 J. Derrida, *Aporias*, London, 1993, p. 16.
20 See also B. Parry, 'On the critique of resistance literature', for similar points, made from a somewhat different perspective.
21 M. Langa, *The Naked Song*, p. 83.
22 Ibid., p. 83.
23 Ibid., p. 84.
24 Ibid., p. 85.
25 Ibid., p. 91.
26 J. Butler, *Excitable Speech: A Politics of the Performative*, New York, 1997, p. 9.
27 P. Wilhelm, *The Mask of Freedom*, Johannesburg, 1994, p. 23. This novel is one of the more interesting published recently in South Africa and deserves far greater attention than I have space for here.
28 M. Behr, *The Smell of Apples*, London, 1995.

10 Paradigms Gained?
A Critique of Theories and Explanations of Democratic Transition in South Africa[1]
David R. Howarth

F. W. de Klerk's decision on 2 February 1990 to begin negotiating the demise of apartheid, followed by South Africa's first democratic elections in April 1994, has provoked numerous attempts at narration and explanation.[2] It has also resulted in a welcome pluralization of the theoretical idioms used to analyse South African politics and society.[3] There is still, however, little scholarly consensus regarding the explanation of democratic transition, and little critical discussion of the theoretical approaches deployed to examine it. Given this, I do not aim to provide another chronological survey of events during the period under discussion. Sufficient empirical information already exists.[4] Rather, I evaluate current interpretations by problematizing the theoretical frameworks and argumentative logics which underpin them.[5]

I begin by identifying and presenting five different ways of analysing democratization in South Africa. These are the constitutionalist, institutional rational choice, pactological, Marxist and discursive approaches. I then pinpoint a number of problems which are not adequately addressed, or even broached, by any of the available interpretations. These concern the relationship between social structures, political agents and the construction of democratic institutions, and the clarification of key concepts such as democracy, democratic transition and democratization. Drawing on Ernesto Laclau and Chantal Mouffe's materialist theory of discourse, I conclude by outlining an alternative research agenda, which may facilitate the further analysis of democratization in South Africa.

 CONSTITUTIONALISM

Proposals for constitutional reform have a long history in the South Africa context.[6] They have also had a particular resonance for those political parties, especially the National Party (NP), which have sought transformist solutions to South Africa's political malaise.[7] Understandably, however, it is only recently that constitutional matters have been tied explicitly to the actual dynamics of democratic transition.[8] This connection is clearly evident in Donald Horowitz's book *A Democratic South Africa?*, significantly sub-titled 'Constitutional Engineering in a Divided Society', which constitutes an exemplary case of this type of thinking. Rejecting the likelihood of an 'inclusive democracy', most of the analysis and prescriptive force of the book centres on suggesting appropriate constitutional and institutional forms likely to facilitate democracy in South Africa. These include an electoral system built around the alternative vote, so as to make politicians more 'reciprocally dependent on the votes of members of groups other than their own',[9] a separately and directly elected presidency, which will be powerful enough to offset the expectedly fragmented and incoherent party system, a federal state structure designed to counter drives towards hegemony by any party, and to foster greater group accommodation at the national level (while proliferating the various points of power in the overall political system), the restructuring of the armed forces to bring them under civilian control, thereby lessening the possibility of a military *coup d'état*, and efforts to reduce the extreme degrees of economic inequality between racial and ethnic groups.[10]

Importantly, however, Horowitz also includes a series of supplementary theses that relate constitutional questions to the underlying divisions, antagonisms and interests in society. These serve as the means of evaluating the prospects for a future democratic order in South Africa, while providing courses of action likely to increase the probability of democratic transition. His diagnosis of the roots of conflict, and the potential pitfalls they bequeath a post-apartheid order, centres on two factors: the pervasive presence of ascriptive racial and ethnic hierarchies, which have political salience, and the propensity to hegemony by aspirant political groups. These obstacles are exacerbated by the fact that the transition process itself was a product of a 'liberation struggle' fought by the majority against authoritarian rule, a factor which militates against an accommodation of those forces struggled against.[11] In short, Horowitz is pessimistic about the process and eventual prospects for democratization: 'South Africa already has several competing parties, with varying ethnic bases, and is as plausible a candidate as any other for a one-party, hegemonic regime.'[12]

Horowitz considers and rejects four overlapping solutions to this crucial problem of avoiding a 'one-party, hegemonic regime'. These are deterrence, habituation, reciprocity, and 'changing belief through learning'. Deterrence facilitates democratic transition either because there is a relative balance of power between contending forces, or because one major power serves as the guarantor of transition, coercing any forces which endeavour to disrupt it.[13] Processes of habituation contribute to the perpetuation of democratic rules by making 'backsliding less tempting' and 'more aberrational and less legitimate than it would otherwise seem'.[14] Reciprocity depends on the formation of pacts, which guarantee mutual security and provide tangible benefits for co-operation, rather than conflict amongst elites. The final solution centres on the acquisition of democratic beliefs through learning during the democratic transition process itself.[15] Horowitz correctly rejects the first three models as tautological, in that they presuppose what has to be achieved by the process of democratic transition, and by extension rejects the combined deployment of the different models discussed.[16] His rejection of the fourth is on empirical, rather than logical, grounds, and centres on its excessive optimism in asserting that changed values could be achieved in the fraught and contingent circumstances of a negotiation process.

Horowitz's alternative solution begins with the idea that there are three stages of the democratic negotiation process: 'bargaining about bargaining', 'preliminary bargaining' and 'substantive bargaining',[17] in which the vital first stage constitutes a key context for different actors to learn of the costs of conflict as against the benefits of democratic power sharing.[18] The difference with the learning model is that Horowitz substitutes a concern with changing *incentives* rather than changing beliefs. His reformulated model thus focuses on the need for incentives to adopt democratic institutions which, in turn, contain incentives to adopt and maintain democratic practices. This way of putting things, he argues, has three advantages. It focuses on the *self-interest* of actors involved in the process, rather than unrealistic cognitive changes; it concentrates on the *preferences* of agents, thus encompassing those approaches concerned with deterrence, reciprocity and belief; and, finally, its analysis of incentives brings out the *contingent* and *reversible* process of democratic transition.[19]

Horowitz's analysis of the South African situation in the period before agreement suggests that the incentive structure is not propitious for the installation of democracy, mainly because the interests of the parties involved in the conflict, especially the ANC, are at odds with the public interest. He does, however, suggest a remedy for 'improving the odds', which centres on the changing structure of incentives during the transition process itself. This is because 'larger democratic entailments . . . sometimes flow from ostensibly more limited commitments', a situation which is made possible because, as Giuseppe Di Palma puts it, 'actors come to comply with the results of actions that they had taken earlier in the process with other intentions and expectations'.[20] This dynamic of greater agreement as the negotiations unfold is hastened and stabilized, argues Horowitz, with the emergence of a moderate centre flanked in the South African case by racial extremists.

INSTITUTIONAL RATIONAL CHOICE

Timothy Sisk's institutional rational choice account of transition in his *Democratization in South Africa* consists of four interrelated arguments. Firstly, he explains the causes of transition by stressing an important shift in perceptions amongst the major political actors in South Africa from a zero-sum to a positive-sum game. Thus the costs of a winner-take-all scenario, whereby either the ANC or the NP could completely subordinate its adversary, were viewed as greater than the benefits of co-operating to create a jointly determined set of institutions to govern a common society.[21] This change, he argues, arose from two important factors: the growing awareness of a 'shared destiny' and 'recognition of interdependence', as well as growing parity, amongst the major parties to the conflict. In addition to these underlying determinants of change, Nelson Mandela's March 1989 memorandum, suggesting talks between the ANC and the government, constituted one of the precipitating set of events, which enabled opposed groups to break the political gridlock, and initiate democratic change.

Secondly, Sisk focuses on what he calls the inevitable period of uncertainty following the initial drive to negotiation, which arises from the need to create and adopt untried sets of institutional rules. Here he argues that the formation of pacts amongst the major protagonists, such as the signing of the National Peace Accord in September 1991, were vital in maintaining the negotiating process, as they reduced uncertainty about a possible return to zero-sum politics, and provided minority forces with incentives not to exclude themselves from negotiations, thereby jeopardizing the negotiation process as a whole. In this respect, Sisk argues that once the negotiation process was underway, uncertainty about respective parties' vital interests ceased to be a constraint on negotiation, and gave way to indeterminacy about the prospects of winning the game according to new rules. In this way, it performed the positive function of sustaining the democratization process. This was doubly so, he argues, because the presence of extremist forces, such as the Inkatha Freedom Party, the white Right and the PAC, strengthened the common interests of the centrist, negotiating parties.

Thirdly, Sisk considers the dynamics of the negotiation process itself, arguing that the strongly divergent interests of the opposed parties were increasingly modified as a result of the search for an agreed outcome. This convergence is seen to focus on the articulation of a new social contract designed to 'institutionalise and maximise cooperation among the moderate centre in order to avoid violent conflict'.[22] This is made possible by the overall context in which the discussions take place. As he puts it: 'Institutional choices in divided societies can converge on a social contract which eschews ethnic politics if there exists a centrist core of political parties with sufficient uncertainty about their potential to win outright in the new game, and if there is a roughly balanced, mutually dependent power relationship among them.'[23]

Lastly, Sisk addresses the kind of social contract which is likely to emerge in South Africa, and the prospects for its consolidation. According to Sisk, the establishment and consolidation of a social contract in South Africa entails a removal of the main causes of conflict – the politics of identity and the unfairness of race discrimination – and the establishment of what he calls an 'inclusive hegemony', as opposed to an initial period of severely 'limited democracy' or 'hegemonic exchange', which is limited to those moderate elites involved in the negotiation process. Borrowing from John Rawls, he argues that the former is more likely if the social contract freely chosen by actors is 'just' and 'fair', that is, 'the arbitrary distinction of race is replaced by a democracy that regulates "a proper balance or equilibrium" between the competing claims of the diverse elements of South Africa's divided society', and if there is 'shared sense of common destiny and the realization that hegemonic aims are self-defeating'.[24] In this case, the prospect for what he calls a 'limited but inclusive democracy' is a possible, indeed likely, outcome of South Africa's transition process.[25]

'PACTOLOGY', OR SOUTH AFRICA IN THE LIGHT OF COMPARATIVE DEMOCRATIZATION

In the search for a coherent model of democratic transition, a number of South African scholars[26] have drawn on comparative studies of democratization in Latin America and Southern Europe.[27] Frederik Van Zyl Slabbert's *The Quest for Democracy: South Africa in Transition* is a beautifully paradigmatic example. The book was written in 1992 as a practical and theoretical contribution to the transition process. Uncharacteristically and refreshingly, though, he begins with a series of definitions and concepts which orientate his account. At the outset, he argues that interna-

tional debates about democracy have witnessed a growing ideological convergence around two fundamental trends. These are a 'demonstrable predominance of market-driven economies', and a growing consensus of
belief about the meaning of democracy.[28] The latter, which is of central
importance to his investigation, centres on two fundamental principles: the
idea of contingent consent, in which victors and losers in electoral contests
conform to the established 'rules of the game', and the principle of
bounded uncertainty, in which the inevitable precariousness of democratic
political systems are bounded by clear constitutional principles that guarantee the rights and privileges of citizenship. Both of these principles ensure
transparent rules of democratic procedure.[29]

In order to analyse and predict the course of democratic transition in the
South African case, he rejects approaches which emphasize certain institutional and structural prerequisites for democracy, as advocated by theorists
of democratic modernization,[30] arguing that the supposed preconditions
may turn out to be the consequences of democratization. His alternative
focuses on

> the critical role of *key political actors* and their *strategic choices* con-
> cerning democracy, democratization and each other; to locate these
> choices within the context of *opportunities and obstacles* that have to
> be exploited or overcome; and then plot a *probable outcome* to the pro-
> cess. In this way structural factors are seen as interacting with the stra-
> tegic choices of key actors rather than predetermining them, which
> provides a more reliable picture of the dynamics of transition.[31]

He then identifies four ideal-typical modes of transition – a pact between
leaders within and outside the regime to be democratized, a unilateral
imposition by one particular force, reform as a result of mass pressure from
below, and revolution.[32] These different modes of transition are important
determinants of the likely outcomes of the democratization process, in
which 'top-down' modes of transition – a leadership pact or imposition –
have a better chance of stabilizing into a democratic regime than 'bottom-
up' modes of transition based on reform or revolution.[33]

With regard to the South African case, Van Zyl Slabbert characterizes
the particular form of apartheid domination as colonial (minority settler
domination), though not resoluble by white withdrawal or an imposed and
monitored solution by external agencies.[34] He then provides a fourfold
categorization of the causes for negotiation in the South African context
charted along two set of axes: planned/unplanned and internal/external
pressures for change. In this regard, unplanned *internal* pressures include

the process of black urbanization, whereas planned *internal* pressures include the growing black revolt against apartheid during the 1980s; the unplanned *external* pressures consist of the *rapprochement* between the Cold War superpowers, while planned *external* pressures consist of the gathering international campaign to isolate the apartheid state.[35]

Van Zyl Slabbert's analysis of democratic transition centres on three problems that have to be dealt with in the corresponding historical phases of the negotiating process. These are the problems of *normalization* (or *liberalization*), *democratization* and *consolidation*. The first refers to the process of restoring or granting rights and privileges to those denied them by the existing authoritarian state, thus ensuring an appropriate legal and political context for negotiations. In the South African context, the questions of political violence and security are of prime importance.[36] The second refers to the involvement of previously excluded groups in various levels of actual policy-making, and centres on four aspects of South Africa's social system. These are the democratization of the constitution, the state, the budget and the economy.[37]

While Van Zyl Slabbert's analysis is more concerned with the problems of normalization and democratization, he does argue that successful consolidation depends on the decisions taken about democratic institutions in the early part of the transition process. These should 'reward moderation and prevent racial outbidding'. However, the ultimate success of a transition to democracy does *not* depend on political elites reaching 'consensus on mechanisms of transition and the outlines of a constitution', but only if the democratic system can be sustained 'after the negotiated transition is over'.[38] In this respect, Van Zyl Slabbert highlights a number of important obstacles, and unintended consequences, surrounding the negotiation process, which means that there are various possible outcomes to the democratization process in South Africa, ranging from a 'clampdown' to a fully fledged democratic order.[39] Despite this, he remains relatively optimistic about the possibility of a successful democratic transition in South Africa.[40] This involves a successful movement from a 'government of transitional unity' (GTU) to a democratic settlement. Whether or not this is possible, depends on the regime's willingness 'to sacrifice exclusive control over the (negotiating) agenda' and the 'mutual bargaining by the regime and its opponents . . . on mechanisms for achieving transitional legitimacy for all parties coalescing at the centre'.[41] In short, Van Zyl Slabbert's model depends on the GTU following a double agenda of 'negotiating not only the outcome of a transition to democracy, but the conditions for a successful transition towards it as well'.[42] It is here that the centrality of pacts comes into play for the establishment of the 'conditions for a successful transition' involves the founding of four agreements amongst the main actors. These include a civil–military pact; an economic contract; an agreement on redistribution and development; and consensus on a new democratic constitution.[43]

MARXISM

By the 1970s and 1980s, Marxist accounts of South African society had come to dominate much of social science discourse. John Saul's account of democratization in the articles collected together in his book *Recolonization and Resistance in Southern Africa in the 1990s* continues their materialist analysis of South African politics.[44] It is predicated on a radical political commitment to a revolutionary socialist transformation of South Africa's 'racial capitalist' society, and a rejection of 'reformist' and 'reactionary' positions. Thus, he argues that a

> democratization of South Africa that remained narrowly political would be a useful achievement in the context of the country's sad history and glowering present. Yet if this levelling impulse were not to be pressed forward to redress the socio-economic inequalities that have been inherent in South Africa's brand of racial capitalism, any new 'freedom' would quickly be rendered very formal indeed for the vast mass of the black population.[45]

His focus thus eschews what he calls the 'lure of elite pacting', and a concern with the 'modalities of democratization', in favour of an analysis of the likely possibilities of 'structural reform' in South Africa. This results in an examination of the political forces engaged in pursuing this objective and the obstacles which such a 'transitional strategy' will have to overcome.

Saul's earlier analyses of apartheid supplemented the standard Marxist picture of a mutually reinforcing system of racial capitalism, with the view that the articulation of racial domination and capitalism was also 'potentially contradictory'.[46] Moreover, he argues that during the 'organic crisis' of apartheid in the post-Soweto period, these two structures were pulling apart in various critical ways,[47] thereby facilitating attempts by business elites and liberal factions of the NP to reform and deracialize South Africa's 'racial Fordist accumulation regime'.[48] These logics provide the background to Saul's analysis of 'De Klerk's flawed deracialization project', which is explained as an attempt to break up the growing political stalemate in South Africa, while simultaneously destablizing the ANC, and preparing a favourable ground upon which to negotiate the end of apartheid rule.[49] Saul emphasizes the contradictory character of this double-edged strategy, and the essentially 'top-down', elitist nature of the process of negotiations which has ensued.

For their part, Saul argues that the ANC and its allies were initially destabilized by de Klerk's dramatic announcements, and he poses the question as to whether the conservative and older ANC leadership will succumb to its worst authoritarian and autocratic style of politics, and consequently the 'lure of elite pacting'. Speculating that this is a possibility, he nevertheless concludes that the internal democracy of the ANC, the creative tensions between the ANC and its working-class allies, principally Cosatu, as well as the popular democratic struggles, such as the civic and community organizations, operating in civil society, still make the ANC the prime focus of democratic and socialist struggle in South Africa. This he claims is shown in the fact that towards the end of 1990, with the ANC's consultative conference, coupled with its more militant campaigns in 1991 and 1992, the negotiation process was being shaped as much by mass actions as elite negotiators.

Saul specifies four possible outcomes of the negotiations process. They are a collapse of negotiations and a return to the chaos and contradictions of the old order; the neo-liberal reformist agenda of the NP and its business allies; the revolutionary outcome favoured by sections of the ANC and the SACP, and what Saul describes as a *tertium quid* between reform and revolution – structural reform. The Hobbesian option is not analysed, but forms an essential backdrop against which the others are evaluated. The likelihood of co-optation, which is Saul's second outcome, is a strong possibility given that 'the strength of capital and entrenched privilege in South Africa . . . will be a pull on actors, both within and without the ANC, to take, in the end, the line of least resistance *vis-à-vis* established power'.[50] This outcome would see de Klerk working hand-in-hand with capital to make the problem of inequality a question of the redistribution of resources *within* a corporatist economic framework conducive to the interests of business, capital and the state, rather than requiring a fundamental restructuring of the means of production.[51] While Saul accepts that part of the ANC and SACP's rhetoric has always included reference to the latter, he concedes that the third option is highly unlikely.[52] This brings him to his preferred choice, that of a project of *structural reform*. This involves a more aggressive political intervention of the state into a mixed economy, which is neither inherently capitalist nor socialist, to ensure a necessary degree of popular control over strategic resources, and the maintenance of a proper balance between the 'private' and 'social' sectors – what the ANC have called the 'market' and the 'plan'

respectively.[53] This strategy of a 'growth through the direction of production' is viewed as the means of ensuring economic development and a more
radical redressing of inequalities in society.

The key to the successful pursuit of this strategy, for Saul, lies in the
concept of *empowerment*, especially as it pertains to the organized working classes at the point of production. More concretely, Saul endorses
Cosatu's idea of a 'reconstruction accord' in which the working classes
themselves bring pressure to bear on capital, as well as the ANC, 'by introducing issues crucially related to economic reconstruction into their various arenas of collective bargaining, at national, industry-wide, and company/
plant levels'.[54] While negotiated accords may carry the potential danger
of co-optation, they could also be vehicles for the advancement of working-
class interests and demands. Saul suggests a similar 'positive dialectic'
of empowerment with respect to struggles for women's rights and education.
This requires that the forces of civil society 'drive the [ANC] forward',
as well as the ANC giving 'focus and effect to the positive urgings
of that civil society'.[55] In sum, according to Saul, if progressive outcomes
are to emerge, then the tension between these two terms 'must *constantly
remain in the process of being struggled over and resolved politically*'.[56]
As to the likelihood of structural transformation, Saul remains ambiguous. Writing at the end of 1992, for instance, he is critical of ANC
concessions to the government on constitutional matters, and of a growing convergence on economic questions between the ANC, the NP and
business interests. As he puts it: 'Critics within the democratic movement have expressed fear that some of the concessions the ANC now
seems prepared to make towards assuaging white minority concerns
threaten to gut the capacity of a post-apartheid government to redress the
socio-economic inequalities of South African society.'[57]

A DISCURSIVE APPROACH

In *The Negotiated Revolution,* Heribert Adam and Koogila Moodley adopt
a hermeneutical approach to social action, inspired by Jürgen Habermas's
theory of communicative action.[58] This account emerges out of a critique
of the four previous approaches we have so far examined. Thus, it is not
concerned with the intricacies of constitutional questions, and the process
of engineering appropriate rules and procedures. For them, it is the 'issues
of future economic control and political power that lie at the heart of the
constitutional wrangling' in South Africa, and they see efforts by the NP to
enshrine constitutional 'principles', such as minority rights, property

rights, taxation levels and financial responsibilities, as attempts to 'freeze economic relations', thereby preventing an ANC-led post-apartheid government and state from intervening to reduce economic inequalities and disparities of wealth.[59] Ultimately, they argue, if democratic systems are unable to address South Africa's 'destablizing inequality', then it is likely that multi-party representation will be replaced by a more authoritarian form of rule.[60]

Moreover, Adam and Moodley do not accept that mass political pressure, or the purported stalemate between the NP and the ANC, caused de Klerk's dramatic decision to begin negotiating the demise of apartheid rule. They contest the view that the NP was *compelled* to negotiate, claiming that those who argue the case for mass working-class and popular political struggle, the armed struggle, the 'defeat' of the SADF in Angola, and international sanctions as the key determinants of change, simply reflect the 'illusionary rhetoric' and 'myth of victory' propagated by the leadership and activists of the ANC and its allies.[61] By contrast, they argue that 'above all else, it was the change in the Soviet Union that emboldened Pretoria to unban the ANC'.[62] In this new context, the 'politics of withstanding threats gave way to the politics of exploiting opportunities', and the 'National Party could . . . project itself as in tune with world trends by liberalizing and promising negotiations for democracy'.[63]

This explanatory focus on the ability of the NP elite to manage conflict and direct change arises logically from their earlier theoretical accounts of South African politics. In his classic account of grand apartheid entitled *Modernizing Racial Domination*, Adam had characterized the political elite of the apartheid system as a flexible 'pragmatic racial oligarchy'.[64] Here, the apartheid system was presented as 'possibly one of the most advanced and effective patterns of rational, oligarchic domination',[65] and he predicted that political change was likely to be the result of gradual reform from above, as the ever pragmatic race oligarchy sought to liberalize itself in order to secure the continued conditions for its economic and political power.[66] This approach is further developed in *South Africa Without Apartheid*, where Adam and Moodley shift their theoretical emphasis from a systemic 'dialectic of enlightenment' to a focus on the strategies of key social actors. Nonetheless, even in the midst of the 1980s' explosion of mass resistance in South Africa's black townships, they still argue that 'South African Blacks find themselves in the role of passive and bemused onlookers to a White struggle over how they should best be subjugated.'[67] Thus, it is the manipulative intent of the white elite which ultimately determines the dynamics of domination in South Africa, leaving little room for the logic and effects of black resistance.

Adam and Moodley consider a number of different scenarios in their speculation about South Africa's future. They reject the view that South Africa will become 'another Zimbabwe', in which the country would descend into 'a pseudodemocratic patronage system . . . characterized by high levels of corruption and little democratic accountability'.[68] This is because there are important structural differences between the two states, largely to do with a too-rapid Africanization of the Zimbabwean state, and the absence of a strong private sector to absorb the new upwardly mobile African elite. Similarly, they are sceptical about the prospects of 'another Yugoslavia' arguing that whereas 'in Yugoslavia artificial units of people were forced together and now aim at being apart, [u]nder apartheid, people were coerced to live apart and now strive to unite in one state'.[69] This is because, as Adam and Moodley put it, despite the traumas of apartheid there exists 'some minimal nationhood' and a feeling of pride about 'being South African', which is absent in situations of 'parochial nationalism',[70] such as the former Yugoslavia, where outsider groups are constructed as 'the embodiment of evil' intent on preventing insider groups from realizing their rightful destinies.[71]

According to Adam and Moodley, 'the most rational and also most likely scenario for South Africa is a social-democratic pact between business, labour and key state bureaucracies, as practiced in postwar Germany'.[72] This possibility arises because of the existence of a powerful trade union movement in South Africa, which was legalized well before the 'granting' of a universal franchise, and which has gradually developed 'a moderate leadership', as well as what they call a 'remarkable pragmatic rationality' amongst the key actors involved in forming a social democratic compact.[73] Accepting that democratic transition has all but been achieved, Adam and Moodley argue that the consolidation of a social democratic model in South Africa, as well as the deepening of democratic institutions and practices, depends largely on the economic performance of the new regime, and whether or not economic growth is compatible with extensive democratic participation. As they conclude, '[t]he chances of a future South African democracy and stability do not falter on incompatible identities but depend mainly on the promise of greater material equality in a common economy'.[74]

THE APPROACHES COMPARED AND EVALUATED

Thus far, I have introduced and described five approaches to democratic transition in South Africa. It is evident that the different texts which have been considered are not on the same level of abstraction, and do not share a common object of analysis. Nevertheless, despite this inevitable uneven-ness, we have witnessed a growing and deepening *contextualization* of the problems under consideration. Donald Horowitz's account focuses on the construction of appropriate constitutional rules and procedures for the installation and consolidation of democracy in South Africa. However, despite his effort to incorporate sociological and political factors, his theo-retical framework exhibits the main problems with constitutionalism.[75] These pertain to the formalistic and abstract character of much constitu-tional theorizing, and the downplaying of the social and political context in which the rules of the political game are established and function.[76] As a number of theorists suggest, constitutional dispensations do not *ground* political processes; rather, legal orders and the state *presuppose* a concept of the political which constitutional settlements endeavour to contain and channel.[77] Thus, the narrow constitutionalist focus tends to exclude an analysis of the deeper political conflicts which constitution-making seeks to domesticate and codify.[78] This is not to argue, as some Marxists have suggested, that constitutional questions can simply be dismissed, espe-cially in cases of major political reconfiguration such as South Africa; it is, however, to place the constitutional issue in the right perspective, which is *after* a consideration of the underlying social struggles, and the discursive forms which make democratization possible.[79]

Timothy Sisk's institutional rational choice model widens the scope of analysis by stressing the changing interests and preferences of rational actors involved in the process of negotiating new institutional structures. However, his analysis is still restricted to a consideration of decon-textualized and self-interested agents with an essentially ahistorical rational-ity. Thus, no real effort is made to locate democratization in relation to the specific historical trajectory of political struggle in the South Africa con-text. Moreover, he tends to *describe* events and processes without deduc-ing explanations from his overall theoretical framework. This is evident in his explanation of the *causes* of democratization in South Africa. Here Sisk presupposes what he must demonstrate, as he provides no explanation of the 'shared common destiny' and 'interrelatedness' which he posits as the (necessary) conditions for a shift from a zero-sum to a positive-sum per-ception. A balance of power between the main political forces does not automatically translate into a recognition of a shared destiny, and is not, therefore, a sufficient condition of de Klerk's dramatic turnabout.[80] More-over, it does not show *how* and in what *form* these conditions resulted in altered perceptions amongst the major actors. Addressing these questions would require an analysis of the different discourses articulated by the major forces engaged in conflict, and the different ways in which identities were constituted before and during the transition process. It also raises questions about the requisite values and norms, especially the production of a democratic *ethos,* necessary for the creation and stabilization of democracy.[81]

Van Zyl Slabbert's explanation of democratic transition in South Africa hinges on the strategic interactions of four main actors involved in the transition process. These are the 'reformers' (or 'softliners') and 'hardliners' in the ruling bloc of forces, and the 'moderates' and 'radicals' in the pro-democracy camp.[82] If reformers and moderates are able to create and institutionalize founding pacts, in opposition to the other actors, then it is more likely that political democracy can be established. However, there are a number of problems with this approach, at both a general theoretical level, and in its application to the South African case. A major theoretical weakness concerns the *nature* of the founding pacts, and the *process* by which they are agreed. It is clear that the 'foundational' pacts proposed by pactologists are aimed at engineering a restrictive and procedural form of democratic rule. As Karl and Schmitter make clear, 'foundational pacts serve to ensure survivability [of the new regime] because, despite their inclusionary nature, they are also and simultaneously aimed at restricting the scope of representation in order to reassure traditional dominant classes that their vital interests will be respected. In essence, they are anti-democratic mechanisms, bargained by elites.'[83] Further, the conception of the process of democratization tends to neglect the vital impact of popular and working-class agents on the transition to democracy. Though O'Donnell and Schmitter accept in their original formulation of the model that popular mobilizations are important in bringing down authoritarian regimes, and even broach the idea that normalization and democratization *may* lead to a 'resurrection of civil society', and what they call a process of *'socialization',*[84] it is, as Daniel Levine suggests, the 'short-term manoeuvring'[85] of elites, which is the central dynamic of the transition process. Thus, the democratization process is insulated from the impact of popular forces, and the transition itself becomes primarily a technical question to be resolved by elite actors.[86] There are also difficulties in applying the comparative model to the South African situation. These concern the peculiarities of South Africa's colonial history, institutions and experience. Not only did South Africa have a functioning, though racially restrictive, democracy and civil society,[87] the ethnic and racial divisions pose particular problems which need to be addressed. Not the least of these is the massively skewed distribution of resources, which will constitute a central obstacle to democratic consolidation.[88]

Saul's perspective widens the scope of analysis further by bringing into play the material conditions and socio-economic factors which shaped the causes and logic of democratization. One of the key problems with this perspective, however, is the tendency to ignore the actual processes of negotiations in favour of mass political action, while neglecting the requisite democratic procedures and ethos necessary for the creation and consolidation of a democratic order. Thus, the formal and procedural considerations of democratic rule, whose achievement Saul revealingly refers to as 'narrowly political', 'useful' in 'the glowering present', and 'very formal', are neglected in favour of a concern with *structural reform*. The latter, borrowed from André Gorz,[89] involves a rejection of democratic reformism as a 'self-contained' strategy, and a move towards the total structural transformation of society, as well as a process of empowerment, which aims at the complete *emancipation* of the working classes. In short, the exigencies of structural change along socialist lines trumps the (important) concern with the creation of democratic institutions and practices in the short and medium term. Moreover, while Saul endeavours to break with some of the rigidities of Marxist theory, his theoretical framework still assumes the *a priori* primacy of economic logics as the means of analysing and investigating politics and ideology, an unquestioned identification of working-class struggles and the achievement of socialism, and a conception of socialism founded on state ownership and the nationalization of the means of production. Without rehearsing the numerous criticisms of these paradigmatic assumptions, it is worth noting the difficulties of successfully negotiating the problems of economic determinism and class reductionism, as well as accounting for the role and character of political agency, and avoiding the authoritarian and undemocratic implications of its political philosophy, while remaining firmly *within* the Marxist model of society and politics.[90]

Adam and Moodley correctly problematize deterministic and reductionist accounts of social action, focusing instead on 'actors' interpretations of the world', as they are 'discursively negotiated through reasoned argumentation'.[91] Thus, 'history' is not 'the inevitable unfolding of predetermined antagonistic class or racial forces', but 'far more open-ended [and] susceptible to intelligent intervention by progressive actors'.[92] However, while their discursive approach has the *potential* to overcome the problems identified in the other perspectives – especially their focus on the changing identities and perceptions of social actors engaged in political struggle – and though their freely admitted theoretical eclecticism is welcome in the name of a greater pluralization of intellectual traditions, it is frustratingly underdeveloped. It remains for the most part a disparate series of insights and opinions, which are not structured and coherently organized. Moreover, in keeping with their view that 'Habermas fails to specify how conflicting claims to validity are adjudicated – how we decide which is the "better" argument', the result is a study which offers no clear solutions to many of the key issues it raises.[93] For instance, while they dispel many of the existing accounts of the causes of de Klerk's 'redefinition of the enemy', they do not articulate a theoretically informed alternative, arguing that 'there is insufficient space to weigh all the causes of this shift in strategy'.[94]

UNDERLYING THEORETICAL PROBLEMS AND OMISSIONS

Having noted some of the strengths and deficiencies of these explanatory models, it is also important to isolate two *common* theoretical problems and omissions in these five perspectives. The first concerns the relationship between structure and agency. The existing accounts of democratization reflect the classical 'either/or' dichotomy, which contemporary dialectical theories have endeavoured to overcome.[95] From differing viewpoints, Horowitz, Sisk, Van Zyl Slabbert, and Adam and Moodley, all concentrate on the decisive role of political agents in initiating and executing democratic transition in South Africa. Using rational choice theory, Horowitz and Sisk focus on the calculative decisions of self-interested individuals pursuing their chosen preferences to explore the processes of democratic transition. They both conclude, Horowitz predictively and Sisk descriptively, that these preferences undergo change during the processes of negotiation, as their calculations are altered by the changing environment in which they operate. This focus is replicated in Van Zyl Slabbert's account, though his pactological model concentrates on the strategic interactions of historically specific actors ('moderates', 'reformers', and so on), and does not make use of the more rigorous assumptions of rational choice theory. However, these agency-based accounts neglect the role of social structures in creating the terrain in which decisions are taken, and the preferences from which agents must choose. Moreover, social agents themselves are regarded as little more than instrumentally rational self-maximizers, whose historically forged identities are unproblematically assumed. In the South African context, this focus results in a top-down, elite-motivated account of democratization, in which agents not directly involved in the bargaining processes are excluded from consideration.

John Saul's Marxist account directly opposes agency-centred models of social action. Rather than starting with the strategic calculations of disembodied agents, he is concerned with the structured context of constraints within which decisions can be taken. Moreover, he argues that the social actors who formulate strategies and take decisions are historical artefacts, and not decontextualised abstractions, in which case their decisions are constrained by the context in which they function, and by their previous historical and political constitution. As we have seen, however, Saul's structuralist perspective is in danger of bending the stick too far in the other direction, as the agency focus is replaced with a framework in which the identity and autonomy of agents are strongly shaped (even determined) by economic logics and processes beyond their control. In short, the different accounts provide no means of explaining the relationship between social structures and political agents.

The second is the striking lack of conceptual clarification in the accounts considered. Concepts are bandied around in these analyses, but their essentially contested definitions and meanings are not spelled out. This is true of concepts such as hegemony, ethnicity and 'race', but is particularly evident in the conceptualization of democracy, democratic transition and democratization. For the most part, it is Robert Dahl's concept of *polyarchy* which implicitly informs many of the accounts examined.[96] Thus, political democracy consists of three elements. These are *pluralism,* or the existence of multiple socio-economic strata, which tends to offset deep conflicts of interest in favour of consultation and compromise; *multipartisanism,* that is, the existence of competition and alteration in power of pluralist rather than structurally based interests and political parties (class, race, etc.); and, finally, *effective guarantees of fundamental individual and collective rights and freedoms* (elections, rule of law, constitutionalism, etc.). These formal, rather than substantive, features of democratic rule serve as the criteria for characterizing and criticizing authoritarian regimes, as well as assessing the outcomes and prospects of democratization.

This minimal and essentially formal definition of democracy is replicated in the concept of democratization deployed in the analyses considered. For Horowitz, Sisk, Adam and Moodley, democratic transition and democratization are virtually synonymous, such that democratization refers to the process of a successfully negotiated transition to democracy. For Saul, on the other hand, the concept of democratization is similarly undeveloped, as he is clearly sceptical about its deployment, usually using scare-quotes to denote the term, and equating it with formal political institutional arrangements; instead, he prefers his concept of structural reform.[97] It is left to Van Zyl Slabbert, who employs a slightly broader concept of democratization to capture the processes of changing not only the constitutiuonal rules, but the state, budget and economy, to provide a distinct conception of democratization. Nonetheless, in line with pacto-logy, this process remains firmly under the control of key elites.

AN ALTERNATIVE AGENDA: THE CAUSES AND PROCESS OF DEMOCRATIC TRANSITION

I turn now to an alternative problematization of democratic transition and democratization in South Africa. Though my aim is not to provide a new substantive account of the problems isolated, I do want to specify more clearly the questions that have to be answered, while endeavouring to provide the theoretical resources with which to answer them. Five main questions can be distilled from the existing accounts. The first concerns the *causes* of democratic transition and raises important methodological and substantive questions about the precise theoretical relationship between structure and agency. The second concerns the *process* of democratization, and poses questions regarding the character of the de Klerk strategy and the negotiations which ensued. The third centres on the *kind* of transition which has taken place in South Africa, while the fourth concerns the *reasons* for the relative success of democratic transition, and the fifth the *prospects* for its consolidation. While the first two questions require the elaboration of an alternative theoretical model to resolve questions surrounding the structure/agency problematic, the last three entail an elaboration of key concepts surrounding democratization, which can serve as *criteria* by which the South African transition can be evaluated. Let us begin with the first set of questions.

The causes

Why did democratic transition take place in South Africa? In this form, the first question is too general, and thus potentially misleading. In fact, it can only be analysed at four disaggregated levels of analysis. At an *individual* level, the question concerns the decision which F. W. de Klerk reached as South Africa's President to unban the ANC and begin negotiations. The questions to be explored at this level include the particular timing of the decision, the alternatives which were weighed up before the decision was taken, and the crucially important question as to whether the decision was imposed by forces beyond his control, or a 'daring gamble'[98] designed to seize the initiative and determine the terms of negotiation itself. Secondly, the decision must be explored within the pertinent *institutional* contexts in which de Klerk functioned, such as the cabinet, party and state levels. Here the focus concerns the varying balances of forces in the key decison-making forums, and the different strategies articulated and pursued by opposed forces. Such an investigation would centre on the debates between (and within) 'hardliners' in the security establishment, and 'softliners' in the more liberal Departments of Foreign Affairs and Constitutional Development respectively.[99] Thirdly, at a deeper level still, the question has to consider the role and impact of significant *collective actors*, such as the ANC, UDF, Cosatu and Inkatha on the structuring of the decision-making contexts, and the decisions taken.[100] The focus of such an investigation would concentrate on which forces made a greater impact on the causes and process of negotiations.

The problems posed at the first three levels presume an agency-centred perspective, which generally excludes a consideration of structural factors. At the *structural* level, attention has to be directed at the national and global economic conditions shaping the processes of democratization, as well as the changing dynamics of the international political system. With respect to the former, it would be necessary to clarify the underlying causes of apartheid's emergence and failure. In the South African context, this has centred mainly on the Marxist and liberal modernization interpretations of South African history, in which Marxists such as Saul have stressed the internal contradictions of racial capitalism, whereas liberals such as Michael O'Dowd and Merle Lipton the progressive development of capitalist social relations.[101] With regard to the latter, the developments in the former Soviet Union, especially the end of the Cold War and the waning fortunes of state-directed socialism, would have to be assessed.[102]

The process

The problem to be addressed regarding the *process* of democratic transition can be resolved into two principal components. What determined its dynamic? Why was it successful? The first component concerns the relationship between the bargaining process conducted within the negotiations framework, and the actions of collective actors outside the process. Two positions are evident in this regard. On the one hand, most analyses focus on the evolving relationship between the negotiating actors, and their changing preferences and interests in the bargaining process. On the other hand, there are those that focus on the movements and forces of civil society, and their effects on the overall contours of negotiations.

The second component is related to the first, as those that focus on the internal dynamics of negotiations explain the success of negotiations in terms of a growing overlapping of interests between the major parties, whereas those that stress external pressures focus on the crises and mass actions which concentrated the minds of those conducting negotiations. What is missing in both perspectives is a consideration of the different identities of the main actors involved in the negotiating process – their different ideological traditions and styles of political practice – and the precise impact of external pressures, principally in the form of powerful collective actors such as Cosatu, on the bargaining agents.

Towards an alternative theoretical model and account

While the disaggregation of these four levels of analysis is essential, it still does not address and resolve the structure/agency dichotomy. Laclau's post-structuralist theory of discourse moves some way in deconstructing and reinscribing this dualism. Simplifying somewhat, he distinguishes between *subject positions* interpellated by a discursive structure, and *political subjectivities* which actively constitute structures.[103] Whereas the identity of the former is fixed by the ensemble of social relations within which the subject is immersed, the latter emerges in the context of a *failed* structure that can no longer confer identity on to a subject. The latter arises because of the *dislocation* of social structures, which in turn is a consequence of processes such as the uneven development of capitalism, the tension between economic logics and political institutions, antagonistic relations between opposed social forces, and so forth. In the case of dislocated social structures, subjects are literally *compelled* to become collective political agents intent on reconstituting a new order within which identities can be stabilized.[104]

At a high level of abstraction, this formulation constitutes an improved conceptualization of the structure/agency dialectic. However, Laclau's conception of agency is overly restricted to those 'heroic' moments of decision when subjects are 'forced' to reconstitute discursive orders in situations of extreme crisis and social breakdown. While this conception might be applicable to those limit situations such as social revolutions – and even here these 'pure' moments of reconfiguration are necessarily conditioned by available ideological traditions and sedimented practices – in actual historical situations this is seldom the case. In most concrete processes of social transformation, we might posit a dialectical relationship between two kinds of decision – decisions taken *about* the structure and decisions taken *within* the structure – which correspond to the split in subjectivity which Laclau has introduced. Whereas the former kind of decision is taken by strong political subjectivities destined to create new 'rules of the game', the latter captures the kinds of decision which actors make within a (developing) system of rules.[105]

One further question has to be considered. Laclau's rethinking of the structure/agency dialectic is premised on the emergence of strong political subjectivities 'filling the gap' left by the dislocation of social structures. This involves the construction of antagonistic relations between forces and the articulation of hegemonic political projects. Laclau and Mouffe theorize this process by introducing the logics of equivalence and difference.[106] These logics are analogous to what Gramsci would call 'revolution from below' and 'revolution from above' or 'transformism', in which the logic of equivalence entails the construction and institution of a political frontier in society dividing 'friends' and 'foes', whereas the logic of difference involves the expansion of a given order through the disarticulation of antagonistic relations and the incorporation of the excluded.

Laclau and Mouffe's approach enables us to chart the causes and processes of democratic transition by focusing on the dialectics of structure and agency. The dislocatory rhythms and crises of 'racial capitalism' in the post-Soweto conjuncture form the structural backdrop against which the various transformist initiatives of the NP must be viewed. Moreover, this attempted logic of difference was negated by the proto-revolutionary political practices of the popular and working classes, who created a set of equivalences between the different sectors of the oppressed and the apartheid state.[107] In short, the period witnessed the emergence and construction of strong political subjectivities intent on undermining apartheid and elaborating new forms of social structure in an effort to resolve the dislocations and contradictions of the failed system.

Seen in this light, de Klerk's 1990 initiative is best viewed as the NP's boldest attempt to resolve the crises of the apartheid state by incorporating and domesticating those anatagonistic forces opposing it. Much of the ensuing political struggle centred as much on the shaping of the terrain of negotiations, as on the actual outcomes produced by them. In this way, the crucial interventions of collective actors, such as Cosatu, in the form of stayaways and mass protest, drove the negotiation process forward. The negotiation process itself, however, involved decision-making and bargaining within the confines of the negotiation framework. It is only within this strongly constrained set of possibilities that most of the agency-centred existing accounts of democratization in South Africa become relevant. In other words, it is only at this level of analysis that the rational choice models of Horowitz and Sisk are effective.

DEMOCRACY, DEMOCRATIC TRANSITION AND DEMOCRAT-IZATION

The second set of questions concern the assessment of the prospects for democratic consolidation in South Africa. They presuppose, moreover, the adumbration of requisite criteria for evaluating these prospects, which in turn entails rethinking the concepts of democratic transition and democratization, and the specification of the required conditions for democratic governance. Let us begin with the former.

Democratic transition, democratic transformation and 'the democratic revolution'

To clarify the concept of democratization, it is important, at the outset, to distinguish between democratic *transition* and democratic *transformation*. The former refers to the process by which negotiating elites manage to oversee the installation of formal liberal democratic procedures, whereas the latter designates the longer-term process of restructuring the underlying social relations of a given society.[108] Furthermore, it is useful to locate this twofold characterization of democratization within the broader logic of what Laclau and Mouffe, borrowing from de Tocqueville, call the *democratic revolution*.[109] For them, the democratic revolution involves an equivalential extension of the democratic logic – demands for liberty and equality – to different sets of social relations. Thus, for example, socialist demands are understood as the extension of greater equality and freedom in the relations of production, and with respect to the economic sphere. This view of democratization enables us to conceptualize the process of democratic transitions as a political project involving the interaction of political agents other than simply state and bureaucratic elites, as its construction and installation would involve the articulation of interests and demands from a wide variety of political forces and agents.

The conditions for democracy

In order to specify the *conditions* for democracy, it is necessary to begin with a more adequate definition of democracy itself. One possible starting point can be found in the path-breaking writings of Claude Lefort.[110] He attempts to theorize democracy as a specific institution of social relations in which the place of power is an 'empty space'. This specific form of the social is intimately connected with the advent of *modernity*, in fact it is its distinctive characteristic. As Lefort puts it in his book *The Political Forms of Modern Society*, a modern democracy is a 'society in which power, law and knowledge are exposed to a radical indetermination, a society that has become the theatre of an uncontrollable adventure, so that what is instituted never becomes established, the known remains undetermined by the unknown, the present proves to be undefinable'.[111] In this way, democracy is characterized by what he elsewhere calls 'the dissolution of the markers of certainty'.[112]

This specification of democracy in its modern form is extremely suggestive. It is a view shared by Adam Przeworski, who has characterized the establishment of democracy as 'a process of institutionalizing uncertainty, of subjecting all interests to uncertainty'.[113] Lefort, however, does not confine his discussion of democracy to this affirmation of its contingency. There is a darker side to modern societies which is an essential possibility of the democratic form itself. It is not coincidental that Lefort discusses modern democracy in relation to his analysis of the logic of totalitarianism: for totalitarianism is democracy's other. Hence, the advent of a space of indeterminacy in democratic societies, always exposes this space to complete occupation and embodiment by a totalizing force or agent ('the working class', 'the people', 'the Party'). Whereas pre-modern forms were constrained to some extent by the presence of something external to the system of power (God or Nature), this is not the case in our secularized age.

This ever-present potential for the empty space of democracy being completely occupied suggests three conditions for the construction and stabilization of democratic rule. The first would be the presence of a democratic *ethos* which consists of a recognition of the *contingency* of social agents and political projects; a finitude which is essential for the fostering of a pluralist political culture. In this regard, Bill Connolly has explored some of the necessary ontological conditions for the creation of a democratic ethics centred on the cultivation of 'agonistic respect' between politically opposed agents.[114] In the South African context, for example, this would involve the production of a common national identity, which both allows for the expression of difference between social agents, while ensuring that these differences do not result in the fragmentation of the state. The second concerns the requisite institutional conditions of possibility for democratic governance. The most obvious element in this regard is the particular constitutional settlement underpinning the operation of the state institutions. However, of equal importance is the establishment of a division between the state and civil society, which does not involve the mutual subsumption of one by the other.[115] As Lefort suggests, the erosion of this division results in either an apolitical liberalism, or an overpoliticized totalitarianism. Finally, as modernization theorists have long insisted, there are important structural conditions which encourage the maintenance and success of democracy. Clearly the most important variable in this regard is the level of economic growth and development underlying democratic institutions and practices.

Prospects for consolidation and further democratization

In light of the above remarks, it is evident that the process of democratic transition in South Africa is well underway. What is disputable are the overall prospects for democratic consolidation, and the extent of democratic transformation. A few concluding remarks are necessary in this regard. As we have seen, a key structural condition of democratic stability is the degree of economic development.[116] South Africa's starkly uneven economic development, coupled with the 'social legacy' of apartheid,[117] has led to commentators such as Herman Giliomee questioning the ultimate viability of democratic consolidation. Moreover, the recent downgrading of the ANC's state-directed development strategy – the Reconstruction and Development Programme (RDP) – in favour of a more neo-liberal economic orientation, throws into doubt the ability of the new state to meet its overwhelming development needs and objectives.[118] This is a result of the growing pressures of financial and business interests, at both the global and national levels, but also certain institutional deficiencies, especially locally and regionally, which have made it difficult to implement development policies in an efficient fashion.[119]

The latter set of considerations raises questions about the institutional conditions of democratic rule in South Africa. Though the constitutional rules which have emerged have proved functional and legitimate in the short and medium term, the relationship between the state and civil society is more problematic. Remarkably, during the 1970s and 1980s South Africa witnessed the painful emergence of an active and relatively resilient civil society, consisting of popular community organizations, trade unions, support groups, and so forth.[120] These popular forces provided much of the sustenance for mass political resistance during these years. Moreover, as I have noted, they also contributed much-needed momentum to the brokering of a negotiated settlement during the 1990s. However, while the formal separation of the state and civil society still exists, the great danger in the current phase of democratization, and for the future consolidation and extension of democracy, is the possible depoliticization of those forces operating in civil society, as well as the sclerosis of the space of civil society itself. Finally, while a functioning and pluralistic party system has been established in South Africa, a key danger is the ANC's stranglehold over political power and its potential in sustaining a *de facto* one-party system. (It ought to be noted that these tendencies are offset by its commitment to implement a Bill of Rights, proportional representation and a federal state structure.)

The production of the required democratic ethos to sustain democratic institutions and practices in South Africa is rather more difficult to assess. Positive developments include the 'Truth and Reconciliation Commission', which has moved a little way in healing the wounds of apartheid, demonstrating some readiness by South Africans to come to terms with the past. Moreover, the ANC's inclusive discourse of non-racialism, coupled with its pragmatic political style, has made it possible to begin to construct a common South African national identity, which is both open to difference, while retaining some overall coherence and unity. However, the discourse of non-racialism does carry the danger of assimilating, and thus erasing, ethnic particularities,[121] and there has been the historical difficulty of realizing non-racialism in practice. Further, as a number of writers have suggested, one of the dangers to the construction of a pluralistic democratic ethos is the continued presence of ethnic identities, particularly the existence of Zulu and Afrikaner identities, which exhibit potentially separatist or secessionist tendencies. One of the crucial tests for the consolidation and extension of democracy in South Africa is the way in which these ethnic differences are negotiated in the future.[122]

NOTES

1   A much earlier version of this chapter was presented in the School of Social Sciences at the University of Kingston. My thanks to the participants in this seminar, as well as Aletta Norval, Graeme Herd and Steve Griggs, for their helpful comments.

2   The range of views expressed reflects the circumstances in which these texts emerged. Many were produced during the late 1980s and early 1990s, and thus embody the contingency of the period of transition itself. They include H. Adam, 'Transition to democracy: South Africa and Eastern Europe', *Telos*, 1990, pp. 33–55; H. Adam and K. Moodley, *The Negotiated Revolution: Society & Politics in Post-Apartheid South Africa*, Johannesburg, 1993; G. Adler and E. Webster, 'Challenging transition theory: the labor movement, radical reform, and transition to democracy in South Africa', *Politics & Society*, vol. 23, no. 1, 1995, pp. 75–106; A. Du Toit, *South Africa as Another Case of Transition from Authoritarian Rule*, Cape Town, 1990; P. Du Toit, *Power Plays: Bargaining Tactics for Transforming South Africa*, Johannesburg, 1991; A. M. Faure and J.-M. Lane, *South Africa: Designing New Political Institutions*, London, 1996; S. Friedman (ed.), *The Long Jour-*

ney: South Africa's Quest for a Negotiated Settlement, Johannesburg, 1993; S. Friedman and D. Atkinson (eds.), *South Africa Review 7: The Small Miracle: South Africa's Negotiated Settlement*, Johannesburg, 1994; M. Frost, 'Preparing for democracy in an authoritarian state', in R. W. Johnson and L. Schlemmer (eds.), *Launching Democracy in South Africa: The First Open Election, April 1994*, New Haven, 1996; H. Giliomee, 'Democratization in South Africa', *Political Science Quarterly*, vol. 10, no. 1, 1995, pp. 83–104; H. Giliomee and L. Schlemmer (with S. Hauptfleish) (eds.), *The Bold Experiment: South Africa's New Democracy*, Southern, 1994; R. J. Griffiths, 'Democratization and civil-military relations in Namibia, South Africa and Mozambique', *Third World Quarterly*, vol. 17, no. 3, 1996, pp. 473–85; D. L. Horowitz, *A Democratic South Africa? Constitutional Engineering in a Divided Society*, Berkeley, 1991; A. Johnston, 'South Africa: the election and the transition process – five contradictions in search of a resolution', *Third World Quarterly*, vol. 15, no. 2, 1994, pp. 187–204; M. Kiloh, 'South Africa: democracy delayed', in D. Potter, D. Goldblatt, M. Kiloh and P. Lewis (eds.), *Democratization*, Cambridge, 1997; H. Klug, 'Extending democracy in South Africa', in J. Cohen and J. Rogers (eds.), *Associations and Democracy: The Real Utopias Project*, vol. 1, London, 1995; R. Lee and L. Schlemmer (eds.), *Transition to Democracy: Policy Perspectives 1991*, Cape Town, 1991; S. Malby, *After Apartheid*, London, 1992; G. Moss and I. Obery (eds.), *South Africa Review 6: From "Red Friday" to CODESA*, Johannesburg, 1992; M. Motlhabi, *Toward a New South Africa: Issues and Objects in the ANC/Government Negotiation for a Non-Racial Democratic South Africa*, Johannesburg, 1992; M. Murray, *The Revolution Deferred: The Painful Birth of Post-Apartheid South Africa*, London, 1994; M. Ottaway, *South Africa: The Struggle for a New Order*, Washington, 1993; J. Rantete and H. Giliomee, 'Transition to democracy through transaction?: bilateral negotiations between the ANC and NP in South Africa', *African Affairs*, no. 91, 1992, pp. 515–42; J. Saul, 'South Africa: the ANC put to the test', *New Left Review*, no. 188, 1991, pp. 3–44; J. S. Saul, *Recolonization and Resistance in South Africa in the 1990s*, Trenton, 1993. T. D. Sisk, *Democratization in South Africa: The Elusive Social Contract*, Princeton, 1995; S. J. Stedman (ed.), *South Africa: The Political Economy of Transformation*, Boulder, 1994; B. Tucker and B. Scott (eds.), *South Africa: Prospects for Successful Transition*, Cape Town, 1992; W. Van Vuuren, 'Transition politics and the prospects for democratic consolidation in South Africa', *Politikon*, vol. 22, no. 1, 1995, pp. 5–23; F. Van Zyl Slabbert, *The Quest for Democracy: South Africa in Transition*, London 1992.

3   As is well known, intellectual debate in South Africa has been dominated by the so-called race/class(/gender) debate. Though now outdated, there has not yet developed an alternative set of reference points to organize discussion on South African politics. Part of the task of this essay is to examine to what extent theoretical differences around the concepts of democracy and democratization form a new terrain of theoretical investigation and, thus, a welcome advance in our conceptualization of South African politics. For a summation of many of the themes of the race/class exchanges, see H. Wolpe, *Race, Class and the Apartheid State*, London, 1988.

4   For a clear overview of the events of the 1990s, see S. Friedman (ed.), *The Long Journey: South Africa's Quest for a Negotiated Settlement*, Johannesburg, 1993.

5   In Wittgensteinian terms, the available evidence needs to be rearranged so as to provide a 'more synoptic' and clearer account. See L. Witgenstein, *Philosophical Investigations*, Oxford, 1953.

6   See A. Lijphart, *Democracy in Plural Societies*, New Haven, 1977; A. Lijphart, 'Majority rule versus constitutionalism in deeply divided societies', *Politikon*, no. 4, 1977, pp. 113–26. For important critiques of this style of thinking and its particular prescriptions, see S. C. Nolutshungu, *Changing South Africa: Political Considerations*, Manchester, 1982, pp. 26–32; R. Taylor, South Africa: consociation or democracy?', *Telos*, 1990, pp. 17–32.

7   The clearest example is the baroque 'Tri-cameral' parliamentary system in 1977, which was eventually installed in 1984 against the backdrop of major mass political protest. See R. M. Price, *The Apartheid State in Crisis: Political Transformations in South Africa 1975–1990*, Oxford, 1991. Numerous constitutional 'fixes' were also put forward by other opposition parties, including the Progressive Federal Party, the New Republican Party and the Conservative Party. See R. Schrire, *Adapt or Die: White Politics in South Africa*, London, 1992, pp. 57–75.

8   In an influential article in the early 1980s, Samuel Huntington had prematurely connected 'reform from above' with its requisite political dynamics. See S. Huntington, 'Reform and stability in a modernizing, multi-ethnic society', *Politikon*, vol. 8, no. 2, 1981, pp. 8–26.

9   Horowitz, *A Democratic South Africa?*, p. 196.

10   Ibid., chapters 5, 6.

11   Ibid., p. 246.

12   Ibid., p. 248.

13   Ibid., pp. 249–50.

14   Ibid., p. 250.

15   Ibid., p. 250.

16   Ibid., pp. 250–6.

17   See P. Du Toit, 'Bargaining about bargaining: inducing the self-negating prediction in deepy divided societies – the case of South Africa', *Journal of Conflict Resolution*, vol. 33, no. 2, 1989, pp. 210–30; P. Du Toit and J. Gagiano, 'Contending regime models and the contest for the middle ground in South African politics', *Politikon*, vol. 15, no. 2, 1988, pp. 5–18.

18   Horowitz, *A Democratic South Africa?*, p. 258.

19   Ibid., p. 261.

20   G. Di Palma, *To Craft Democracies: An Essay on Democratic Transitions*, Berkeley and Los Angeles, 1990, pp. 111–12.

21   Sisk, *Democratization in South Africa*, pp. 284–8.

22   Ibid., p. 291.

23   Ibid., p. 289.

24   Ibid., p. 291.

25   Ibid., p. 292.

26   See Du Toit, *South Africa as Another Case of Transition from Authoritarian Rule*; H. Giliomee, 'Democratization in South Africa'; Van Vuuren,

'Transition politics and the prospects for democratic consolidation in South Africa'; Van Zyl Slabbert, *The Quest for Democracy;* Lee and Schlemmer, *Transition to Democracy: Policy Perspectives*; Rantete and Giliomee, 'Transition to democracy through transaction?: bilateral negotiations between the ANC and NP in South Africa'. It should be noted that while these different writers share a common framework, they differ with regard to the substantive conclusions they reach in using the framework.

27   See T. Karl and P. Schmitter, 'Modes of transition in Latin America and Eastern Europe', *International Social Science Journal*, no. 128, 1991, pp. 269–284; G. O'Donnell, L. Whitehead and P. Schmitter (eds.), *Transitions from Authoritarian Rule*, vols. I–IV, Baltimore, 1987; G. O'Donnell and P. C. Schmitter, *Transitions from Authoritarian Rule: Tentative Conclusions about Uncertain Democracies*, Baltimore, 1986; P. Schmitter and T. Karl, 'What democracy is . . . and is not', *Journal of Democracy*, 1991, pp. 75–88; A. Przeworski, 'Some problems in the study of the transition to democracy', in G. O'Donnell, L. Whitehead and P. Schmitter (eds.), *Transitions from Authoritarian Rule*, vol. III, Baltimore, 1987; A. Przeworski, *Democracy and the Market: Political and Economic Reforms in Eastern Europe and Latin America*, Cambridge, 1991.

28   Van Zyl Slabbert, *The Quest for Democracy*, p. 1.

29   Ibid., pp. 3–4.

30   See L. Diamond, 'Economic development and democracy reconsidered', *American Behavioural Scientist*, no. 35, 1992; S. M. Lipset, *Political Man, The Social Bases of Politics*, Baltimore, 1960; S. Huntington, *The Third Wave: Democratization in the Late Twentieth Century*, Norman, 1991.

31   Van Zyl Slabbert, *The Quest for Democracy*, pp. 5–6.

32   Ibid., pp. 6–8.

33   See Karl and Schmitter, 'Modes of transition in Latin America and Eastern Europe', p. 280.

34   Van Zyl Slabbert, *The Quest for Democracy*, pp. 12–17.

35   Ibid., pp. 32–7.

36   Ibid., p. 59.

37   Ibid., pp. 61–70.

38   Ibid., p. 71.

39   Ibid.

40   Whereas Van Zyl Slabbert is confident about the possibility of a successful transition to democracy, other 'pactologists' have used comparative insights to question the likelihood of liberal democracy in South Africa. Herman Giliomee, for instance, argues against the likely inauguration and consolidation of liberal democracy in South Africa because of the absence of two key structural prerequisites for the installation and sustenance of democratization: 'broad-based economic development' and 'national unity'. He also draws on O'Donnell and Schmitter's comparative conclusions about democratic transition in Latin America and Southern Europe to predict a non-democratic outcome in South Africa, arguing that the political gridlock between opposed forces, the hybrid political forms that inevitably emerge from transition, and the substantive economic inequalities in the South African context, strongly jeapordize the possibility of consolidating democratic institutions and practices.

Giliomee suggests two likely alternatives to liberal democracy in South Africa. These are a *durable racial power-sharing pact*, in which government is based on consensus rather than the principle that the strongest party can impose its will, and a *one-party-dominant system* in which the line between the ruling party, government and the state becomes blurred (as is the case with states such as Taiwan and Mexico). The former outcome is likely to be an unstable compromise between contending forces in which the different elements will be forced 'to cooperate under conditions of anarchy – that is, without the sovereign temporary majority that is the essence of a liberal democracy', whereas the latter has become more likely following the successes during the 1994 elections, and its subsequent actions in strengthening its grip on power. In this case, as Giliomee puts it, 'South Africa may be heading for a one-party dominant system, along Mexican and Taiwanese lines, sooner than most analysts expected.' See Giliomee, 'Democratization in South Africa', pp. 95, 103–4.

41   Van Zyl Slabbert, *The Quest for Democracy*, p. 87.
42   Ibid., p. 90.
43   Ibid., p. 90–2.
44   See J. Saul and Stephen Gelb, *The Crisis in South Africa*, 2nd edn., London 1986; J. Saul, 'South Africa: the question of strategy', *New Left Review*, no. 160, 1986, pp. 3–22; J. Saul, 'The Southern African revolution', *Socialist Register 1989*, London, 1989; J. Saul, 'South Africa: between "barbarism" and "structural reform" ', *New Left Review*, no. 188, pp. 3–44.
45   Saul, 'South Africa: between "barbarism" and "structural reform" ', p. 5.
46   Saul, 'South Africa: the question of strategy', p. 5.
47   Saul, 'South Africa: between "barbarism" and "structural reform" ', p. 7.
48   Ibid., p. 8. The latter concept drawn from Stephen Gelb's analysis of South Africa's political economy. See S. Gelb, 'South Africa's economic crisis: an overview', in S. Gelb (ed.), *South Africa's Economic Crisis*, Cape Town, 1991.
49   Saul, 'South Africa: between "barbarism" and "structural reform" ', p. 9.
50   Ibid., p. 7.
51   Ibid., pp. 30–2.
52   See A. Callinicos, 'Reform and revolution in South Africa: a reply to John Saul', *New Left Review*, no. 195, 1992, pp. 111–15.
53   These ideas are drawn from economists such as Manfred Bienefeld, Stephen Gelb, and Lawrence Harris, as well as ANC intellectuals and activists, such as Max Sisulu, Tito Mboweni and Ketso Gordhan.
54   Saul, 'South Africa: between "barbarism" and "structural reform" ', p. 37.
55   Ibid., p. 40.
56   Saul, *Resistance in Southern Africa in the 1990s*, p. 129.
57   Ibid., p. 170.
58   Adam and Moodley, *The Negotiated Revolution*, pp. 6–7.
59   Ibid., pp. 34–5.
60   Ibid., p. 32.
61   Ibid., pp. 49, 45.
62   Ibid., p. 44.
63   Ibid., p. 45.

64 H. Adam, *Modernizing Racial Domination: South Africa's Political Dynamics*, Berkeley, 1971, pp. 18–31, 37–9, 145–59.
65 Adam, *Modernizing Racial Domination*, p. 16.
66 Adam, *Modernizing Racial Domination*, pp. 181–2.
67 H. Adam and K. Moodley, *South Africa Without Apartheid*, Berkeley, 1986, pp. 163–4.
68 Adam and Moodley, *The Negotiated Revolution*, p. 203.
69 Ibid., p. 206.
70 Ibid., p. 219.
71 Ibid., p. 208.
72 Ibid., p. 210.
73 Ibid., p. 213.
74 Ibid., p. 222.
75 For an extended critique of the 'constitutionalist fallacy', see I. Shapiro, *Democracy's Place*, Ithaca, 1996, pp. 30–42.
76 Though it should be noted that, along with the rise of 'new institutionalism', there has also been a 'rediscovery' of constitutions, and their importance to other branches of political theory and political science. See J.-E. Lane, *Constitutions and Political Theory*, Manchester, 1996. See also the special issue of *Political Studies* (vol. 44, no. 3, 1996), edited by R. Bellamy and D. Castiglone, and entitled 'Constitutionalism in Transformation: European and Theoretical Perspectives'.
77 See M. Foucault, 'Governmentality', in G. Burchell, C. Gordon and P. Miller (eds.), *The Foucault Effect: Studies in Governmentality*, London, 1991; K. Marx, 'On the Jewish question', in D. McLellan (ed.), *Karl Marx: Selected Writings*, Oxford, 1977, pp. 39–62; C. Schmitt, *The Concept of the Political*, Chicago, 1996; C. Schmitt, *Political Theology*, Cambridge, 1985. For attempts to mediate between the critique of constitutionalism and the 'constitutionalist fallacy', see P. Q. Hirst, *Representative Democracy and its Limits*, Cambridge, 1990.
78 As Robert Goodin notes perceptively, 'there is no particular reason to suppose that a political constitution itself can necessarily conjure up the social conditions which serve as preconditions for its won success. There are many things a constitution can do: it can prescribe for all in the eyes of the law; its electoral laws can be structured so as to encourage parties to appeal to members of other ethnic groups as well as to their own natural constituencies. But all that is just to say that the constitution can lay down principles and invite people to internalise them. And it might so happen that people actually go for it. . . . If they do, the constitution will have succeeded in bootstrapping itself to sociological viability.' See R. E. Goodin, 'Designing constitutions: the political constitution of a mixed commonwealth', *Political Studies*, vol. 44, no. 3, 1996, pp. 637–8.
79 See in this regard Dick Howard's stimulating discussions of constitutionalism in the French and American revolutions. See D. Howard, *Political Judgements*, London, 1996.
80 Indeed, writers such as Herman Giliomee doubt the existence of a shared destiny even after the successful conduct of elections in 1994. Even though I do not agree with Giliomee, his argument does place the onus on Sisk to

provide reasons for his claims. See Giliomee, 'Democratization in South Africa', pp. 100–1.

81 These questions have, of course, been raised by theorists of political culture, such as Gabriel Almond and Sidney Verba, though Brian Barry has, quite correctly, drawn attention to the vicious circularity involved in suggesting that a requisite civic culture *causes* a democratic polity. More recently, this focus on the requisite values and norms for democracy has been revived by writers such as Edvardsen following the anthropological theories of Mary Douglas. See G. Almond and S. Verba, *The Civic Culture: Political Attitudes and Democracy in Five Nations*, Boston, 1965; B. Barry, *Sociologists, Economists and Democracy*, Chicago, 1978; U. Edvardsen, 'A cultural approach to understanding modes of transition to democracy', *Journal of Theoretical Politics*, vol. 9, no. 1, 1997, pp. 211–34.

82 See O'Donnell and Schmitter, *Transitions from Authoritarian Rule*, pp. 15–17; A. Przeworski, *Democracy and the Market*, p. 69.

83 Karl and Schmitter, 'Modes of transition in Latin America and Eastern Europe', p. 281.

84 O'Donnell and Schmitter, *Transitions from Authoritarian Rule*, pp. 11–14.

85 D. Levine, 'Paradigm lost: dependency to democracy', *World Politics*, vol. 40, no. 3, p. 385, quoted in J. Foweraker and T. Landman, *Citizenship Rights and Social Movements: A Comparative and Statistical Analysis*, Oxford, 1997, p. 234.

86 As Glenn Adler and Eddie Webster note in their perceptive critique of 'transition theory', it is not the case that pactologists necessarily embrace ideologically the conservative conclusions and prescriptions they advance; rather, they flow from the conceptual and theoretical limitations of their approach when *applied* to cases like South Africa. Developing an element of O'Donnell and Schmitter's original argument, they argue that once the transition is underway the threat posed by hardliners 'recedes the more it is invoked and the further along the transition progresses'. This is because it would be extremely costly for moderates were there to be a return to authoritarianism. Moreover, they argue, the rational response by pro-democratic forces *ought* to be to mobilize their forces so as to prevent the likelihood of this occurring. A second limitation emanates from the *functionalist* understanding of the relationship between popular movements and elite pacting. Whereas, in this view, political movements are significant only to the extent that they are functional or dysfunctional to the success of creating pacts, Adler and Webster draw on recent social movement theory to give greater prominence to the role and impact of the labour movement, embodied in Cosatu for example, in shaping outcomes. See Adler and Webster, 'Challenging transition theory', pp. 83–91.

87 See S. P. Huntington, 'How countries democratize', *Political Science Quarterly*, vol. 106, no. 4, 1991–92, p. 581.

88 Adam and Moodley, *The Negotiated Revolution*, pp. 15–16.

89 See A. Gorz, 'Reform and revolution', in *Socialism and Revolution*, New York, 1973.

90 For a sustained consideration of these issues from a post-Marxist perspective, see E. Laclau and C. Mouffe, *Hegemony and Socialist Strategy: Towards a Radical Democratic Politics*, London, 1985.

91   Adam and Moodley, *The Negotiated Revolution*, p. 6.
92   Ibid., p. 7.
93   Ibid., p. 6.
94   Ibid., p. 44.
95   See R. Bhaskar, *The Possibility of Naturalism*, Hemel Hempstead, 1979;
     A. Giddens, *The Constitution of Society*, Cambridge, 1984; C. Hay,
     'Structure and agency', in D. Marsh and G. Stoker (eds.), *Theory and
     Methods in Political Science*, London, 1995; B. Jessop, *State Theory:
     Putting the Capitalist State in Its Place*, Cambridge, 1990.
96   R. Dahl, *Polyarchy: Participation and Opposition*, New Haven, 1971.
97   Saul, *Recolonization and Resistance*, pp. 173, 176.
98   Ottaway, *South Africa*, p. 13.
99   See Adam and Moodley, *The Negotiated Revolution*, pp. 41–2; Giliomee,
     'Democratization in South Africa', pp. 84–6.
100 See Adler and Webster, 'Challenging transition theory', pp. 91–100;
     Murray, *The Revolution Deferred*, pp. 177–8, 182–4.
101 M. Lipton, *Capitalism and Apartheid*, London, 1985; M. C. O'Dowd,
     'The stages of economic growth and the future of South Africa', in
     L. Schlemmer and E. Webster (eds.), *Change, Reform and Economic
     Growth in South Africa*, Johannesburg, 1978. For a critical assessment of
     these debates, see Wolpe, *Race, Class and the Apartheid State*, pp. 24–35.
102 These questions are raised in Adam and Moodley, *The Negotiated Revolu-
     tion*, pp. 44, 80–101.
103 See Laclau, *New Reflections on the Revolution of Our Time*, pp. 30–41.
104 This conceptualization of the structure/agency dualism is predicated on a
     materialist theory of discourse. See D. Howarth, 'Discourse Theory', in
     D. Marsh and G. Stoker (eds.), *Theory and Methods in Political Science*,
     London, 1995; D. Howarth, 'Post-foundationalism and the social sci-
     ences', in E. Scarborough and E. Tanenbaum (eds.), *Research Methods in
     the Social Sciences*, Oxford, 1998.
105 These arguments have been developed further in D. Howarth, 'Theorising
     Hegemony', in G. Stoker and J. Stanyer (eds.), *Contemporary Political
     Studies 1996*, Glasgow, pp. 971–83.
106 Laclau and Mouffe, *Hegemony and Socialist Strategy*, pp. 127–34.
107 In this vein, I have analysed the logic of the Black Consciousness Move-
     ment during the 1960s and 1970s in D. Howarth, 'Logics of identity/dif-
     ference: black consciousness ideology in South Africa', *Journal of
     Political Ideologies*, vol. 2, no. 1, pp. 51–78.
108 See J. Foweraker, *Making Democracy in Spain: Grass-roots Struggle in
     the South, 1955–1975*, Cambridge, 1989, p. 2.
109 Laclau and Mouffe, *Hegemony and Socialist Strategy*, pp. 152–9.
110 See C. Lefort, *The Political Forms of Modern Society*, Cambridge, 1986;
     C. Lefort, *Democracy and Political Theory*, Cambridge, 1988.
111 Lefort, *The Political Forms of Modern Society*, p. 305.
112 Lefort, *Democracy and Political Theory*, p. 19.
113 Przeworski, 'Some problems in the study of the transition to democracy',
     p. 58.
114 W. E. Connolly, *Identity/Difference: Democratic Negotiations of Polit-
     ical Paradox*, Ithaca, 1991; W. E. Connolly, *The Ethos of Pluralization*,

Minnesota, 1995. This view has also been articulated by Chantal Mouffe, who has endeavoured to articulate the conditions for what she calls an 'agonistic pluralism'. See C. Mouffe, *The Return of the Political*, London, 1993.

115 See J. Keane, 'Despotism and democracy: the origins and development of the distinction between civil society and the state 1750–1850', in *idem.*, (ed.), *Civil Society and the State: New European Perspectives*, London, 1988; M. Walzer, 'The concept of civil society', in M. Walzer (ed.), *Towards a Global Civil Society*, Oxford, 1995. In the South African context, these questions have been considered in B. Fine, 'Civil society theory and the politics of transition in South Africa', *Review of African Political Economy*, no. 55, 1992, pp. 71–82.

116 For a recent and important discussion of the relationship between economic development and democratization, see A. Leftwich (ed.), *Democracy and Development: Theory and Practice*, Cambridge, 1996.

117 See T. Lodge, 'South Africa: democracy and development in a postapartheid society', in A. Leftwich (ed.), *Democracy and Development: Theory and Practice*, Cambridge, 1996, pp. 197–202; B. Munslow and P. Fitzgerald, 'South Africa: the sustainable development challenge', *Third World Quarterly*, vol. 15, no. 2, 1994, pp. 227–42.

118 For an overview of economic debates in the 1990s, see R. Munck, 'South Africa: "the great economic debate"', *Third World Quarterly,* vol. 15, no. 2, pp. 205–17.

119 For critical discussions of the RDP, see R. Cameron, 'The Reconstruction and Development Programme', *Journal of Theoretical Politics*, vol. 8, no. 2, 1996, pp. 283–94; M. MacDonald, 'Power politics in the new South Africa', *Journal of Southern African Studies*, vol. 22, no. 2, 1996, pp. 221–34; N. Nattrass, 'Economic restructuring in South Africa: the debate continues', *Journal of Southern African Studies*, vol. 22, no. 4, 1994, pp. 517–32.

120 T. Lodge and B. Nasson, *All, Here, and Now: Black Politics in South Africa in the 1980s*, London, 1991; A. Marx, *Lessons of Struggle: South Africa's Internal Opposition, 1960–1990*, Cape Town, 1990.

121 See F. Johnstone, 'Quebec, Apartheid, Lithuania and Tibet: the politics of group rights', *Telos*, no. 85, 1990, pp. 56–62.

122 See T. M. Shaw, 'South Africa: the corporatist/regionalist conjuncture', *Third World Quarterly*, vol. 15, no. 2, pp. 252–4.

Index